CALLED (TO) TEACH

CALLED ⟨TO⟩ TEACH

An Introduction to the Ministry of Teaching

WILLIAM R. YOUNT

ACADEMIC

Nashville, Tennessee

978-0-8054-1199-7

Published by B&H Publishing Group, Nashville, Tennessee
Acquisitions & Development Editor: Leonard G. Goss
Page Design and Typography: TF Designs, Mt. Juliet, Tennessee

Dewey Decimal Classification: 370
Subject Heading: TEACHING/CHRISTIAN EDUCATION
Library of Congress Card Catalog Number: 98-37379

Library of Congress Cataloging-in-Publication Data
Yount, William R.
    Called to Teach / William R. Yount.
        p.   cm.
    Includes bibliographical references and indexes.
    ISBN 978-0-8054-1199-7 (pbk.)
    1.Teaching. 2. Educational psychology. 3. Classroom management.
4. Christian education   I. Title.
LB10253.3Y68
370.15—dc21   98-37379
                                                                      CIP

24 25 26 27 28   22 21 20 19 18

Contents

Preface

Of making many books there is no end,
and much study wearies the body.

Ecclesiastes 12:12b

hy another book on teaching? Many already exist. There are general books that attempt to cover the whole spectrum of teaching. There are specialty books that take one part of the spectrum and give their full attention to it. Teaching manuals abound, written by committees and work groups of teachers, covering every conceivable topic related to teaching. So why write another?

I suppose the most honest answer would be that I have a teaching book in me that has to be written. In 1970, as a Sunday school teacher of deaf college students, a question riveted my heart: How can I teach so that learners grow in the Lord? The One who put that question in my heart also led me to study at Southwestern Seminary in Fort Worth and minister to the deaf (people group) at First Baptist Church, Irving, Texas. Through seminary studies and practical teaching experiences he began to put together the pieces of the answer. Over the past twenty-five years I've shared my heart and mind with Sunday school teachers in church and state conferences, through videotape, and in the seminary classroom. But beyond the driving desire to get this book out of my heart and head and onto paper, there is another reason. Writing this book has been a challenge—a challenge to convey a four-dimensional reality in a two-dimensional medium. Here's what I mean.

Books are by nature two-dimensional and sequential. We read them page by page over time. Step by step, books on teaching deal with preparation (before readers know what they're preparing to do), writing objectives (before they've learned how to select content, or translate content into a form best assimilated by students), or learning readiness (before they know what they're readying them to do). By the time readers study methods like lecture, question and answer, and small group discussion, they may well have forgotten most of what they learned about objectives. So they see "methods" as disjointed activities that can be selected like Chinese food—one from column A and two from column B—without a sense of direction or purpose. The conclusion, disjointed from "objectives," is reduced to a challenge to "do better." Or worse, the conclusion's a nice pithy saying by which we send learners off into the world until the next class session. Even the best books are two-dimensional and sequential.

Unlike books, teaching is four-dimensional and global. Teaching is four-dimensional in that it occurs in the three-dimensional space of thinking, feeling, and doing—the Christian Teachers' Triad—and in real time. It is global because everything related to the teaching process happens simultaneously. Learner backgrounds and prejudices, teacher goals, content, questions, learning difficulties, directions, skill levels—it all comes together in that mystical experience of teaching and learning.

So the challenge is to translate a four-dimensional, global process into a two-dimensional, sequential format. I have attempted to overcome this problem by dealing in triad and time. By introducing the three-dimensional triad in the first chapter, the global nature of teaching is emphasized even as we deal sequentially with the topics. Then, through time, we'll add elements to the mix, strengthening the whole as we go. Here's a road map through the entire text:

Part 1 emphasizes the teacher as a person at center stage, and focuses on the personal characteristics of teachers.

Chapter 1. The Teacher as Dynamic Synergist
- The Triad of Teaching
- What Learners Think
- What Learners Experience and Value
- What Learners Do
- Three-in-One Teaching
- Jesus, the Dynamic Synergist

~❖~ Becoming a Synergisic Teacher

Chapter 2. The Teacher as Mature Person
   ~❖~ The Triad of Maturity
   ~❖~ Mature Thinking
   ~❖~ Mature Emotion
   ~❖~ Mature Action
   ~❖~ The Teacher as Exemplar
   ~❖~ The Teacher Growing in Christlikeness

Part 2 emphasizes the teacher as instructor. Chapters in this unit focus on instructional activities that focus directly on student learning.

Chapter 3. The Teacher as Clear Communicator
   ~❖~ The Teacher as Teller
   ~❖~ The Teacher as Facilitator
   ~❖~ The Teacher as Provocateur
   ~❖~ The Teacher as Instructional Technician

Chapter 4. The Teacher as Motivator
   ~❖~ The Teacher as Shaper
   ~❖~ The Teacher as Social Model
   ~❖~ The Teacher as Curositeur
   ~❖~ The Teacher as Friend
   ~❖~ The Teacher as Success Agent

Chapter 5. The Teacher as Dramatic Performer
   ~❖~ The Teacher as Personal Presence
   ~❖~ The Teacher as Speaker
   ~❖~ The Teacher as Storyteller
   ~❖~ The Teacher as Enchanter
   ~❖~ The Flawed Dramatic Performer

Part 3 emphasizes the teacher as educational manager. Chapters in this unit focus on managing the classroom environment in order to enhance learning.

Chapter 6. The Teacher as Creative Designer
   ~❖~ The Teacher as Researcher
   ~❖~ The Teacher as Course Architect

Part 4 emphasizes the teacher as "minister." This single chapter focuses on the ministry aspects of teaching in a Christian context, whether it be in a church, college, or Christian school.

Whether this text delivers these high-sounding objectives depends on what happens in your heart and mind as you read these pages. If you come to the end and have no sense of being better prepared to teach in church or Christian school, college, or seminary, then I will have failed.

If you come to the end with clearer understanding of how to teach, a deeper conviction for teaching ministry, and confidence that you possess the skills to make it happen, then I will have succeeded, making my dream a reality.

Before she died in the *Challenger* disaster, Christa McAuliffe expressed her love for teaching this way: "To be a teacher is to touch the future." She was right.

But to be a teacher in the service of the Lord is to touch eternity. He enables us to do this as we allow him freedom to change us, shape us, mold us into the kind of teacher who can. He wants you to succeed. He will help you succeed. He will teach you as you give him freedom in your life—hold back nothing. "Humble yourselves, therefore, under God's mighty hand, that he may lift you up in due time" (1 Pet. 5:6).

Right here at the beginning of our journey together, will you humble yourself under God's hand as a teacher? Will you submit your experiences and fears to him, and let him lift you up to be one who touches eternity in the now? To teach, in Jesus' name? I hope and pray so. Because this book was written just for you, beloved. Just for you.

W.R.Y.
1999

The Teacher as Person

Chapter 1

The Teacher as Dynamic Synergist

*T*he eight of us sat on sofas clustered around a fireplace in the conference room. Beyond plate glass windows lay the verdant countryside of western Virginia—pine trees and Blue Ridge Mountains. A warm fire softly crackled in the background. The staff of Columbia Baptist Church had gathered, calendars and notepads in hand, to dream together about the new year. Our pastor, Neal Jones, had already planned the year's preaching emphasis around the themes of togetherness, mutual support, and the family of God. He captured the essence of the year in the term *dynamic synergism*—"many elements working together." Perhaps it was the synergistic effect of lush trees, mountain mist, warm fire, and close staff relationships that filled me with wonder. Even now I can with closed eyes travel back twenty years and still feel the impact of the term.

The American Heritage Dictionary defines synergism as an alloy of elements whose "combined effect is greater than the sum of their individual effects." The word comes from the Greek *ergon*, "to work," and *syn-*, "with," and literally means "to work together." The word *dynamic* comes from the Greek *dynamis*, "power," and refers to a "moving or driving force." A dynamic synergism is composed of elements that normally exist independent of one another. They push at each other, or escape to go their own way. Holding them together is difficult, but the resulting effect is powerful.

In a previous book, *Created to Learn*,[1] I described three major learning theory systems: the behavioral (doing skillfully), the cognitive (understanding clearly), and the affective (experiencing and valuing personally). In introducing the Teachers' Triad, I wrote, "Educational problems do not fall neatly into any one system. . . . Effective teachers move freely from system to system, engaging learners where they are, helping them to master the subject and grow as a result."[2]

But I would go farther now. The best teachers are like parallel processors[3] who operate in all three systems simultaneously, conscious in-the-now of behaviors, concepts, and values. Dynamic synergists make the best teachers.

The Triad of Teaching

The diagram represents the three systems of learning. Each circle is independent of the others, and so their relationship to each other is variable. Each circle can be any size, representing varying degrees of importance. Here we see an ideal balance: all three circles are the same size, and all three intersect equally. I'll briefly define the elements, then describe the distortion in learning that's caused when we overem-

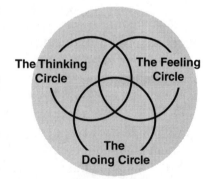

The Teachers' Triad

phasize any one of them. Finally, I'll describe the benefits of synergistic teaching.

What Learners Think

The thinking circle represents the cognitive aspect of learning and includes such elements as knowing (recalling) facts, comprehending concepts, solving problems, analyzing case studies, writing conceptual essays,[4] and judging situations by established criteria. Cognitive learning is objective, cerebral, logical, and rational. Without helping learners think clearly, we open them to confused frustration: "Whutduzallthisstuffmean?!"

How can we help our learners to think more clearly? We will do well if we focus on concepts more than words, ask questions rather than provide answers, pose problems rather than give reasons, and present examples rather than isolated facts. Let's look more closely at each of these.

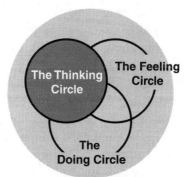

The Teachers' Triad

Concepts vs. Words. I once asked a class to write down at least eight sentences using the word *run*. Here are some of their examples:

- Johnny runs (moves swiftly) to second base.
- Barbara runs (manages) her business efficiently.
- Tim runs (operates) the printing press well.
- Jeannie has a run (defect) in her hose.
- Peter's team scored a run (score) in the second inning.
- Water always runs (flows) downhill.
- Members of Congress run (campaign) for office.
- Fido was kept in a nice dog run (outdoor enclosure).

The word is singular: *run*. The meanings are multiple: move swiftly, manage, operate, and so forth. These meanings reflect the different concepts referenced by the word *run*.

When Jesus said "Do not judge, or you too will be judged" (Matt. 7:1), he was condemning the nagging, carping, censorious spirit of the Pharisees and religious leaders of his time. He was saying that when we live like this, we will be criticized by others. Citizens of the kingdom are to avoid the hypercritical, judgmental spirit of religious bigotry. It is not enough to say "Jesus said, 'Don't judge.'" Unless you explain what Jesus meant by the word *judge*, you leave your learners to define it out of their own imaginations. For instance, here's one such misinterpretation: Two people at church are overheard discussing a prominent television evangelist. One of them says, "I would never send money to him. He's just a crook.

He's taking advantage of poor people." The other replied, "Oh, honey, you shouldn't say such things. Remember, Jesus said we aren't to judge people."

As teachers we must help our learners develop the concepts represented by the words. One day a seminary student of mine led the class in a Bible study of the fruit of the Spirit. He explained "joy" this way: "Joy is another one of the fruits of the Spirit. Joy is the kind of joy that only God can give. It's the kind of joy we'll experience in heaven. Ohhhh. The joy of the Lord is wonderful!"

This student didn't have a clue about the meaning of "joy." He talked about it. Said nice words about it. Said those words with deep feeling. But in terms of explanation, his words were empty.

If he had compared biblical joy with the similar concepts of fun or pleasure or happiness, he would have accomplished much more in helping his students understand it. All these terms reflect a sense of delight, or bliss, or elation. The distinction is that biblical joy is not dependent on life circumstances. We can experience God's joy whether we meet success or trouble. As we walk with him, he produces joy-from-within by his Spirit, in good times and bad. For example, my first experience with biblical joy in bad times occurred as I sat alone in a hospital waiting room. I had ridden in the ambulance with my mostly comatose wife. From time to time she had sat up, screamed, and passed out. They had taken her back into the emergency area—and pointed me to the waiting room. An hour had passed. I sat in silence, trying to breathe despite clouds of cigarette smoke being produced by nervous floor-pacers. Then in the stillness of my aloneness, out of the quiet, came the unspoken words: "Do not worry. Everything will be all right." *Then she'll live?* I asked within myself. "Whether she lives or not, everything will be all right." And with that assurance, felt from within, came peace. And on the heels of peace, joy. I certainly was not having fun. There was nothing pleasurable about it. I wasn't happy. But I was filled with joy. For the next two hours I sat calmly, eyes closed, at peace, giving thanks for what the Lord would do.

Questions vs. Answers. Help learners think by asking conceptual questions based on their readings or your explanations. A "conceptual question" is one that focuses on the essential meaning of a concept or principle. Answers go beyond fixed or memorized definitions. Different answers can correctly define or explain the meaning of a concept simultaneously. The question "What is a conceptual question?" may ask for nothing more than simple recall of a definition previously given. The question "What is an example of a conceptual question?" requires understanding of the term as well as the ability to create an illustrative example. A hundred different "examples" can all be correct, if, in fact, students give correct examples.

Giving learners pat answers and simple facts can produce little more than noise in the air. As one deaf student of mine once said, "In one eye and out the other." It's all forgotten by tomorrow's lunch. But ask a thoughtful question after an explanation, and you drive learners into their own understanding for answers. For example, you might ask, "So, how would you explain the meaning of Paul's phrase 'express image of the Father' in referring to Jesus?" The idea is to teach, then question. Ask questions and give fewer "pat" answers. Listen to responses and make adjustments in their understanding.

Problems vs. Reasons. Help learners think by posing problems rather than giving reasons. Giving your students "five reasons why Christians ought to forgive" will do less to develop an understanding of "forgiveness" than presenting them with problems that can be solved by a forgiving spirit and then prompting them by asking, "Based on our study this morning, how would you handle this situation?" Listen to their solutions. Correct misunderstandings. Suggest or call for alternatives. Lead the class to see the relevance of "forgiveness" to the contemporary situation.

Examples vs. Facts. Help learners think by emphasizing examples over isolated facts. Paul wrote that love is—and I'm paraphrasing here—patient, kind; it does not envy, boast; it is not proud, rude, self-seeking, easily angered; it keeps no record of wrongs; does not delight in evil but rejoices with the truth (see 1 Cor. 13:4–6).

These are facts, but what do they mean? Elaborate on *patient* and *kind*. Illustrate *envy* and *boasting*. Explain "proud, rude, self-seeking, and easily angered." How might someone keep a "record of wrongs"? Why would anyone "delight in evil," and what is the "truth" that I am to rejoice with? We must clearly explain the meanings of biblical words—in modern translations, but even more so with the King James Version, which uses language unfamiliar to the modern layman: "Charity suffereth long, and is kind; charity envieth not; charity vaunteth not itself, is not puffed up, Doth not behave itself unseemly, seeketh not her own, is not easily provoked, thinketh no evil; Rejoiceth not in iniquity, but rejoiceth in the truth" (1 Cor. 13:4–5 KJV).

Whatever translation of Scripture you use, focus on correctly translating the words on the page so that the message comes through clearly. Paul said it this way: "Do your best to present yourself to God as one approved, a workman who does not need to be ashamed and *who correctly handles the word of truth*" (2 Tim. 2:15, italics mine).

In summary, we help our learners think when we focus on concepts more than words, on questions more than pat religious answers, problems more than reasons, examples more than sterile facts.

However, too much thinking is dangerous. Excessive emphasis on the rational can produce an atmosphere that is dry and impersonal. It is one thing to understand the concept of honesty, but quite another to live honestly; one thing to understand salvation, but quite another to commit your life to Jesus Christ; one thing to know the teacher's triad diagram, but quite another to use it correctly. Knowledge and understanding are necessary but not sufficient for synergistic learning. So, what else do we need?

What Learners Experience and Value

The feeling circle represents the affective aspect of teaching and learning. This circle includes sharing personal experiences, developing positive attitudes, establishing values, reorganizing priorities, and living out the truths of the subject. It is personal, emotional, spontaneous, and warm. Without openness and freedom, we lead learners into isolated boredom: "Howduzthisstuffrelatetome?!"

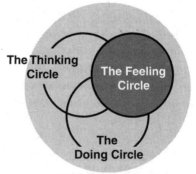

The Teachers' Triad

As teachers we should help students develop positive attitudes and values. We will make good progress toward emotional warmth in the classroom if we focus on sharing ourselves and the experiences of the learners, accepting them as they are (while helping them grow), using humor appropriately, and building trust. Let's look at each of these more closely.

Personal Experiences vs. Wooden Stories. Stories are wonderful tools to make concepts more personal and real to learners. However, fictitious testimonies, contrived case studies, and artificial anecdotes may do little to warm up a class. These devices are wooden, stilted, and forced—no matter how good they are—because they are not related to the life experiences of you or your class.

Far better are stories that flow out of the personal experiences of teacher and learners. All of us have experiences of success and growth related to the subject at hand. Weave these experiences into the fabric of the class to personalize learning.

"Earn the Right" vs. "Put on the Spot." Teachers add to the warmth of a class when they earn the right to ask students to share personal experiences. We do this by sharing ourselves first. Christian teachers "prepare God's people for works of service, so that the body of Christ may be built up" (Eph. 4:12). It is not for us to tear down learners through guilt or embarrassment.[5] However, it is a natural tendency to put learners on the spot. Once a seminary student of mine began his ten-minute MicroTeach[6] exercise this way: "Okay, how many of you haven't had a daily time of prayer and Bible study this week [pause]. Just lift your hands [uncomfortable pause]. Well, now I know that in a class this size there's someone who hasn't had a regular time of Bible study and prayer this week [tension building]. Remember, God is watching and he knows who you are [angry pause]." Finally, a young man in the back of the room bowed his head and slowly lifted his hand. The student teacher then proceeded to talk about how to have a quality quiet time.

In my opinion, the student teacher had no right to do this. It humiliated the learner and angered the class. It certainly killed any sense of openness toward the student teacher (a fact his evaluations from the class clearly pointed out to him).

Yet if this student had "earned the right" to ask that question by sharing his own struggles with having a daily quiet time, there would have been no problem. For instance, look at the difference if he had said it this way: "This past week I've not spent as much time in prayer and Bible study as I normally do. I mean, things have gotten so busy and hectic—and I've let them push my devotional time aside. Are any of you struggling with this problem? [several heads nod in agreement]. Let's see what we can discover that will help us give top priority to the Lord."

Such an approach increases openness. It warms the class because "we have a common struggle" and "we're working together" to find answers from God's Word. Share yourself before you ask others to share. Earn the right.

Acceptance vs. Judgment. We discussed Jesus' command "Judge not, lest ye be judged" earlier in this chapter. Jesus was condemning the carping, nagging, nit-picking, censorious spirit of the Pharisees. As teachers we need to pray through our own attitudes toward those we teach, or we will move in this same direction.

I often hear comments such as "I can't get anyone in my class to answer a question" or "Projects? Are you kidding? I can't get anyone to do anything in my class!" I wonder if these teachers tell their classes these things!

The disciples failed in many ways, but Jesus forgave them, loved them, and continued to teach them. Accept those you teach where they are. Then love them, teach them, and allow them to grow in the Lord. Some will take longer than others. The commitment level of a few may never please us, but that is not our concern. Our concern is to be faithful in our loving ministry toward those we teach. If your focus is on acceptance rather than judgment, openness and warmth will grow in your class or church.

Humor vs. Solemnity. The apostle Paul was a philosopher. His writings are deep and often hard to understand. Even Peter had trouble understanding him sometimes (see 2 Pet. 3:16). But the evidence of a Christ-filled life for Paul is not found in philosophical reasoning or theological expertise, but in the joy that comes from knowing him (see Rom. 12:12; 14:17; 15:13; Phil. 1:25; Col. 1:11–12). The Bible is a solemn book, and declares a solemn message. We approach Scripture study with reverence. But this reverence differs from the stoic, stern, dispassionate logic of those false teachers whom Paul wrote against in his letters to the Colossians. Where the Spirit is free to produce fruit, there we find joy among the harvest (see Gal. 5:22–23).

The super-serious have little warmth. The super-silly little depth. But proper use of humor can both warm up and settle down a class. Humor can enhance the openness of the class. People who honestly laugh together can also honestly share together. If you can use humor naturally, you will find an effective technique for building openness in the classroom.

One last word on humor. Be sure that the humor is positive and uplifting. Avoid crude or vulgar jokes, stories with double meanings, and even lighthearted pranks or gags. Humor is wrong when it denigrates others or demeans the sacred task at hand. "Nor should there be obscenity, foolish talk or coarse joking, which are out of place, but rather thanksgiving" (Eph. 5:4).

Trust vs. Guilt. I would make one last suggestion here on improving the warmth of a class: avoid guilt and strengthen trust. Guilt is a strong motivator; perhaps that is why so many immature leaders use it. It produces quick results but undermines the glue that holds human relationships together—trust.

B. F. Skinner conducted many experiments in which he taught rats to run mazes. In some cases he used a positive reinforcer: food. In others he used punishment: electric shock. He found that electric shock motivated the rats to learn the maze faster than food. But the shock also taught the rats to fear the maze. Eventually, rats refused to move, regardless of the degree of shock applied, even to the point of death. Guilt is like an electric shock to the personality. It produces quick results but leads to fear of the cage—be it a Sunday school class, college or seminary class, or congregation. Such motivational techniques are toxic to learners.

Did Jesus, the Lord of Lords, teach this way? No. Rather, he said, "*For God did not send his Son into the world to condemn the world,* but to save the world through him" (John 3:17, italics mine). Did Paul, strong personality that he was, teach this way? No. Paul countered his enemies in Corinth, who claimed Paul was strong in his letters but weak in person (see 2 Cor. 10:10), by saying, "You even put up with anyone who enslaves you or exploits you or takes advantage of you or pushes himself forward or slaps you in the face. To my shame I admit that we were too weak for that!" (2 Cor. 11:20–21a).

Rather, Paul loved the church at Corinth, and grieved over their problems: "For I wrote you out of great distress and anguish of heart and with many tears, not to grieve you but to let you know the depth of my love for you" (2 Cor. 2:4). By his clear teaching and his firm but loving exhortation, Paul led the church at Corinth away from her problems and into a more focused relationship to Christ.

Trust grows among people as they live and work and pray together, as they share needs together, as they forgive one another. If we were to take Paul's words as marching orders for our classrooms, we would find a great increase in the trust level among our students. Experiences rather than wooden case studies, earning the right, accepting more than judging, humor more than super-solemnity, trust more than guilt—these distinctives will help you create a climate for the growth of Christian values.

But beware: too much emphasis on personal experience can be dangerous. Too much emphasis on the affective can produce an atmosphere that is shallow, purely subjective, self-centered, and speculative. Students may feel they've mastered a subject, but their "mastery" may bear little correspondence to the truth. Such a class emphasizes what students like over what they need, or how much they enjoy the class over how competent they are, or how much they love the teacher over how much they actually learn. Personal sharing and valuing are necessary but not sufficient for synergistic learning.

What Learners Do

The "doing" circle represents the behavioral aspect of teaching and learning. Learners may understand *agape* love, but do they love? They may value missions, but do they support missions tangibly with time and money? They may know how to write essays, but do they write well?

Learning in this circle develops competence in putting learning

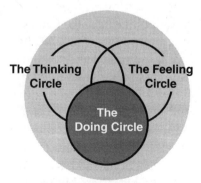

The Teachers' Triad

into practice. It is hands-on, interactive, and task oriented. Without helping students develop the skills required to do their work successfully, we consign them to inactive helplessness: "Sohowdoahdoit?"

Years ago I taught a Sunday school class for deaf college students. One day I met one of the students on campus and, after a few minutes of conversation, asked him what discoveries he'd made during our study the previous Sunday. "Ohhh," he said, "that was a long time ago." Yes, I agreed, this is Wednesday and our study was Sunday, but what did you get out of the study? "Well, ummmm, we were studying the Old Testament, right?" Well, no, actually, we studied a passage out of Ephesians. "Ephesians! That's right! I remember now!" So what did he discover? What did he learn? "Ohhhh, well, I don't remember. That was a long time ago!" I had spent five or six hours preparing to teach. I had given the presentation all I had. Now, on Wednesday, he couldn't remember the first thing about what we'd studied. What discouragement! How could he possibly *act* on what we studied if he couldn't remember it? Without giving attention to what learners can and should do with what we teach, we may lead them into discontented inactivity.

How can we help our learners put what they learn into practice? Let me suggest two general ways and then focus on a third specific way to do this. One general way to encourage practical application is to engage *learners in thinking* (as we discussed previously under "What Learners Think"). Learners cannot transfer learning from classroom to life unless they clearly understand the subject. Solving problems in class, based on assigned materials, is an excellent way to build bridges into the daily lives of learners.

A second general way to lead learners to put truth into practice is to *lead them to value the subject and its implications* (see previous section "What Learners Experience and Value"). When learners see for themselves the value of the subject, they are far more likely to use it in facing situations in their own lives.

A third, and more specific, way to encourage learners to put leaning into practice is to *make assignments* to be done outside of class. These assignments can vary in their intensity and scope: selected materials to read, specific questions to answer, projects to do, journals to keep, words to analyze, and the list goes on. By making such assignments, you prompt learners to think of your class and its subject during the week. You share part of the teaching responsibility with learners as they share the results of their study the following class period. Assignments can be done individually, in pairs, or in groups of various kinds. By focusing learners on things to be done between sessions, you move learning outside the classroom and help them take greater responsibility for their own learning.

Provide learners with guidelines for doing their work skillfully. This can be done through discussion, overhead projection, or printed handouts. Shape skillful work in your learners by showing both good and bad examples of previous classes' efforts. Explain clearly your basis for grading assignments. Make helpful comments on submitted work so that learners can improve their skills throughout the semester.

Use assignments in future class sessions. Let students volunteer to share what they've learned through the graded assignments. Work will be more carefully done if students know they will have opportunity to share it in class.

It is important to note that too much emphasis on outside assignments, projects, and papers can be dangerous. It can produce an atmosphere of busyness, overwork, and, eventually, exhaustion. Students may finish their work, but do they understand how facts, concepts, and principles interrelate? Do they value the work they are doing, or are they simply going through the motions? They write out their assignments for class discussion, but do they thoughtfully consider their answers? Do they reflect on personal experiences associated with the questions? Skillful "doing" is necessary but not sufficient for synergistic learning.

Three-in-One Teaching

We face a constant dilemma, in real time, as we stand before our classes and teach. Productive teaching engages the thinking processes of learners. But too much emphasis on *thinking* leads to a dry, cold, idealistic intellectualism. Productive teaching also touches the hearts of students, generating positive

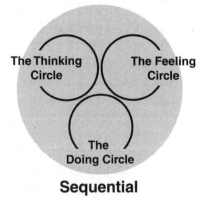

Sequential

14

feelings toward the class, the subject, and the teacher. But too much emphasis on *feeling* leads to mindless, sentimental, impractical fluff. Productive teaching challenges learners to do their best, motivating them to practice skillfully what they're learning. But too much focus on *doing* leads to mindless, personally irrelevant ritual. Sequential and disjointed application of think-feel-do produces these wobbles which shake the class even if each part is done well!

The answer to the dilemma is to integrate the rational, emotional, and behavioral into a single teaching style that communicates concepts clearly, warms students personally, and engages students productively. Such a teaching style is global rather than overly specific. Dynamic synergists know where they're going with the class. They know their material, but they integrate student needs into the way they process the material in-the-now. They are not deterred by student comments or questions that are off the mark. They are not deterred by disagreeable facial expressions or thin whiney voices. Synergists take it all in, and move learners forward.

Such a teaching style is spontaneous rather than overly programmed. Synergists are not deterred from chasing a momentary "rabbit"[7] by an overly rigid teaching plan. They can laugh with students and can laugh at themselves. Synergists do not fear the consequences of considering new ideas in front of the class. If they respond well, they model good thinking

skills in real time. If they respond poorly (and the class is free enough to point it out), they model humility and the fallibility of human thinking—even among teachers!

Jesus, the Dynamic Synergist

Jesus reflected this triad of rational, emotional, and behavioral elements in his teaching. Jesus reflected cognitive elements of teaching as a prophet, proclaiming and explaining by way of stories and illustrations the kingdom of God (see Matt. 13:57; 21:11; Luke 24:19; John 6:14). As prophet, Jesus focused on the eternal Truth and objective standards of Kingdom living.

Jesus reflected affective elements of teaching as priest (see Heb. 3:1; 4:14). He loved and cared for his disciples and followers. He healed and fed them, calming their fears and ministering to them. He nurtured them, wept over them, and prayed for them. He taught them with compassion and retaught them with patience. He forgave them when they failed. Ultimately he gave his own life for them—and

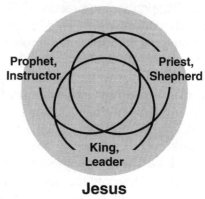

us. As priest, Jesus cared for his learners as a mother hen cares for her chicks, or a family doctor his dear friends, and focused on the affective elements of Kingdom living.

Jesus reflected behavioral elements of teaching as a leader or king (see Mark 15:2; Luke 23:3; John 18:37; Acts 17:7). He chose twelve apprentices and trained them for action. He sent his followers into the whole world to make disciples. He is Leader, Lord. As King, Jesus focused on the action element of Kingdom living.

Jesus demonstrated in his own teaching ministry, in his own life, the balance we raise as our standard. He is our Model, our Guide, and our Helper as we seek to emulate this balance in our own life and ministry.

Becoming a Synergistic Teacher

Becoming a synergistic teacher is much like learning to drive a car. Look left; look right; check rearview mirror; check left-hand mirror; check speed; watch for traffic signals, pedestrians, and other cars. When I was fifteen and practicing with my learner's permit, I remember trying to do all this sequentially: 1-2-3. Tension was high. As I practiced more, I became more global in my driving. I found I could glance at the speedometer as I shifted from left mirror to right, from windshield to rearview mirror. Now, nearly thirty-five years later, I do all of these things without consciously thinking of them. I can carry on a conversation, eat a hamburger, or plan out my next teaching series—all the while checking right, left, rear, speed, cars, pedestrians, and so on.

Dynamic synergists have practiced all three elements of teaching long enough that they no longer consciously say to themselves, "I need to ask a conceptual question here." They simply ask one. They no longer think, *Whoa! From the expressions on all these faces, I believe I've rocked their boats a little too much. I'd better lighten up.* They sense the uneasiness and instinctively lighten up. Throughout the text, we'll emphasize concepts, values, and skills that will help you grow as a dynamic synergist. Through case studies and video clips, suggestions and examples, we hope to lead you through a learning experience that will literally transform your presence in the classroom.

This textbook is dedicated to helping you become more synergistic in your teaching. Understanding the elements of the dynamic synergism of teaching is a beginning point. Growing in those elements—the subject of chapter 2—is a journey of a lifetime.

Chapter 2

The Teacher as
Mature Person

Then we will no longer be infants,
tossed back and forth by the waves,
and blown here and there
by every wind of teaching and by the cunning and craftiness
of men in their deceitful scheming. Instead,
speaking the truth in love, we will in all things
grow up into him who is the Head,
that is, Christ.

Ephesians 4:14–15

Mrs. Grace, a Sunday school teacher, scowls at the offending reader and says with disgust, "Oh, somebody with the right version of the Bible read that verse!" Dr. I. M. Tender, a seminary professor, grips his podium and flames his questioner, "Your

19

question is so shallow, so devoid of meaning, that I will not stoop to grace it with an answer. Let's get back to the point." Mr. Nurture, a teacher in a Christian college, responds to a student's concern about a recent exam this way: "If you had been serious about your study, you would have known to study the footnotes. How long must I spoon-feed you?" Sister Sweet, a teacher in a private Christian school, whacks a seven-year-old across the knuckles with a ruler, saying, "Whoever saw a flower with purple leaves!"

What had the learners done in these situations to warrant this kind of treatment at the hands of these Christian teachers? The Bible reader, a visitor in the class, read a verse from the Revised Standard Version (RSV) instead of the King James Version (KJV)—which was the preferred version Mrs. Grace used. The seminary student asked a question about the reading assigned for the day. The college student missed several items on the exam that had been taken from footnotes and unassigned chapters in the course text. The child drew a flower as he imagined it—one with purple leaves.

The visitor never returned to that Sunday school class or our church again. The seminary student never asked another question in Dr. Tender's class—and it was two months into the next semester before he risked asking a question in any of his classes. The college student learned not to question exam items, no matter how poorly they were conceived or written. The child decided that pleasing the neo-scholastic teacher was not as important as having an active imagination. A few years later he began attending another church, committed his life to the Lord, and became a leading Christian educator and pragmatic leader.

Each of these actual instances of toxic teaching happened because of the immaturity of the teachers. Four instances. Two men and two women. Two older and two younger. All of them Christian. All of them immature. Mrs. Grace could not think clearly enough to relate the RSV translation to the King's English, and so was embarrassed because she didn't know how to explain the words in the RSV. Immature thinking. Dr. Tender could not relate to the frustrations of a confused student, and was irritated by the interruption. Immature emotion. Mr. Nurture and Sister Sweet were frustrated by the failure of their students to perform according to expectations. Mr. Nurture "expected" students to study everything and be ready for any question. After all, he had done that as a student. Why should he make learning any easier for his students? Sister Sweet "expected" students to color leaves green. Why should she have to tell students how to color flowers? Both teachers were immature guides.

The Sunday school teacher had studied her lesson. She was prepared and knew her stuff—at least in the King James. But her teaching was toxic. It not only drove off this fragile visitor, but its consistency over time nearly destroyed the class. The professor delivered a brilliant lecture, providing for his students a framework, a structure, for the semester. But his teaching was toxic. It not only silenced this student for the semester and longer, in his class and beyond, but it silenced everyone else as well. (The teacher was actually grateful for the additional lecture time his passive students gave him by their silence.) The college teacher cared enough about his students to go over the exam with them, to answer their questions and clarify learning. But his teaching was toxic. He taught his class that questions about exam item quality are off limits to students, that to raise a question about the appropriateness of a question is a sign of rebellion. So students did the best they could to study, and accepted whatever grade was handed out, even though it was based on invalid and unreliable test scores. The church school teacher engaged her children in activity and allowed them to create a flower. But her teaching was toxic. She did not give ample instructions. She did not set boundaries. And when her ungiven instructions were ignored and her unset boundaries violated, she responded with physical abuse. Mature teachers would have responded very differently in each case.

The *American Heritage Dictionary* defines maturity in two ways. One emphasizes the completion of maturity and uses synonyms like *grown-up, full-fledged, full-grown,* and *developed.* Such a perspective defines a destination to be attained, a mountain to be scaled, a work of art to be fashioned, as in *matured.* A second meaning emphasizes the process of maturity and uses synonyms like *develop, grow,* and *ripen.* This perspective defines a process of traveling, climbing, and fashioning, as in *maturing.* In this chapter we consider both the destination and the journey.

The Triad of Maturity

In chapter 1 we defined the effective teacher as a dynamic synergist, as one who integrates thinking, feeling, and doing elements together in a single, global, balanced teaching style. The focus there was on the balance among the three circles—the interrelationship among the elements. Maturing teachers strain toward the balance. Immature teachers produce a detectable wobble in their classes because of a triadic imbalance that can produce intellectual icies, warm fuzzies, or detached busyness. (Truth be known, we all need to be spin-balanced periodically.)

In this chapter we deal with the *size* of the circles. Given our desire to avoid toxic teaching, how do we grow in these areas? Just what *is* mature thinking? Mature emotion? Mature action? How do we move away from immaturity—and the toxic teaching it produces—and toward maturity and teaching that transforms our students—head, heart, and hand?

Mature Thinking

The thinking element of the triad emphasizes the rational and logical. Growth in thinking is energized by the principles of conceptualization, decentration, and metacognition.

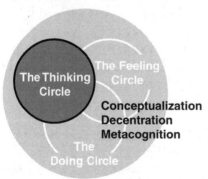

Conceptualization. Conceptualization moves us beyond specific words to general meanings. Mrs. Grace displayed immature thinking by her inability to see that both the RSV and KJV translations express the same concepts, even though they use different words to express those concepts. She identified King James words, and those words alone, with explanations she prepared from her study materials. Had she studied several different translations, she would have understood the important concepts in the passage and could have discussed them no matter what translation was read in class.

Many times I have heard banquet speakers extol the virtues of Sunday school by quoting 2 Timothy 2:15 (KJV): "Study to show thyself approved." But Paul didn't mean *study* the way we use the term: attending class to acquire knowledge or understanding. And he certainly wasn't thinking of present-day Sunday school work. The word he used means "to make effort" or "be diligent."[1] The NIV translates the original meaning very well: "Do your best to present yourself. . . ." By using multiple translations, we expand our thinking from words and simple definitions to complex definitions. We conceptualize the words in the passage, giving the words broader meaning than any one word can contain—flexible, yet focused, meanings.

If we read one book on a subject, we can present little more than a fragile reflection of one view. Such shallow preparation leaves us open to embarrassing questions. Since we have not gone beyond the text itself, it is difficult to answer questions that do, such as "Just what did the author mean . . . ?" My wife once asked a question like this in a statistics class. The teacher, unable to answer the question, simply said, "Well, I wouldn't worry about that, little lady, that's not on the test." He was teaching material he himself had not conceptualized, and his "little lady" comment underscored his irritation at the question.

On the other hand, if we read two or three books on a subject, we can become confused. Authors present different perspectives, emphasize different elements. One writer may be positive; the other two, negative. We end up wondering what the true meaning is.

But as we read a dozen or so books on a subject, we begin to detect commonalities among the writers. We begin to see categories of thinking, differences of opinion. As we conceptualize the subject for ourselves, we step outside of any one author and see a picture larger than any one of them, or even any group of them. We can determine strong points and weak points in the arguments of all sides. We wrap our minds around all the writers' ideas and conceive of the subject on a different plane than any one of them. In class, we can take any position, positive or negative. We can take any student's question and answer it from the perspective of any of the writers—or our own. We can defend a "faulty position" with arguments made by those who support it, and then raise questions from another perspective. The conceptualization of the subject gives us freedom to think in broader terms than the student's textbook.

Without conceptualization, we walk into a mine field every time we enter the classroom. Once while presenting a research paper in one of my seminars, a doctoral student said, "Multiple regression serves the cause of scientific parsimony. It reduces the multiplicity of tests and measures with greater simplicity. . . ." I had reason to believe some of my students might be unfamiliar with the scientific term *parsimony*, so I spoke up and asked him to explain it. "Uh . . . it's in a quote," he replied. Yes, that's fine, I said. So, what does "parsimony" mean in your quote? "Uh . . . uuuuhhh . . . well, Dr. Yount, I didn't look it up." *Boom!* Stepped on a mine. He was embarrassed and I was frustrated, but it was a moment, as my old Scottish pastor would say, "prrrrreyg-nunt"[2] with potential for learning. So I called him by name and said, "For future reference, I would make this suggestion to you: never write anything in a research paper or book or sermon that you cannot explain. Transferring words from one piece of paper to another is not research. And it certainly isn't the basis for teaching." He had not conceptualized his paper. He used words he could not explain, and it mangled his presentation.

Decentration. The second term, *decentration*, refers to the ability to see all the elements of a problem, not just the most obvious. In Jean Piaget's most popular experiment[3] in cognitive development, children were shown two tall vials filled equally with water. Then the water in one of the vials was poured into a shallow pan. Piaget asked, "Which has more water—the vial or the pan?" Younger children would point to the vial. "Why?" he would ask. "Because the water is taller in the vial." They *centered* on height— taller water is more water. They could not *decenter*, could not take into account the broader, longer dimensions of the pan. When he poured the water back into the tall vial, younger children perceived it became—magically—the same as it had been before. Piaget found that older children understood three-dimensional volume and were not deceived by the "taller water" in the vial. Though the water took a new shape, it was perceived as having the same amount as that in the vial.

Adults are susceptible to "centration" as well. If a television evangelist quotes a few Bible verses as he asks for donations to buy

"Holy Spirit hot tubs," the money will come rolling in. For some, quoting Scripture guarantees the honesty of the quoter. Apparently these people missed Paul's meaning in the "tossed back and forth by the waves, and blown here and there by every wind of teaching and by the cunning and craftiness of men in their deceitful scheming" (Eph. 4:14) passage. Otherwise they would understand how Paul agonized over the gullibility of believers who followed and supported false teachers.

Some of my students in educational psychology have a single, decidedly negative, perspective on "humanism." Godless, self-centered, evil, dangerous, pervasive—they often personify it as an enemy to be avoided, if not overthrown. But the truth of the matter is that humanism exists in many forms: secular humanism, classical humanism (which includes the Reformation and its focus on Scripture), and educational humanism, the feeling element of the triad. "Little-h" humanism is found in "humanitarian" and "humane," in "meeting the needs of people," and in "personalizing the classroom," all of which Christians should embrace. "Capital-H" Humanism is a philosophy centered in man and generally opposed to religion and the supernatural. When students finish our class's study of humanistic learning theory, they have a global view of what it is and where it fits into the larger picture of teaching. They understand its dangers, but can appreciate and use its strengths. Rather than seeing humanistic learning as an enemy to be avoided, they see it as a tool to be used by pastors and Christian teachers to solve specific problems in learning. They achieve all of this without compromising their faith or undermining their foundation in the Lord or his Word.

Piaget's "three-cone problem" illustrates the concepts of decentration and egocentrism[4] clearly. A table was set with two smaller cones, side by side, with a larger cone behind them. A child was placed on the side facing the two smaller cones. Dolls and stuffed animals were placed on the three remaining sides of the table. Piaget asked children to describe or draw what they saw. Then he asked them to describe or draw what a doll or stuffed animal saw. Young children described the cones the same. They could not mentally move around the table to "see" the three cones as they actually appear in the other positions. They could not decenter from their own view. Older children, having developed the ability to think three-dimensionally, could correctly draw the three cones at any position around the table.

The cones did not move. Their size, position, and interrelationship were constant. This was the *truth* of the cones. But the *perception* of the cones—the way they looked—changed depending on the position around the table.

Most classroom disagreements erupt between students who view the "cones" from different points around the table. Each student centers on his or her own perception of the "cones." Since others see the "cones" differently, they must be wrong. There is no basis for discussion because "it is obvious" that the "cones are as I see them." The only real solution to this dilemma is to step back from the various perceptions and focus on the truth-of-the-whole. If each position could see the "cones and their relationships" as the truth-of-the-whole, then each could recognize the truth of the other's view—different, perhaps, but not wrong.[5]

Immature thinkers are chained to their own perspective, unable to move around the table. The result is toxic teaching. Some browbeat students into compliance: "If you'd get right with God, you'd agree with me!" or "Everyone move to position 'A,' please. Position 'A' is the only true position." Others timidly resign themselves to letting students think whatever they want to: "Isn't it wonderful that God has made each of us as individuals, to decide for ourselves what is true!" or "Okay, everybody. Just sit wherever you want to. And feel free to move the cones around any way you please." None of these responses are acceptable.

Mature thinkers have the ability to help students from a variety of backgrounds, from a range of perspectives, because they can decenter from their own view and see the whole truth from various perspectives. They can teach with confidence, helping every student to grow in their understanding of the truth of the subject because they understand the truth-as-a-whole, regardless of where around the table they may sit.

Metacognition. Metacognition is a term used in information processing theory[6] to refer to the awareness and control of how we process information, which includes the elements of attending, recognizing, encoding, and retrieving. We process information that arrests our attention, or that we intentionally attend to. If what we attend to is recognized—linked in some way to what we already know—we can process it. We encode the information so that it can be integrated and stored with what we already know. We retrieve the information for later use by decoding this stored information. Metacognition enables us to step back mentally from our own processing in order to evaluate it and improve it. Level 1 metacognition is the learning process itself, in which information is recognized, encoded, and stored.

Level 2 metacognition allows us to observe *how we attend* to new information, how we encode and retrieve. Level 2 allows us to evaluate how we learn. Should I sit in the front of the class or in the back? Should I take detailed notes, or should I focus on listening? What distracts me from paying attention to the classroom activities? Does it help or hinder me to study with music playing in the background? Do I understand things better when studying alone or in a group? Such questions as these focus on level 2 metacognition.

Level 2 metacognition also helps us as class leaders. Do I do better with a detailed manuscript or loosely structured notes? Do students give better attention when I stand at my podium or when I walk around the room? Does my use of the chalkboard help or hinder student learning?

If we've evaluated our approach to learning, and yet do not learn better, then our evaluation process is faulty. Level 3 metacognition allows us to step back again and *evaluate how we evaluate* our own learning. If I've evaluated my own teaching but do not seem to be able to teach better, I need to concentrate on how I'm evaluating myself.

The point of this rather technical discussion is to underscore the way thinking grows as we move from level 1 to 2 to 3: learning the subject, learning how to learn the subject better, learning how to improve the way we evaluate our learning. My perception, other perceptions, truth-as-a-whole. Facts, concepts, interrelated principles. Words, phrases, language.

Mrs. Grace operated at level 1. She saw only her own embarrassment because "some stranger" had read the "wrong" translation. She was unable or unwilling to consider the feelings of the visitor, or the embarrassment of the class. Teachers must move to level 2 metacognition to consider these kind of things. And she certainly did not evaluate the exchange, analyzing it dispassionately as one might dissect a case study, in order to prevent such damage in the future. That's level 3.

Conceptualization, decentration, and metacognition: these cognitive processes move us away from "my truth" to the truths-as-wholes in our subjects. But Paul says we are to do more than speak the truth in order to "grow up into . . . Christ" (Eph. 4:15). We are to speak the truth "in love" (v. 15), the affective dimension of the triad.

Mature Emotion

The feeling element of the triad emphasizes personal experiences, values, priorities, and character of students. Mature emotion is personal, spontaneous, and warm, creating a classroom atmosphere of openness and even love. Growth in emotional maturity is reflected in sensitivity, flexibility, and grace.

Sensitivity. Dr. Tender demonstrated blunt insensitivity to his student. Not only did he fail to help someone in need—the essence of agape love—but he went the extra mile in the wrong direction by ridiculing the question and the student. Sensitivity consists of tolerance, patience, tenderness, nurture, and teachableness.

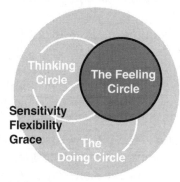

Tolerance, as defined in the *American Heritage Dictionary*, is the "practice of recognizing and respecting the beliefs or practices of others" or "the capacity to endure hardship or pain." Teaching is sometimes painful for teachers. We confront ignorance,[7] confusion, and prejudice every day. But we must first hear the perspective of our students before we can lead them to a broader or deeper understanding of the subject. If we do not respect our students as persons of worth, regardless of the ideas they have, how can we expect them to respect us? Why should they listen to us if we refuse to listen to them?

Just think for a moment of how tolerant Jesus was with impulsive Peter; with James and John, the sons of thunder; with Judas, the thief and betrayer. Tolerant, so he might teach them. Mature teachers show their sensitivity by being tolerant of students' ideas and actions.

Patience is "bearing or enduring pain, difficulty, provocation, or annoyance with calmness." Teaching is messy. Even when we have our lesson plans and goals and materials nicely prepared and in order, things happen in-the-now of teaching to make waves and rock our teaching boat. Interruptions are irritating to teachers when "the lesson" is more important than their students.

Jesus, however, viewed interruptions as part of the Father's plan, not antithetical to it, as shown by his patient demeanor with the outcast woman who touched him (see Matt. 9:18–25; Mark 5:21–43; Luke 8:40–56).[8]

Tenderness is the state of being "considerate and protective, and is characterized by gentle emotions." Immature teachers have difficulty being tender in the classroom because they often feel small and vulnerable: "What if students ask a question I can't answer? What if they disagree with my explanation?" Little people resort to blustering power plays and are much more likely to abuse their students. Tenderness seems like weakness to these folks.

Mature teachers know their subject and understand learners. Questions do not intimidate them. Rather, questions enable teachers to teach, or more specifically, *to minister to the needs* of their students. They can be tender. When Jesus appeared to John on Patmos, in all his resurrection glory, John—worshiping the Lord at the time—fainted from fear, so great was the impact of his presence. And what did the all-powerful King of Kings and Lord of Lords *do* before giving John a commission to write? He put his right hand on John's shoulder and told him he had nothing to fear (see Rev. 1:17). Mature teachers are like that. They have power, but they touch their students with tenderness and assure them they have nothing to fear.

Nurture refers to "something that nourishes" or "feeds." Students are not enemies to be conquered by our lessons. They are hungry "little ones" (Matt. 10:42) whom we feed by teaching. Some foods are more pleasing than others, but mature teachers provide a healthy balance of concepts and values and skills so that their learners can grow strong. Three times Jesus asked Peter, "Do you love me?" When he answered in the affirmative, Jesus said,

"Feed my lambs," "Take care of my sheep," and "Feed my sheep" (John 21:15–17). Nurture them, Peter.

Immature teachers worry about themselves, about feeding themselves, about protecting themselves. They do not have the emotional energy to feed others because they consume it feeding themselves. Mature teachers, on the other hand, nourish their learners by providing the best in educational food, care, and protection.

Teachableness refers to the willingness to be taught by another and is a sign of humility and wisdom. After seventeen years of teaching and more than five thousand students, there are few questions that surprise me. Even so, there are times when a question blindsides me, a question that connects the dots of our material in a way I've not seen before. These times bring the flow of the class to a halt while I sort through what I know. My first challenge is to determine if the student has found something I need to learn, or if the something is merely confusion in a clever disguise. I do not hide my thinking, fumbling as it often is in these times—like trying to find a light switch in a darkened room. I expose my feeble attempts, my failed starts, my first efforts at forming an answer. (Some students, usually those repressed by sit-still-while-I-instill teachers, smell the blood in the water and nip at these dead-end efforts. Their excitement rises as they fight for the kill, but beyond them sits the rest of the class, wondering where I'm headed.) We dialogue until most of us come to common ground and see the answer together.

I actually love these times, these serendipitous romps through thinking. I'm stretched, and students are lifted from mere listeners to participants. But such romps would never take place if I did not see myself as a learner, open to instruction from those I teach. I know how *I* see things, but when I see it through others' eyes, it is like seeing it for the first time. It is a blessing, a thrill, for teachers who are not afraid to be taught by learners. Solomon wrote, "Listen to advice and accept instruction, and in the end you will be wise" (Prov. 19:20). His words apply to those of us who teach, as well as to our students.

But immature teachers are unteachable. Their fragile egos cannot bear to be questioned or challenged. Therefore, they turn toxic in their teaching to defend themselves. Mature teachers, on the other hand, long for moments when students take the material seriously enough to line it up to their own experience and raise questions. It is only then that real life-changing learning begins. We, as mature teachers, help when we shuck off the garments of established knowledge, roll up our sleeves, and work up a sweat considering the consequences of theory and concept.

All of these elements—tolerance, patience, tenderness, nurture, and teachableness—make us sensitive to our learners as they speak from their own triad of concepts, values, and behaviors.

Flexibility. Part of Dr. Tender's frustration may have been due to time constraints. He had planned his lecture for the day. He knew where he wanted to go with the class. The last thing he wanted was for students to begin asking him "foolish" questions about the assigned readings. Still, his inflexibility led to toxic teaching.

Structure and flexibility are complementary parts of a whole. Well-planned class sessions are necessary but not sufficient for good teaching. Plans are static, lifeless, and cold in and of themselves. It is the dynamic of teacher, plan, and learners that brings life to teaching. Mature teachers balance structured planning with flexible execution. Too much structure leads to mind-numbing, mechanistic learning: "We have four objectives to achieve today, so please pay close attention." [Translation: please don't interrupt my plan.]

Too much flexibility, however, leads to confusion and hopeless wandering: "So, class, what would you like to discuss today?" [Translation: I have little or nothing planned, so you set the agenda.] Structure and flexibility live best in balance. Such balance, as in marriage, is not consistently a fifty-fifty proposition. Some situations call for greater structure; others, for greater flexibility. In the long run, however, structure and flexibility must complement each other, balance out each other. Otherwise, we veer off our teaching tarmac, sliding into ditches of overly rigid requirements to the right or overly loose vagueness on the left. It is the *art* of teaching that keeps us between the ditches and on the road to learning and growth.

Let's look at flexibility in our courses, in our lesson plans, and "in-the-moment." A *course* is a prescribed series of class sessions, or lessons, that make up a semester's study in a particular subject. A course includes an introduction to the subject, several units that emphasize major topics in the subject, and some means to evaluate student learning. A particular course is developed from subject content, the needs of students, and learning goals set by the teacher. This is structure. Mature teachers build flexibility into this structure by varying methods (lecture, question and answer, small group work) and evaluation tools (tests, individual written work, and group projects). From the first day, mature teachers present students with a rich mix of structure and flexibility.

Further, flexibility calls for adjusting courses from time to time. Content changes; learner skills and perspectives change. An effective course, like any living thing, must grow and adjust or it will die. What works well in the classroom this semester may be completely obsolete in five years. Flexibility demands that structure change over time.

Finally, flexibility calls for plans made at the beginning of a semester to be altered during the semester due to unexpected events. Bad weather may close the school. A particular class of students may have more difficulty with the material than expected, requiring additional, unplanned time. The school may cancel all classes for a special emphasis during the semester. Life happens; and when it does, mature teachers make the adjustments necessary to ensure a good course regardless. There must be flexibility in structure.

The structure of a *lesson plan* is softened by flexibility. Individual lesson plans, usually grouped into units of study, make up courses of study. Lesson plans consist of instructional objectives, learning readiness activities,[9] a variety of instructional activities, a conclusion and, if appropriate, an assignment for the next class session. These lesson plans contain lecture notes and specific questions to be asked, group work ideas, overhead cels—the bits and pieces of daily classwork that make up learning.

Yet classes have personalities just as individual students do. A plan that works with one class may fail in another. A question that produces enthusiastic discussion in one group may be met with eerie silence in another. A teacher's personal experience, received in awe and rapt attention in one class, may produce little more than bored yawns and drooping eyes in another. There is a science to writing quality teaching plans, but the art of teaching is found in knowing when to change the plan to meet the needs of the persons sitting in front of you. Once again, we need flexibility in structure.

The structure of teaching *in-the-moment* is softened by flexibility. At any given time during a class period you may sense that things are not going as you had anticipated them. A growing sense of uneasiness confronts you with the need to decide: "Is this a time for continued structure, or flexibility? Do I stay with my plan and ride out the uneasiness? Or do I make changes and move into uncharted waters—risking far more than boredom?" We all make mistakes in-the-moment. We chase a rabbit, thinking it a fruitful side trip into learning, only to find we've wasted time for no obvious good. Or, we stay the course and remain with the plan, thinking a question's just another empty tangent, only to find at the end of class that we missed the best opportunity for real learning that day. Some days persistence pays the best wage; on others, impulsiveness. But neither is a sure bet—every day, in every class. These in-the-moment flashes of decision make teaching the wonder it really is. Structured flexibility. Flexible structure.

Grace. Dr. Tender's response lacked any semblance of grace, defined in the *American Heritage Dictionary* as a "disposition to be generous or helpful." His response reflects the raw material out of which Satan spawns the popular image that "Christian teaching" is graceless, autocratic, judgmental, and censorious. Jesus asked, "Which of you, if his son asks for bread, will give him a stone? Or if he asks for a fish, will give him a snake?" (Matt. 7:9–10). The obvious, unspoken answer was, "No one." Why? Because even "evil fathers" love their children and know how to grace them.

What about teachers? "Which of you, if your student asks a question, will give him a rebuke? Or if he asks for help, will give him a slap?" We should just as readily say, "No one!"

The apostle John wrote, "If anyone says, 'I love God,' yet hates his brother, he is a liar. For anyone who does not love his brother, whom he has seen, cannot love God, whom he has not seen. And he has given us this command: Whoever loves God must also love his brother" (1 John 4:20–21).

Husbands who love their wives make it far easier for wives to love back. Masters (employers) who love their servants (employees) make it far easier for servants (employees) to love back. Teachers who love their students . . . See? *Grace.*

Jesus spoke directly to the necessity of grace when dealing with "little ones." He said, "And whoever welcomes a little child like this in my name welcomes me. But if anyone causes one of these little ones who believe in me to sin, it would be better for him to have a large millstone hung around his neck and to be drowned in the depths of the sea" (Matt. 18:5–6).

Even in cases where students are adults, they are "little ones," in terms of position and power, with respect to the teacher. We teachers are to welcome them, not rebuke them. And if, by our toxic teaching, we cause them to sin, we will answer to the Supreme Headmaster.

Sensitivity, flexibility, and grace: these affective elements move us away from rash comments, fickle feelings, irritability, fear, anxiety, and short temper and toward mature emotion. In the process we find we are able to work more easily with others, manage impulses and outbursts better, express good feelings without embarrassment, refrain from worry, and cordially accept constructive criticism.

Such growth certainly makes the classroom a more pleasant place. But pleasant learning is not the chief end of our efforts. Jesus said that those who are truly wise "hear these words of mine and put them into practice" (Matt. 7:24). Mature teachers guide students to skillfully master their subjects.

Mature Action

We defined the *doing* element as emphasizing skills, competence, and the ability to put learning into practice. It is hands-on, interactive, and task oriented. Skillful doing in the classroom, rooted in clear thinking and warm conviction, should produce the fruit of competence in ministry. Growth in skills is reflected in teacher expectations and student mastery.

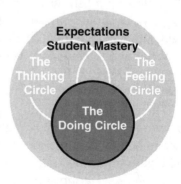

Teacher Expectations. Mr. Nurture, the college teacher, had unreasonable expectations of his students' ability to figure out how to study for his exams. He provided no structure for their preparation and was frustrated at their confusion. Sister Sweet, the schoolteacher, expected her students to color leaves green, and was frustrated with creativity. Had either teacher thought to explain their hidden expectations, their silent guidelines, their unspoken basis for evaluation, their students would have achieved at higher levels. Their understanding would have been clearer, and their feelings toward the teachers more positive. In the last section we emphasized flexibility in the structure of teaching. Here we emphasize the need for clear structure—in terms of expectations—so that students have a knowable framework in which to work. Without this framework, a classroom is a frightening, confusing place.

While flexibility in classroom *activities* is desirable, making last-minute changes in graded assignments and exams is not. It causes students unnecessary anxiety. Paul used the common image of the battle trumpet to make a case for speaking intelligibly, clearly, with understanding: "If the trumpet does not sound a clear call, who will get ready for battle? So it is with you. Unless you speak intelligible words with your tongue, how will anyone know what you are saying? You will just be speaking into the air" (1 Cor. 14:8–9). The context of Paul's words is ecstatic speech, but his principle applies to the classroom. From Greek to Statistics, from Bible to Biology, from Philosophy to Counseling we can sound as if we are speaking in an unknown tongue to our students.

Immature teachers disparage structured expectations: "My teachers never told *me* what to expect!" So their students flail about in confusion, battling their teachers as much as their subjects. These teachers are retroactive. The better ones may attempt to repair the damage done by unclear directions and unnecessary dead ends, but it's too late. Others merely blame students for the confusion and mediocre performance. If such incompetence were displayed in the heat of battle, the trumpeter would be convicted of dereliction of duty.

Mature teachers are proactive. They provide a clear description of course expectations and requirements at the beginning of a semester. Assignments are listed and explained. Examination dates are set. Criteria are set for course grades. They sound a clear trumpet of expectations so that their students can ready themselves for battle against ignorance, confusion, and misplaced values. These teachers establish the basis for success. This is mature action.

Student Mastery. Immature teachers focus on themselves—what they do, how they're perceived, what they've read and experienced. Students exist to provide receptacles for their knowledge and experience: "If the students are not able to keep up, if they cannot understand the lectures, if the reading is too confusing, if the exams are too much for them, it is merely evidence that they fall below standard and need to work harder." Success and failure lie solely in the hands of students.

Mature teachers certainly understand that ultimately it is up to learners to learn, and that there is only so much a teacher can do to stimulate learning. Still their focus is on helping students learn, not how they themselves appear. Mature teachers focus on what students do, what students perceive, what students read and experience. Teachers exist, they believe, because students need guides to help them find their way through personally uncharted waters: "If students can't keep up, if they don't understand the lectures, if the reading is confusing, if the exams are too much for them, it is evidence that my course is misdirected." As skillful observers and listeners, mature teachers detect student signals of frustration and confusion. They make changes in the flow of the course, the assignments, the use of class time in order to chart the path to success. Paul writes, "Do your best to present yourself to God as one approved, a workman who does not need to be ashamed and who correctly handles the word of truth" (2 Tim. 2:15). The triad of student mastery—clear understanding, positive values, and honed skills—is the goal of mature action—and of mature teachers.

The Teacher as Exemplar

An exemplar, as defined by the *American Heritage Dictionary*, is "one that is worthy of imitation; an ideal that serves as a pattern." In this section we refer to teachers as persons who provide an "excellent example" to those they teach.

Immature teachers see teaching as a *job*. Read books, make notes, gather materials, go to class, give lectures and tests, answer questions as they arise. They see their work much as they might view the work of farmers: plowing, planting, repairing fences, maintaining equipment, harvesting. Or architects: planning, drawing, presenting. Some do these things better than others, but they all get the job done. They put in the time.

Mature teachers see teaching as a *mission*. They challenge students with new ideas, new priorities, and new skills in order to change them, grow them, mature them. The mission is greater than reading and lecturing and answering questions—It is to stimulate a desire for excellence, first in the subject at hand, but beyond that, in life itself. Mature teachers see the work of farmers as

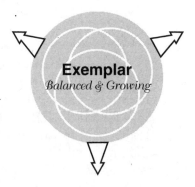

Exemplar
Balanced & Growing

focused, not on the specific tasks of farming, but on the bountiful harvest. The work of the architect is focused, not on the specific tasks of architecture, but on a beautiful building. What they do in order to fulfill their mission is important, but secondary, to the mission itself. What's more, they pay whatever price it takes to insure that the mission is accomplished.

If we expect excellence in our students, we must display excellence in our own work. Immature teachers reflect confused thinking when they stumble over student questions; confused values when they humiliate learners; and mediocre performance through faulty tests, disorganized sessions, or inability to handle interruptions. Students who make their way to excellence under such teachers do so in spite of them.

Jesus condemned the Pharisees as blind guides (see Matt. 15:14; 23:16; and 23:24). Should we expect him to do less with us, who teach in his name? The apostle Peter, first among the disciples,[10] wrote: "Be shepherds of God's flock that is under your care . . . not lording it over those entrusted to you, but being examples to the flock" (1 Pet. 5:2–3).

Mature teachers understand that they serve as examples to those they teach—whether in the role of pastor, staff minister, seminary professor, or church school teacher. They strive to be examples of godly thinking, godly priorities, and godly behavior, thereby setting the stage for student growth toward excellence.

Of course. Yet, none of us has "arrived." We are all "in process." Every one of us is a sinner, saved by grace. Even Paul, second only to Jesus in his maturity as a teacher-missionary, recognized his need for continued growth. He wrote,

Not that I have already obtained all this, or have already been made perfect, but I press on to take hold of that for which Christ Jesus took hold of me. Brothers, I do not consider myself yet to have taken hold of it. But one thing I do: Forgetting what is behind and straining toward what is ahead, I press on toward the goal to win the prize for which God has called me heavenward in Christ Jesus. All of us who are mature should take such a view of things. And if on some point you think differently, that too God will make clear to you (Phil. 3:12–15).

Paul's focus was, of course, growth in Christ. And it is towards him that we turn our attention.

The Teacher Growing in Christlikeness

At the center of the triad, all three circles overlap. This is the domain of the will, the executive of the personality. Jesus declared that our spiritual fruitfulness is dependent on being attached to the Vine (see John 15:4–5). Paul declares that any hope we have of glory comes as a result of Christ living in and through us (see Col. 1:27). He further wrote that Christians live in a battle with self. That battle is whether Christ will rule, and lead us into spiritual understanding, values, and actions—or we will rule ourselves and drift into carnal thinking, worldly values, and sinful actions (see Rom. 7:14–8:2; 1 Cor. 2:14–3:3).

How do teachers grow up, or mature, in Christ-centered thinking? We must ask the Lord, who will—if we let him—establish knowledge, spiritual understanding, and wisdom so that we can teach in a manner worthy of the Lord (see Col. 1:9–10). He will renew our minds so that, rather than conforming to the world's way of living and working, we can be fashioned by his teaching (see Rom. 12:1, 2).

How do teachers grow up, or mature, in Christ-centered attitudes and values? We must ask the Lord, who will—if we let him—give us a heart for these things. He will make us both willing and able (see Phil. 2:13) to teach in a way that serves, encourages, gives generously, and leads diligently. To teach in a way that is merciful, sincere, and devoted to others, zealous in serving the Lord, hospitable, blessing those who curse us, and empathizing with students, living in harmony with others, not proud or conceited (see Rom. 12:7–16). Much toxic teaching would be elimi-nated if Christian teachers lived Paul's words.

How do teachers grow up, or mature, in Christ-centered actions and ministry? We must ask the Lord, who will—if we let him—hone our skills for his service. He said, "Take [a voluntary action] my yoke [Jesus' ministry carved just for us] upon you and learn from me [Jesus will teach us himself], for I am gentle and humble in heart [not a taskmaster], and you will find rest [refreshment] for your souls. For my yoke is easy [to be carried] and my burden is light [it fits, does not chafe]" (Matt. 11:29–30). The Lord himself, the Master Teacher, will pull with us in the yoke of teaching min-istry, helping us mature into a master teacher in his image as we give him freedom.

In Conclusion

Maturity is the destination, the mountaintop, the masterpiece. Maturing is the journey, the climb, the fashioning. The challenge is to develop bifocal vision. Let us fix our eyes on both the destination and the journey, the mountaintop and the climb, the finished mas-terpiece and the fashioning.

We quote Paul again: "Forgetting what is behind and straining toward what is ahead, I press on toward the goal to win the prize for which God has called me heavenward in Christ Jesus" (Phil. 3:13–14). May we honor his name and his example by the way we learn, the way we teach, and the way we grow—head, heart, and hand.

As you move through this text, use the Teacher's Triad defined in this unit as the organizing structure for your study . . .

- concepts, attitudes and values, actions
- understanding, commitment, skills
- thinking, personalizing, doing
- prophet, priest, king

. . . with Jesus at the center, in the yoke with us, teaching us even as we teach others. "And you will find rest for your souls" (Matt. 11:29).

The Teacher as Instructor

Chapter 3

The Teacher as Clear Communicator

*Even in the case of lifeless things that make sounds,
such as the flute or harp,
how will anyone know what tune is being played
unless there is a distinction in the notes?
Again, if the trumpet does not sound a clear call,
who will get ready for battle? So it is with you.
Unless you speak intelligible words with your tongue,
how will anyone know what you are saying?
You will just be speaking into the air.
Undoubtedly there are all sorts of languages in the world,
yet none of them is without meaning.
If then I do not grasp the meaning of what someone is saying,
I am a foreigner to the speaker, and he is a foreigner to me.*

1 Corinthians 14:7–11

I felt like a foreigner in Dr. Stats's class. He said words that
I recognized; but when I put them together, they melted into

linguistic mush. I had read the assigned chapter on chi-square, but the present trumpet sounds played a very different, indecipherable tune. I had even taught material very similar to the day's topic in my own statistics class at Southwestern. But the detailed descriptions of cel percents and minimum E values left me bewildered. For three hours Dr. Stats played his chi-square trumpet, and I left understanding less than I did when I arrived.

If teachers are anything, they are communicators. Of what value is an encyclopedic knowledge of a subject if we cannot express that knowledge in ways that learners understand? Teachers are catalysts for learning—active agents providing the sparks that ignite explosive thoughts and values. We are bridges between subjects and learners, scholars who express profound ideas in learner-language. We tell and explain; we facilitate discussions; we challenge the status quo; we illustrate cogent points with chalk, light, and computer graphics. Yet the crucial question that must be answered when the telling and discussing are over, when the chalk dust has been rubbed off the board and the computer put away, is: Did I communicate in a meaningful way with my students today?

Mr. Shoulow (pronounced "shallow"), a graduate student, usually began class like this: "Well, students, what would you like to discuss today?" There followed fifty minutes of random discussion on topics ranging from a personal family illness to which version of the Bible one ought to use for devotions. Had he not prepared? He participated in the discussions, but to what end? The "feelers" enjoyed the sharing, but the "thinkers" and "doers" left with a sense that class time had been a waste. Shoulow saw himself as a facilitator, encouraging students to open up to one another, to communicate with each other. But what had been communicated? He was a facilitator without direction.

Ms. Blunt enjoyed shocking her classes—particularly about women's issues. One day she walked into her Biblical Backgrounds class and said, "I spoke with God today, and she said . . ." Ms. Blunt continued to express some of the impressions she'd gleaned from her time with God. But many of her students were upset by her use of "she" in referring to God. Several complained to her dean. When asked about the incident, Ms. Blunt shrugged it off as being inconsequential and petty: "Doesn't everyone know that God is Spirit, and therefore neither masculine or feminine? My use of 'she' simply points out the common error of thinking of God as a man." Provocative, yes. Sensitive to learners? No. Meaningful communication? Certainly not. We will offend students often enough without having to do so intentionally. Intentional provocation for provocation's sake communicates little more than a teacher's disdain for student "narrow-mindedness." Ms. Blunt wanted to stretch her students, but she lost any real chance to do so with most of them.[1]

Dr. Computer had the educational technician's dream classroom. We sat in a controlled-environment classroom with theater-type seats. A large rear-projection screen covered the front wall. Dr. Computer stood at his control console, stage left. From that locked position he addressed us directly through the built-in public-address system, and indirectly with color slides, computer presentations, video clips, and even overhead transparencies. He was able to write on a digitizer tablet, which converted his markings to electronic images, which were in turn displayed on the rear-projection screen. He could operate any of the equipment—including the ambient light intensity of the room—remotely from his console. The class was Instructional Computing 101, and he certainly had the hardware to show us how to develop effective illustrations and presentations. Heady stuff in the 1980s.

I was fascinated by the potential, but by the third day of class I was frustrated by the reality. Slide show after slide show, video clip by video clip, computer graphic by graphic, Dr. Computer lost the humanity inherent in teaching. The professor was anchored to his console and had little interaction with students. We were served, coldly and mechanically, one cluster of flashy facts after another. A good textbook would have served us better for self-pacing and personal review. For most of the hour—hour after class hour—we sat silently in darkness while the professor displayed his multimedia talents. The medium was the message. We were treated to a factual stage show with little substance. The latest in instructional technology was reduced to shallow gimmickry. It actually hindered real instruction.

Up to date? Yes. Visually stimulating? Absolutely. Meaningful communication? Hardly. Dr. Computer's media blitz did not enhance his course content; rather, it *was* his content—static, rigid, canned, predictable. He thought he was providing a rich resource of examples, but examples was all he had. Teacher and class never established meaningful contact.

Regardless of the technique, the real goal of teaching is balanced and mature communication. Clear directions. Understandable principles. Crisp distinctives. Relevant illustrations. Lucid examples. Explicit explanations. Thoughtful insights. Personal links. A sense of going somewhere. An enjoyable trip. How is it done? Let's look at how we can become clear communicators even as we function as tellers, group facilitators, provocateurs, and instructional technicians.

The Teacher as Teller

Dr. Stats was a teller, but not a communicator. He said words that the class recognized, but left us unable to put them together in a meaningful way. The descriptions were technical, detailed, and impressive. But they also consisted of disjointed, unconnected facts without any conceptual framework. His explanations simply left the class bewildered.

Each semester, I begin my Principles of Teaching classes by asking students to define *teaching* and *learning*. I find that most of my students define teaching as "telling." "Teachers just tell what they know" is a pervasive misconception—pervasive because we certainly want those who tell us things to know what they're saying; misconception because teaching is far more than telling. The danger with "teacher as teller" is that those who define teaching this way put more emphasis on "knowing" than "telling." The best teacher in this view is the one who knows the most, has the most credentials, has written the most books, or has done the most research. But while scholarship is essential to effective teaching (see chap. 6), the emphasis in effective teaching is more on telling than knowing. As I said earlier in the chapter, encyclopedic knowledge is useless in a teacher who cannot convey that knowledge in a meaningful way to those who need to learn it. The problem with "toxic telling" is its love for discrete bits of information and its lack of appreciation for structure and meaning. Dr. Stats told us many facts about chi-square, but the facts did not fit what we had read, nor did they form any structure of their own. The result of these conditions is always confusion. So how do we "tell with meaning"? Like a trip to an unfamiliar city, we need a known destination, a route to get us there, and landmarks to mark our progress. We may, at times, take the scenic route because we'll enjoy the trip more if we savor the sights along the way. We may even decide in-the-moment to take a side trip or two if we discover something unexpected.

Destination: Where Are We Going?

An old rocking chair philosopher once remarked, "If'n ya don't know wharya goin', yer li'bulta end up som'ers else." A successful journey begins with a known destination.

What do you want your students to know as a result of your telling them about a subject? The answer must be more specific than "Paul's Third Missionary Journey" or "Principles of Behavioral Learning"—more specific, but not trivial. The educational destination has to be more than remembering trivia such as "Lottie Moon's cabin number[2] as she sailed to China" or the "animal that figured prominently in the story of missionaries John and Alice Smith."[3] Less extreme examples, but ones still considered to be educational trivia, include the year that B. F. Skinner published *Walden II*, or the bibliographical references of "twenty leading texts in the field of . . . ," or how many Baptist churches existed in 1625.

Be specific, but not trivial. As you gather material for your course, you will find numerous cross references—common essentials among the endless words—that reflect the structure of your subject. These are the elements worth talking about because they form the skeleton on which all the other words hang. These essential elements cluster in conceptual networks. Some clusters are foundational and must be understood before other clusters make sense. Some clusters are functional and can be properly understood only after the foundation has been laid. Some clusters are conceptual; still others, illustrative. These conceptual clusters are powerful—by them we strip away the noise of nonessentials and reveal pure meaning.[4] Students not only recognize these conceptual diamonds, but are electrified by them: "Ohhh. So *that's* what the term means!" When we've delivered our students to the desired destination, they can read the textbook with clearer understanding; they can write research papers and essays with clearer perceptions. Telling must do more than rearrange the words of the course text.

The Start: Do I Have Your Attention?

All packed. Picnic materials are in the ice box. Favorite books, magazines, and computer games loaded as well as a cassette player and headphones. Car's prepped with an oil change and full gas tank. Preparation for a good start is no small matter.

The educational trip begins by *establishing contact*—human contact—with members of the class. Review key ideas from the last session, or tell a humorous story or current event related to the topic. Gain student attention by engaging the interest of learners. If you are teaching an academic course, discuss ways students can use the day's material to prepare for exams or papers. Regardless of the class, link the day's activities to the study at large. Relate the material to particular student goals: achieving a measure of success in life, solving a problem, satisfying curiosity, or helping others. Or, raise a conceptual question.[5] Let students know the destination of your study. Use instructional objectives,[6] a general outline or hand-out,[7] or a quiz to expose the students to the key concept clusters. What will they understand or experience or do during class? What will they be able to do as a result of class time? Such preparation insures a good start.[8]

The Route: How Will We Get to Where We're Going?

Knowing that we're headed for Chicago is one thing; planning which route to take is quite another. The plan should include cities and sights along the way, famous landmarks, and the best roads. Choices may need to be made when landmarks and good roads don't coexist. In the end, the best route is the one that gets us to the destination with some combination of efficiency and enjoyment.

Sequencing. Conceptual clusters make up the route to our educational destination. Part of the preparation for teaching includes deciding how to sequence these clusters for optimal learning. *Analytic learners* prefer to move from foundational clusters (Why do I need to know this?), to conceptual (What do the terms mean?), to illustrative (How does all this work?), to functional (What can I do with this now?).[9] *Global learners* prefer to begin with problems and play with solutions (functional), defining terms (conceptual), and creating new examples (illustrative), until they discover the relevance to other course learnings and their own learning (foundational).[10]

Regardless of the sequence type you select, spend class time moving toward the destination. Avoid wandering aimlessly in irrelevant detail or unnecessary tangents. Effective telling involves explicit sequencing of conceptual clusters.

Explaining. Clearly explain terms. Create examples of what a concept "is" as well as good nonexamples of what it "is not." Note the following examples:

> *Agape* (love) means meeting the need of another. It is not the same as brotherly love *(phileo)* or sexual love (eros).

> Joy is a spiritual exuberance, a heavenly blessedness, that is produced by the Holy Spirit in a committed believer, regardless of external circumstances. It differs from the similar concepts of fun, or pleasure, or happiness, in that these are determined by life circumstances.

Periodically update examples to relate better with contemporary students. I have used the classic *Star Trek* characters to illustrate the cognitive (Spock), humanistic (McCoy), and behavioral (Scottie) domains of learning. Kirk reflected the balance and maturity of all three. (Just between you and me, I believe Gene Roddenberry, the creator of *Star Trek,* was a student of educational psychology, forming these characters out of the three learning theory systems.) Over the years *Star Trek* movies have kept the characters alive, and I always have ten or twelve students who are *Star Trek* fans. But more and more in recent years I've had to make a trip to the video store for one or two of the movies, a recreational requirement of the course so students unfamiliar with the characters understand the connection. The handwriting is on the wall: there will come a time when the Kirk-ian analogies will lose their meaning and potency, and I'll need to find new ones.

Organizing. Explicitly follow an organized order of concept clusters. Three common organizational structures are part-whole, sequential, and relevance. Use *part-whole organization* to reflect hierarchy, as in the example of "love" as *agape, phileo*, and *eros*.

The English word *love* is the larger, umbrella concept; the three Greek terms are smaller, distinctive parts of the whole. Statistical procedures can be broken down by research design (relationship between variables or difference between groups) and again by data type (nominal, ordinal, interval, and ratio). This is part-whole organization. I used part-whole organization in the discussion of sensitivity and its five descriptive elements in chapter 2.

Use *sequential organization* when the material is chronological, as in history or a specific process, or linked in cause and effect relationships ("if p, then q"). The missionary journeys of Paul could be organized sequentially around cities visited. The scientific method reflects a sequential organization pattern in its step-by-step approach to knowledge-getting.[11]

Use *relevance organization* to build concept clusters, which consist of a central criterion surrounded by positive and negative examples. If the criterion is "New Testament Church" as defined by Revelation 2–3, we might discuss concept clusters like perseverance and "first love" (Ephesus), faithfulness through persecution (Smyrna), loyalty and false teaching (Pergamum), faithful work and sexual immorality (Thyatira), worthy walking and spiritual deadness (Sardis), weakness and missionary activity (Philadelphia), and lukewarmness and self-centered sufficiency in size and wealth (Laodicia). The result of this study would be a clearer understanding of what the Lord praises and condemns in churches.

While a well-organized route minimizes frustration and maximizes enjoyment, too much organization stifles spontaneity. By emphasizing landmarks and allowing side trips, you increase flexibility without losing direction.

Landmarks: Marking Our Progress

As we travel to our vacation destination, we can tick off the landmarks as we experience them. Whether it's a quick stop at a historical marker or a three-hour walk through Colossal Caverns, the landmarks reflect our progress toward the destination. Educational landmarks include transition statements, reflective questions, and synthesis statements.

Transition Statements. These help students understand the divisions between concept clusters. Transitions expressly communicate the end of one cluster and the beginning of another. In *part-*

whole structures, transitions clearly delineate the meanings of individual parts: "So we've defined *phileo* as having tender affection for someone, as in 'brotherly love.' Now we turn our attention to another Greek term used for *love*—the word *agape.*"

In *sequential structures,* transitions delineate the separate steps in the sequence, or causes from effects: "In summary, we need to establish contact with our students and engage their interests before moving into the material for the day. The next step is to . . . ."

In *relevance structures,* transitions differentiate among several concept clusters related to the central criterion: "So Jesus' words to the church in Ephesus teach us . . . what?" (students respond correctly). "Exactly! Now let's look at the church in Smyrna. Who'll read Revelation 2:8–11?"

Reflective Questions. In this last example you find the second type of landmark. Reflective questions allow students to pause and consider key elements of a concept cluster before plunging headlong into the next. Questions slow the pace of delivery and shift emphasis from receiving-interpreting to reflecting-analyzing: "So Jesus' words to the church in Ephesus teach us . . . what?" (students respond). Answers to this question provide immediate feedback to the teacher concerning how well students comprehend the material. Discussion of student answers reinforces correct understanding. It says to students, "Let's be sure we understand this principle well before we move to the next."

Statements of Analysis or Synthesis. If time is a premium, teachers can emphasize key elements in a concept cluster by making statements of *analysis*[12] or *synthesis.*[13] Given the many words and concepts discussed in a given cluster, what essential meanings do we find? What truths can be drawn out of the verbiage? "So we see in the church at Laodecia that size and popularity, wealth and status, may not reflect the spiritual nature of a church. Religious power and spiritual maturity are two very different commodities."

Just as landmarks mark off the miles between home and our destination, so transitions, questions, and summaries mark off the progress we're making toward objectives—not only for those of us who teach, but, more importantly, for those who want to understand our teaching.

The Scenic Route: Enjoying the Journey

My dad understood one law of driving: get to the destination. Averaging fifty miles an hour, including pit stops and quick snacks, it was thirty hours from El Paso, Texas, to Hollandsburg, Indiana. One stop at a Stuckey's meant at least an hour of road time lost forever (and my mom wanted to stop at every Stuckey's we saw).

Dad never drove hard, but I've known some teachers who drive their classes hard. Move through the material. Cover the content. It is as if these teachers want to get the information out of their notebooks and into student notebooks as quickly as possible—regardless of whether or not it passes through the minds of either on the way.

But "covering content" is merely the beginning of good telling. There are elements of the heart that must be nurtured along the way if we are to get the whole person involved in our journey. These elements of the heart include warmth, trust, safety, acceptance, and openness—room to be oneself, express oneself, share oneself with others and vice versa. Don't leave these heart excursions to chance. Plan for them along the way. Model the role by sharing yourself appropriately—the struggles, questions, difficulties, discoveries you've made in your own journeys. This isn't sharing for sharing's sake alone, but real-life human drama that connects with the subject at hand. Let students know they are welcome to share experiences they've had as well. Then treat their personal experiences like the fine gems they really are. It won't take long before hearts open up and integration between subject and student really begins. The real danger then? It's controlling the sharing so that the content structure isn't lost.

Side Trips: Serendipities along the Way

There were times on family trips when we made unplanned stops. Usually these came because of a billboard or a notation on our road atlas. We put off—delayed—our final destination in order to enjoy some of the sights along the way. I loved these "discovery" times that centered in rattlesnakes or crocodiles or salt water taffy. And though it made the trip longer, these serendipities usually made it better. I say "usually" because I've found, in vacation trips as in classroom activities, every serendipity is not positive. Heading out on a spontaneous side trip is a risk. If it turns out badly, it is not only a disappointment but a waste of valuable travel time.

Yet this need for "surprise" is just as true for students riding along in our Greyhound of a classroom. As course content streams into their minds through ears and eyes, it triggers memories of experiences and teachers and friends. Questions ebb and flow in and out of consciousness: "How does this relate to . . . " or "That contradicts something my pastor once said . . ." or "This is all new to me—what does it all mean?" Wise teachers allow for their own telling to be interrupted by the questions, examples, experiences, and reinforcements that spring from student thought. Part of the dynamic of teaching is the serendipitous interplay among the players—content, experienced teacher, and curious students. The unplanned side trip may be a brief roadside break, such as a question or short anecdote, or it may be a longer trek into unknown territory, such as an extended discussion over controversial or problematic implications. Regardless, the occasional surprise infuses the telling with anticipation as students wonder just what might be over the next hill.

In Defense of the Lecture

The lecture is the most reviled method of teaching. Student discussions of methods in my teaching classes quickly degenerate into venting sessions about teachers who punished them by lecture: boring, monotonous, monotone, dry, predictable, detached, lifeless, and painful. But these complaints focus on poor telling, not telling itself. Even a Lexus or an Infinity will deliver a rough ride if one of its wheels is out of balance. Don't blame the car—fix the wheel.

Despite universal teeth gnashing, lecture remains the most prevalent and popular method. There are numerous reasons. If tellers have the platform skills of presence and presentation (see chap. 5), then no other method can so infuse the learning situation with heartfelt enthusiasm, mind-focused clarity, or living personality. Student attention is a given in these classes. If the teller is properly prepared (see chap. 6), instruction is more flexibly focused than in any other method. Emphasizing, rephrasing, explaining, and synthesizing occur in real time and can be custom-fit to the specific questions and difficulties of any student in the class.

If the teller establishes effective contact with the student-persons in the class, then the human needs of warmth, acceptance, humor, and personal worth can be met even as the telling journey unfolds.

If the teller possesses a high level of personal energy related to the subject being taught, and can communicate that energy to students, then telling can sustain student attention and motivate flexible, yet persistent, learning.

If the teller has organized a clear sequence of clusters in the lecture and can execute that sequence effectively, learning the essentials of a subject is more efficient. The preprocessing done by the teller during preparation—developing instructional objectives, advance organizers, and class notes—all focus on essential structure.

If we do it right, the enthusiasm and dynamic generated on the classroom journey provides psychological inertia for outside study and preparation for future sessions. If we do it right, the journey satisfies in a way that cannot be described. Insight. Contact. Community. Shared discovery.

The problem—the eternal, nagging problem—is getting it just right. Too much of the time we fail to get it "just right." Try as we might, the magic of "just right" eludes us more than we'd like. But worse—oh, so much worse—is missing the truth that there's a "just right" to get.

Dr. Stats missed it. "If then I do not grasp the meaning of what someone is saying, I am a foreigner to the speaker, and he is a foreigner to me" (1 Cor. 14:11). Effective tellers communicate as neighbors, not foreigners, to their students.

The Teacher as Facilitator

Another popular role for teachers is group facilitator. Some see "telling" as an autocratic, rigid, and controlling process. They see discussion as softer, more personal, more flexible, and less directive. And it is quite true that group discussion has solid advantages over the more structured "telling" approach. Sharing ideas and molding concepts through discussion helps students develop critical thinking skills. The give and take of ideas and perceptions among students develops democratic skills. Such interaction permits affective learning to happen more naturally than in the more structured "telling" approach.

But there are dangers as well. Low structure invites "going with the flow" of student comments. Open discussion is less efficient in conveying essential content. If the class is broken down into smaller groupings, the teacher relinquishes control to each group. Quality of learning is circumstantial and controlled by the level of maturity in each small group. Unless students *want* to engage each other seriously, small group learning can collapse into a "whadjadoo" session: "So, whadjadoo in your youth group last Sunday?" Remember Mr. Shoulow, the graduate teacher? He saw himself as a discussion facilitator. But there was no direction, no destination, for his class encounter exercise. Most students left frustrated, and little was accomplished because he had no destination.

The Destination

Facilitators must have a destination for group discussion beyond "What would you like to talk about today?" We described the importance of "the scenic route" and "side trips" earlier. These elements take on much more importance in discussions. But the destination is still important. Discussions without an academic destination is like Mom and Dad gathering the family in the car and, while sitting in the driveway, engaging in an hour of small talk. It might be nice, but they'll never get where they're going.

We've defined "destination" as the network of concept clusters—the common elements or essentials—that make up a subject. Group discussion heads toward this same destination but does so with greater flexibility than telling. Sharing one's attitudes and experiences has little academic value unless the sharing is tied to the subject at hand. When it is, personal sharing and participation carry the subject right into the hearts of students. So as part of destination preparation, choose discussion topics wisely. Are they controversial? Are they more cognitive or affective? Determine the common ground between the topics and the students' views. Arrange the classroom in a way that facilitates discussion—semicircle or circle rather than the rows. Essentials. Well-chosen topics. Common ground. Platform.

The Start

In my experience, many a class discussion fails simply because some students have faulty notions about discussion. "Discussion" for them means the teacher is unprepared to "teach." So what we're really doing is filling time. Letting students know something of the product expected, as well as the process to get there, makes for a good start.

Introduce the day's session by describing the destination. Explain guidelines for "good discussion." Pose a problem or ask a question. The question should be drawn from the common ground you established in planning—not too abstract or theoretical. This past semester I asked the following question in my educational psychology class: "So, as you read about Piaget's theory of cognitive development for class today, what implications did you discover for assimilation?" Blank stares. Some students began turning pages in the text looking for *assimilation*. Everyone averted their eyes. Silence. Disaster. They were not the problem. I was the problem—for asking such a question to begin discussion.

Far better would have been a question like this: "I defined *assimilation* as . . . and gave the example of the little boy calling a cow a 'horse.' Take a minute and jot down an instance or two relating encounters you've had with assimilation in your ministry or home (pause). Now then, what did you uncover?" Implications come later. Get students into the topic through the door of their own experiences. Furthermore, be sure to earn the right to ask students to share themselves by sharing yourself first.

The Route

Most of our family vacations have revolved around visiting relatives. Destinations are fixed, and there are only a few alternative routes. Then came our trip to Glorieta. I was teaching ten hours of conferences in each of three "Sunday school weeks" at the Southern Baptist conference center in Glorieta, New Mexico. Our family had a great time while there, but on the way back we decided to follow the wind. The kids had never seen Carlsbad Caverns, so we headed south through the New Mexican desert. We stopped to eat where we pleased. Chris, my then fifteen-year-old son, discovered Guadalupe Pass—the highest point in Texas—and so we headed off to see it. Though we were headed west, and our destination—home—was east, we were going right where we wanted to. After driving over Guadalupe Pass, we came to a fork in the road. To the south lay Van Horn, Texas, where we could pick up Interstate 20 and head home. Or we could continue west 140 miles to El Paso, Texas. I had not been back there since my parents and I left for New York City in November 1961, nearly thirty-five years before.

So off we went on another adventure. When we got to El Paso, I recognized major streets and—straining my memory—made my way to the house where I spent eight years of boyhood. The church where I surrendered to full-time Christian service still stood, but was now a Head-Start school. We found Clardy Fox Elementary as well as the Coliseum where I'd witnessed my first rodeo. There were the huge irrigation ditches and scenic drive and lookout point. Chris was amazed at this bustling city of 800,000 because he'd always imagined El Paso as a small dusty Western town, like he'd seen in the movies. We finally headed back toward home, stopping in Van Horn for a family swim and some of the best Mexican food we've ever had. We arrived at our destination, happy to be home—a day later than we'd planned, but richer for the experience.

Such is the "route" of group discussion. Unfixed. Spontaneous. Random. And yet always with the final destination in mind. The landmarks and side trips, so important to break the mile-by-mile monotony of telling, become the focus of the discussion journey. Any student is free to interject any thought, any memory, any question, any suggestion, any discovery at any time. Sure, it takes longer to get to the destination—the ultimate goal—but everyone is richer for the experience.

The facilitator's responsibility during discussions is to keep the class on track. Aimlessness and disorganization are prime ingredients of toxic discussion. You may choose from a wide range of participation and intervention—from none to dominant. Pose problems or ask questions when student participation lags. Insure that all views are heard. If students begin to digress too far into unrelated topics or experiences, intervene. Exaggerated responses? Mistakes in knowledge or understanding? Faulty reasoning? Intervene. Ask questions to get the class back on track.

Student responsibility during discussions is primarily to participate: to answer questions, pose problems, evaluate the answers of others, defend positions, share relevant experiences illustrating the concepts being discussed. Students are sometimes unwilling to participate for a variety of reasons. Previous bad classroom experiences may make group discussion a risky venture for them—too risky until you can establish a warm, trusting atmosphere in the class. (Remember Dr. Tender?) The risk also increases with class size—the level of participation usually declines in larger classes. Required courses present additional attitude problems to deal with. Students who mentally ride out the course in neutral are common enough—at least until you can establish some personal rapport and make the course meaningful to them. You will also find that students vary in degree of social skill, which may hinder participation. In a highly affective world, having one's ideas challenged and critiqued can hurt. Some seek the safety of silence and let others wage verbal battles. All of the above factors are enemies of good class discussion—enemies that must be overcome by the effective facilitator.

To the facilitators who succeed, there is great joy in watching students wrestle with issues and integrate the subject matter into their own thinking. On the wide screen of the classroom unfolds the drama of understanding and wisdom battling ignorance and misconception. The flashes of insight and bold discovery—acted out in real time and voiced out of the hearts and minds of the very ones we struggle to teach—make all the effort worth it.

Mr. Shoulow saw himself as a facilitator, encouraging students to open up to one another, to communicate with each other. But what had really been communicated? He was a facilitator without direction. Group discussion is more than a loose "rap session." It is more than group catharsis. It is a shepherd gathering his or her sheep and moving together toward greener pastures, each one learning from the others as they go. Mr. Shoulow was no shepherd. He was but one of the sheep, wandering around in search of a convenient patch of grass. It's no surprise that the flock lost their way.

The Teacher as Provocateur

Ms. Blunt interpreted her provocations in the classroom as being educational—causing her students to see things in a different light. However, her words and subsequent actions reflected a personal soapbox more than an academic agenda. Provocation can be positive or negative. The positive flavor—reflected in terms like *arouse, excite, kindle, prompt, activate, stimulate,* and *inspire*—energizes learning, motivates students, and creates a dynamic learning situation. The negative, toxic flavor—reflected in terms like *anger, inflame, irritate, rile, ruffle, goad, incite,* and *prod*—saps learning, offends students, and creates a passive, defensive learning situation.

Wise teachers use their power to help students, not to display themselves. They avoid the negatives and use positive provocation to enhance learning. Such provocation can be cognitive, affective, or behavioral.

Provoking the Mind

We all see things we have learned in specific and personal ways. Our mind-set acts as a filter for what we experience. When we experience something that doesn't seem to fit, we become anxious and uncomfortable. Jean Piaget called this uneasiness "disequilibrium." It can be likened to waves rocking a boat. Our response is to remove the anxiety—to calm the waves and steady the boat. Piaget believed that we do this through the push-pull processes of assimilation and accommodation.[14]

In assimilation we change the disturbing experience to fit our perception. A seminary student may label a professor's provocative, but correct, interpretation "liberal" or "fundamentalist" because it does not fit what he was taught back home. It is easier to reject the professor as "one of them" than to consider spiritual truth in a different way. A child sees a skunk and thinks it's a cat because it's the closest match she can make. Though these changes result in mistaken perception, they do remove anxiety and restore equilibrium between mind-set and experience. But of course this has little to do with learning.

Intentional learning[15] is associated with accommodation, in which either new perceptions[16] are formed or old ones updated. The seminary student accommodates the professor's explanation as a different way of understanding a Scripture passage (whether or not he agrees with it). The little girl creates a new scheme for "skunk" and can now, thankfully, differentiate between skunks and cats.

Provoke the minds of students by presenting explanations and illustrations that differ from the mind-sets of students. Student concepts are sometimes too narrow, too limited. Their perceptions are incomplete and need expanding. Take the example of a boy who sees a dachshund for the first time and calls it a "rat" because it's the closest match he can make. His concept of "dog" is not broad enough to include dachshunds. After this new experience is explained, his concept of "dogness" has been expanded. Learner concepts of biblical truths can be as narrow as their own personal experience with their family, church, and region. Good teachers expand these narrow concepts so they can include the whole counsel of God's Word, the full meaning of biblical terms and principles. Educators call this process of expanding concepts that are too narrow *generalization*.

Student concepts can also be too broad, too inclusive. The boy we mentioned above might see a miniature horse, full grown at eighteen inches, and mistake it for a dog. He is now including elements in his concept of "dogness" that do not belong. After this new experience has been explained, he has a narrowed concept of "dog" and a new concept of "miniature horse." Learner concepts of biblical truths can also be overly broad. Good teachers help learners narrow their concepts to what the Bible actually teaches. Educators call this process of narrowing a concept *discrimination*.

Explanations and illustrations serve the dual purpose of broadening the narrow-minded and narrowing the broad-minded. How do we do this? First, ask questions to determine student perceptions and ideas. Then choose explanations and illustrations appropriately—not too different and not too close—for the purpose of expanding or contracting learner concepts. You must use illustrations that differ enough to arouse, but not so much as to anger; to inspire but not to irritate; to excite but not to incite; to prompt but not to prod; to stimulate but not to stampede. Piaget called this range of difference "optimal discrepancy." Provoke, but not too much.

Oh, I hear some of you: "Why not incite them? I lay it out there for my students. If it offends some of them, that's *their* problem, not mine." The reason is this: toxic provocation robs us of the opportunities to really teach—to get inside the hearts and minds of our students and help them really "see" what we're explaining. Ms. Blunt may have gotten her "non-human-gender" view of God over to a few of her students, but she made others of her class angry enough to complain to the dean's office. This is not teaching. It is browbeating. We should not engage students-as-we-wish-them-to-be, but students-as-they-are.

I was teaching a group of deaf adults one evening. We were studying the early ministry of Jesus. I asked them if Jesus had ever sinned. No, they all replied. They all knew Jesus had lived a sinless life. "Was Jesus ever tempted?" I continued. No, they all replied. Jesus had never been tempted. Then we read the Matthew account of the temptations of Jesus in the wilderness. They read the verses with wide eyes. "So, was Jesus tempted?" Yes, they all replied. "Then, did Jesus sin?" Yes! They all replied—with a mixture of discovery and fear. *Well, if Jesus sinned, then his death on the cross was for his own sins. He could not pay the penalty for ours.* Their boats were rocking.

What was their problem? It was confusion between the concepts of "temptation" and "sin." For those ten deaf adults, "to be tempted" and "to sin" was the same thing. This is dangerous confusion, because once tempted to do something wrong, we have no reason to restrain the wrongdoing if we believe we are already guilty. Jesus was tempted to sin—here and many other times during his life—but did not sin. All of us are tempted. But we choose whether or not to sin, rebel, transgress. We spent most of our study time that evening illustrating the distinction between temptation and sin. Disequilibrium. New or modified schemes. Equilibration with new understanding. That Bible study strengthened those deaf believers because it separated the uncontrollable (temptation) from the controllable (sin) in their lives. It moved them away from futility toward responsibility. They had been mentally provoked.

Provoking the Heart

Education has a way of producing dry bones and calloused hearts. Teaching by mass production—class goals, teacher expectations, required texts, arbitrary test questions—can leave individual students feeling alone and hurting. Jesus chose twelve to be with him, and in that "withness" Jesus taught. At the end of their three years together, he told them, "I shall not call you servants any longer, for a servant does not share his master's confidence. No, I call you friends, now, because I have told you everything that I have heard from the Father" (John 15:15 Phillips). Jesus had provoked the hearts of fishermen and tax collectors. And most of them would die from the provocation to own their Teacher as Lord, die as a result of provoking others to faith in his name.

It is so hard to create "withness"[17] in the Sunday school classroom. Routine religious ritual sets in so easily. Members gather and pray and sing and study, Sunday by Sunday, month after month, year upon year until one can travel through the whole process without ever really touching anyone, or being touched by the realities of life. We can discuss verses, clarify concepts and principles, and produce "practical" applications—all without ever reaching down to where we actually live.

It is hard to create "withness" in the Christian college classroom. Many colleges have difficulty keeping class ratios small enough to permit meaningful interpersonal interaction between teachers and students. Class bells, course overloads, extracurricular activities (like working to feed the family), as well as "course content to be covered" pull us away from each other and build walls of separation.

What can we do to provoke the heart, to move beyond mere information and touch our learners personally, even in the process of teaching our subject matter? How do we get beyond the defensive walls built up over the years by toxic teaching experiences? How do we help our students to really *care* about what we're teaching?

First, we must root out any attitudes or teaching practices that have toxic effects on students. Toxic teaching destroys any sense of "withness" and kills the heart. The following comments were made by Christian teachers as they taught. In every case they wounded students. Worst of all, there was no educational or spiritual reason for the statements. First, in college classrooms:

- "That is the dumbest question I've ever heard."

- "If you people would work, you'd get this stuff!"

- "You earned a 95 percent, but in my class that's a C."

- "So you didn't do your homework? Come to the board and do it in front of the class. Now!"

- "What should you study for the test? Simple—know it all."

In Sunday school classes I've heard such comments as these:

- "Oh, someone who *studied their lesson* answer the question!" (After one of the members answered incorrectly.)

- "If you all were committed to Bible study, you'd arrive on time."

- "Anyone who believes *that* can hardly be a Christian." (After a member expressed an opinion in response to a question.)

These teachers were angry, frustrated, defensive. Their concern in making these statements was self-protection, not student inclusion. "Withness" dies. Wounded hearts become hardened hearts as scar tissue builds a protective barrier. Let us commit ourselves to intentionally remove as much toxicity from our teaching as possible. "Rejoice with them that do rejoice, and weep with them that weep" (Rom. 12:15 KJV). Let us reject any behavior or attitude that humiliates or embarrasses students. Let us rather embrace attitudes and behaviors that nurture students, open students to themselves and others, remove scar tissue, and allow hearts to be shared. Such teachers are more helpful than judgmental, more humorous than somber. By caring about students as persons—Jim and Tom and Carol—we can penetrate layers of scar tissue and in time actually make contact in a meaningful way.

Second, focus on personal transparency before students. By being transparent and honest with our students—in an appropriate way—we invite them to risk openness too. We become real rather than pompous. I have found the most powerful path into students' hearts is to share personal failure-to-success stories that related to the topic at hand. I begin with an area of ministry or personal growth that has caused me to struggle. It is interesting how students grow more quiet and attentive as they relate their own experiences to what I'm describing. Then I move into choices I made and how those choices solved the problems I was facing. Sometimes students share their own stories, which convert cold principles to warm real-life examples, and draw us closer together. The "withness" of the moment lays the foundation for future risk, future sharing, and the continued growth of openness in the class.

Third, relate course content to the needs of students, both general and specific. Over the years my "major points" have shifted with the changing needs of students. I rewrite my syllabi nearly every year. I add content and remove content, add examples and remove examples. Some stories remain year after year because they touch common experiences and create a sense of "withness" despite changing student needs. What issues are my students wrestling with? What fears do they have now? What skills do they need for their ministry? Relevance in a class opens the heart and tells the student that "this teacher cares about *my learning* more than his or her *lecture notes*."

Provoke the heart. "Bind mercy, as well as truth, around your neck, and you will grow in favor with the Father as well as your students" (see Prov. 3:3). Years ago in one of my Principles of Teaching classes, a student shared in class why he was in seminary training for ministry with youth. He said that a friend of his had invited him to Sunday school. He didn't care about going, but went because his friend invited him. Their teacher was a young lady who demonstrated on that Sunday and in the days that followed that she really cared about the teens in her class. This young teen was drawn to her because of her love for them. Then he said he discovered that the reason she was like that was because of her faith in the Bible. She taught the Bible with conviction, with application, and by example in her own life. Later, he discovered that it was not so much the Bible that made the difference, but her personal relationship with Jesus Christ—he made the difference. And so he gave his life to the Lord. He summarized his testimony by saying, "First I loved my teacher. Then I loved my teacher's Bible. Then I loved my teacher's Lord. And here I am. I want to be that kind of youth minister and help others find the joy I found." That unknown Sunday school teacher provoked his heart toward the written Word, and further, to the Living Word. There is no telling what impact her life will have on others as at least one of her students carries the "withness" he found to them.

Provoking to Action

Sir Isaac Newton's second law of motion says that "a body at rest will remain at rest, or a body in motion will remain in motion, unless acted on by some outside force." Bodies at rest. There they sit in your class. Minds on autopilot. Faces reflecting a so-what-else-is-new expression of boredom. They've heard it before. They're putting in their time, as if learning were some kind of prison sentence. They hesitate to answer questions and usually respond with a blasé "I dunno." Rarely do they ask a question.

Bodies in motion. They gather with excitement. A rumbling buzz fills the room as multiple conversations compete to be heard. Lots of activity. An overabundance of agenda items to be completed and checked off. Personal agendas driven by personal values and needs.

In the first case, the will to act, to participate, to put into practice has been snuffed. In the second, the will to act and participate needs to be redirected.

Just do it! We've already suggested two approaches that help learners put their learning into practice. First, provoke the mind! Help learners understand how to apply what they've learned. Help them build bridges from the classroom to where these concepts are lived out in real time.

Second, provoke the heart! Help learners develop a sense of personal connectedness to the truths you've taught. Touch student experiences in some way as you teach. Such personal connectedness channels learnings naturally into action.

Third, engage students directly by making assignments to be done between sessions. Be sure to use assignments in class and demonstrate how students can apply their studies in practical ways. Laboratory work, teacher demonstrations, and practical projects all engage students in meaningful action.

Keep in mind, however, that provoking student action is mere busyness unless they do quality work. Good teachers demand excellence from their students, and then provide the means to achieve that excellence. I see this process worked out every semester in my Principles of Teaching class when we tackle the task of writing instructional objectives. First I explain, using a "living chalkboard,"[18] each of Bloom and Krathwohl's eleven levels of learning.[19] I distribute a detailed handout that reviews the levels and illustrates how to develop instructional objectives to target each of these levels. The assignment for the next class session is to read over the handout and bring questions to class. The second hour I discuss the examples in the handout and answer questions. I caution against the most common mistakes students make in writing objectives—wrong format, incorrect behaviors, misused terminology, and failure to target learning outcomes. "Any questions?" Rarely do they have any. They seem to have a good grasp of the material and its use.

Their assignment for the third hour is to actually write five objectives. At the beginning of class, student volunteers write one of their objectives on the board. I ask for four examples of each of the five assigned objectives—so twenty students place their work on the board. We spend the hour comparing "what they actually wrote" with guidelines they'd already "learned." Few of the statements reflect the guidelines. *Common* mistakes—those I carefully cautioned them against making—*commonly* show up. I ask the students to evaluate each statement first. As I point out mistakes they've overlooked, I hear gasps and sighs and "So *that's* what you meant!" Obviously my students had not understood how to write objectives. They *thought* they did. They *felt good* about their work. I even gave them an assignment so they would put their learning into practice. But it was not until they confronted the work of their own hands in light of the guidelines that they broke through their dusky familiarity to the bright light of real understanding: "Oh, so *that's* what you meant!" I then let them carry their broken pieces of objectives home to be revised and resubmitted. Then I grade them. That is provoking to higher standards!

Interesting, isn't it? By provoking students' minds, hearts, and actions toward course goals, you jump-start stalled learners into focused action and help overactive learners funnel their energy into productive behaviors.

Dr. John Drakeford[20] would often say to his psychology students, "We can't feel our way into a new way of acting. But we can act our way into a new way of feeling." Provoking learners to make use of the material produces Christian action, but it also clarifies their thinking and enhances their appreciation for the material.

Ms. Blunt provoked her students to anger, thus closing, not opening, their minds. She thought she was helping them learn. She did just the opposite. Let us weigh carefully how we provoke our learners, doing so with clear concepts, with positive experiences, and with meaningful hands-on applications. Then our provocations will help clearly communicate our subject.

The Teacher as Instructional Technician

Dr. Computer's multimedia blitz was up-to-date and visually stimulating, but it missed the mark of meaningful communication. He made the mistake of substituting the medium for the message.

The result was a static, rigid, canned, predictable classroom. He thought he was providing a rich resource of examples of high-tech instructional support, but the high-tech examples were all he had. Hidden behind his "Power Console," he was unable to establish meaningful contact with his students.

Low-Tech

Improper use of instructional aids need not be as complicated as Dr. Computer's situation. Two of the most common problems in classroom teaching aids—low-tech and inexpensive—are poor use of a chalk- or markerboard and poorly designed overhead cels.

One day I walked into the classroom to find, scrawled across both slabs of green slate at the front of the room, a detailed outline of the day's lecture. I groaned all the way to my seat. Step by step, line by line, the teacher walked us through the painful outline. No sense of surprise. No side trips or serendipities. It was like counting telephone poles across miles of flat plains. Avoid static diagrams and outlines. Rather, create a "living chalkboard" that grows, develops, and changes throughout your presentation.

Instead of putting bulky lists or lecture outlines on the board before class, use a question or a problem to set the direction for the class. Start with a clean board.[21] Draw and label diagrams as you present material. Write key terms as you discuss them. Write related terms in clusters around the keys. Let the visual unfold on the board as you talk. This, obviously, illustrates your verbal explanations visually. It also slows your rate of presentation, which helps students process the material. Practice writing and drawing on chalk- and markerboards so that your visuals are clean, clear, and attractive. This approach to the chalk- or markerboard enhances comprehension without destroying curiosity.

Poor use of overhead cels is also a common problem. I once attended a seminar on "Use of the Computer in the Classroom." I was amused when the presenter cued his first visual. It was the projected image of a full page of 10-point type, in paragraph form. To those of us sitting twenty feet away, it had the appearance of purple fuzz. Here was a double dose of poor design: a bad fifty-cent overhead cel projected with $10,000 worth of computer and projector.

Overhead cels are notorious for being poorly designed, whether or not they are projected by computer. In an attempt to save money,

I suppose, we put ten cels' worth of information on one. Or we make a cel from a sheet of typewritten information to save xeroxing costs. We save a few dollars but create an overhead cel that is at best educationally useless, and at worst harmful. Placing five or six sub-points on a single cel reduces the type size, making the cel harder to read from the back of a classroom, thereby inviting the same boredom one achieves with a list of items on a chalkboard.

High-Tech

New presentation computer software packages[22] have design elements built into templates, making it difficult to render a poor design. When my daughter turned eighteen, she produced, on her own, a stunning computer presentation designed with color graphics, moving type, and arresting sounds to convince my wife and me to buy her a car. We didn't buy the car immediately, but we thought about it a lot. And when we did purchase her first car, we both remembered Bonnie's presentation.

With various types of "wizards" and "helpers," teachers can produce good computer presentations with little trouble. But beware: programs offer a wide range of bewildering options—3-D type, animations, video, and sound—that confront us with steep learning curves. Last year I spent a month of spare time developing a 3-D animation for a promotional piece for this book. I rendered 300 frames of 800 x 600 full-color animation, complete with lightning and thunder. It was a month of learning how to create type, apply textures, set lights, and position the "camera track" for the dramatic opening. Twelve hours of computer time went into the final rendering for a video that takes fifteen seconds to show on screen. Combining sound, pictures, fades, colors, videos, and animations together in a smooth multimedia presentation requires skill, time, and computing power. Still, the emotional impact of well-designed presentations can take communication beyond clarity to electricity. Multimedia has taken education by storm, but care must be taken to avoid the dead-end of Dr. Computer.

The Target: Clear Communication

Good instructional aids enhance the presentation of essential content. When aids draw too much attention to themselves, however, they lose their usefulness. To the extent they increase the power and economy of a presentation or demonstration, they are helpful. *Power* refers to the focus of a presentation—its ability to convey central concepts in a straightforward manner. *Economy* refers to the efficiency of the presentation, which implies less detail, fewer nonessential facts. Instructional aids should clarify the content by emphasizing its structure—whether you've chosen part-whole relationships, sequence, or relevance ties.

Instructional aids should have *excellent visual quality*. Better to have fewer high-quality aids than many poor-quality aids. Plan and practice "living" chalkboard diagrams. Study books on overhead cel design or use state-of-the-art software to produce slides or presentations that convey information effectively and efficiently. Insure that instructional aids are appropriately configured—font, size, color, content—for the size of the classroom.

Instructional aids should *inject energy* into presentations rather than sap energy from them. A static chalkboard is dull. An overhead cel written in 12-point Courier type is boring. A "cutesy" slide show is tedious. Instead, use aids to punctuate verbal explanations with visual energy.

Instructional aids should *present material simply*. Use decorative fonts and graphics with caution. Some overhead cels and class handouts I've seen look as if they were composed by a kidnapper: two many fonts and too many styles. As I write this, the Internet is exploding with web pages sporting multicolored icons and animated graphics. The cry is building: "Lean is clean!" Keep it simple. Give us information without cutesy images that burn valuable on-line time. The same is true of instructional aids.

Computer-generated presentations are fun to produce. Yet, "computer fun" can rapidly turn productive teachers into inefficient hackers. Overuse of graphic effects can make illustrations more bizarre than effective. What's more, in combination, fun and effects can consume hours of precious preparation time. Better to have a few focused visual aids and rich lecture/discussion material than many detailed visuals that say all you know. The former enhances the human being as teacher; the latter relegates the teacher to a mechanical cel-shifter.

Instructional aids require balance between their helpfulness in presentations and the time required to generate them. Dr. Wes Black, a teaching colleague of mine,[23] generates short presentations with his laptop computer. He uses them at the beginning of class to create learning readiness for other class activities—and does so with flair and pizzaz!

Be sure to surround instructional technology, regardless of its form, with human warmth. Share yourself with students. Display personal enthusiasm for the subject. Reflect your confidence that the content is more than "lesson"—that it will make a positive, personal impact on learners who embrace it. Dr. Computer failed to humanize his technology, and the result was a dead learning environment.

In Conclusion

Teacher as teller, as facilitator, as provocateur, as instructional technician—all for one goal, which is nothing less than transforming dark, foreboding subjects into life-changing bright light experiences for our students. I can see those lights in their eyes when it happens. I hunger for those lights. It is worth all the hours of preparation, all the grading and committee meetings, all the failed attempts to teach. There is nothing like it in the world, and it comes only to those who teach with clarity, who communicate mind and heart and soul, who make meaningful contact with those who desire to learn. "I have meat to eat that ye know not of," Jesus said to his disciples (John 4:32 KJV). I hunger for the eye-light of understanding in my students—and when it comes, oh, when it comes, it satisfies like nothing else I've known in teaching.

How do we motivate learners to pierce the darkness of confusion with the light of understanding? Energizing student learning is the subject of the next chapter.

Chapter 4

The Teacher as Motivator

By faith Moses, when he had grown up,
refused to be known as the son of Pharaoh's daughter.
He chose to be mistreated along with the people of God
rather than to enjoy the pleasures of sin for a short time.
He regarded disgrace for the sake of Christ
as of greater value than the treasures of Egypt,
because he was looking ahead to his reward.

Hebrews 11:24–26

*S*teve sat in the back corner of the Sunday school classroom, his face staring holes into the white wall beside him. His body language communicated his rage, even as he sat in total silence. He did not want to be here, except for the hand that gently held his. The hand belonged to his newfound girlfriend, and she insisted that—if he really wanted to be her boyfriend—he would attend

Sunday school and church. So he sat in the back of the room, cut off aurally from the rest of us by his deafness and visually by his preference for a blank wall.

Week by week he came. Sitting in the same seat. Staring at the same wall. Holding the same hand. He wanted nothing to do with me, or my studies, or my teaching. Attempts to build a bridge to him before and after class were quickly or abruptly blocked.

Other guys in the class, all students at Gallaudet College—a four-year liberal arts college for the deaf in Washington D.C.—made their attempts, with a little more success. Week by week, they invited him to activities, greeted him on campus, befriended him. He was an angry young man, and friends—other than Brenda—were of no interest to him. He certainly wasn't interested in any kind of meaningful Bible study, thank you. He was there because Brenda required it. But he didn't have to listen and he didn't have to learn.

Conveying content *to* a student is one thing. Stimulating desire to learn *in* a student is quite another. In the previous chapter we focused on communicating content—telling, facilitating, provoking, and presenting. Such matters center in "teaching's *what*." Now we turn our attention to stimulating student interest to learn, a matter of the "learning's *why*." Let's look at teachers as shapers, models, "curiousiteurs," friends, and success agents.

The Teacher as Shaper

The term *shaper* comes out of the work of behavioral learning theorists like E. L. Thorndike and B. F. Skinner.[1] Teachers shape the behaviors of their students as they teach—for better or for worse. Good teachers intentionally shape positive behaviors that produce learning, growth, and success. Poor teachers unintentionally shape behaviors that produce confusion, stagnation, and failure.

Dr. Leroy Ford[2] began our first class by handing us a syllabus—four pages of "shaping" information. Assignments, due dates, projects, quizzes, and major examinations were listed and explained. The entire course was laid out. Unlike other classes I'd had, there were no pop quizzes, no surprise examinations, no last-minute research paper assignments. Everyone knew from day one where we were going and what was expected.

Ford included "practice cycles" in each unit to insure we could correctly use what we were learning. These practice cycles helped us convert what we read and heard into practical skills. I quickly learned the difference between *recalling* Ford's definition of "instructional objective" and *writing* one! Or the difference between *defining* "learning readiness" and *developing* one for a specific situation. While other teachers assumed we could properly apply what we were hearing and reading, Ford integrated activities into class sessions that demonstrated our ability (or lack of ability) to use what we were learning.

While Ford's structure of course and session was rather cold and mechanical, he himself was not. His gentle manner, easy smile, helpful suggestions, clear explanations, and warm congratulations softened the journey. The cooperative[3] nature of group activities helped us teach and shape each other in an atmosphere of team-work. Ford was not a distant enigma to be figured out, but a close advisor who showed us the way. Every day, moment by moment, he shaped us toward the essential concepts, values, and skills of the course.

Elements of Shaping

The technical term for shaping is *behavior modification*, which refers to adjusting behaviors of others through direct reinforce-ment. Interest in direct reinforcement strategies, popular in the 1960s, has long since declined. Yet teachers continue to shape student behaviors by the way they conduct their classes. Let's look at the damaging effects of punishment, the limited effects of direct reinforcement, and the liberating effects of teacher praise.

The Damaging Effects of Punishment. Teachers punish students in a wide variety of ways. Specific examples have already been given in this text: verbal abuse, irritation at questions and frus-tration from unclear instructions, arbitrary grading practices, sur-prise assignments, and waste of class time are just a few we've mentioned. The anger and hostility of students are the predictable result of unintentional punishment. I say "unintentional" because I've known few teachers who intentionally meant to hurt students, who intentionally used their position as teacher to wield power for power's sake, who intentionally humiliated or embarrassed stu-dents. But all of these things happen in classrooms every day,

"Christian" or not. The antidote is to intentionally avoid behaviors and attitudes that punish students. What kinds of behaviors and attitudes am I talking about? I asked some of my colleagues to share experiences they'd had that they deemed "punishment"—that is, behaviors or attitudes that hurt them, that hindered their learning, that demotivated them in a class. Here's what they said:

- During the second week of class, my freshman composition instructor stripped the names from our first written assignment—a three-hundred-word theme on any topic—and handed out photocopies to the class as examples of good/bad writing. My paper was handed out as the "bad example" and the professor spent at least twenty minutes pointing out the "terrible" sentences and literally ranted about how horrible the writing was.

- I recall "failing" trigonometry in high school after making 100 percent on all the exams! The teacher explained that I had shown "a questioning attitude" and had "repeatedly asked questions in class."

- My American Literature professor called me in to grill me on how I wrote my first essay. He said it was "unusually good" for a freshman topic and execution. After an hour of grilling, he was convinced that the work was mine, and then he gave me my grade—B-minus!

- I had an algebra teacher who ranted and raved like a madman for more than thirty minutes about how annoyed he was that four of us, out of a class of thirty, had passed the first exam. He was outraged, he said, because usually no one passed his first exam.

- An anthropology professor once told me that my writing was much too "literary." Academic writing should not be clear and easily understandable, he said; people might not take me seriously. I should learn to be as obscure and jargon-laden as possible. And I'm sure that he wasn't kidding; his own writing was absolutely impossible to understand.

- Dr. F routinely chose students to go to the board and work problems. Rather than helping them past their sticking points or soliciting help from other students, he would completely humiliate the student if he or she could not complete the problem.

- At a Christian conference, the group leader ignored my questions and kept talking. This didn't happen just once, but several times throughout the conference. I felt humiliated.

- My preaching professor totally shot down my first sermon outline. My approach was wrong, my exegesis incorrect. But he never explained why, or how, I might improve. I never preached in preaching lab again.

- My pastor, who led our Bible study, told me my thinking was all wrong and his thinking was right "because he is the pastor." Many people in our church were hurt by his autocratic control.

- One of my professors arrived late for class. Because time was short, he stopped a group's class presentation in midstride. Then he blasted the group in front of the entire class for not finishing.

- When I was twenty-one I was in a young adult Bible study class. My thirty-year-old teacher did not like my questioning of one of her explanations. "No, no, no! I don't want to hear it!" she yelled as she shook her finger in my face. I was embarrassed and infuriated.

Avoid Punishing Your Students. B. F. Skinner studied the ability of rats to learn how to run through a maze under two conditions: electric shock (presentation punishment) and food at the end of the maze (positive reinforcement). The electric shock promoted faster learning, but they also learned to fear the maze. Food took longer, but produced no negative side effects. The movie *Full Metal Jacket* includes a subplot in which Marine basic training, designed to build strong attack infantry, breaks a recruit, who then commits suicide. Too much punishment can do as much to psychologically break weaker students as it does to motivate stronger students. At the very least, students should leave our classes more interested in our subject than when they came in. Punishment is an academic shortcut that does more damage than good.

When I use the term *punishment* in this context, I am not in any way condemning academic consequences, even if this fits Skinner's definition of punishment: "giving what one does not want." Docking a student's grade for lateness or failure to follow instructions or submission of poor work is honest feedback to him or her and justice to the rest of the class. Such academic consequences help focus attention on established guidelines. To let late assignments slide or to give full credit for mediocre work is dishonest and will, in the long run, lower motivation. But to humiliate students for lateness, to demean their character, to embarrass them in front of the class, or to write personally derogatory messages on their papers—this is gratuitous punishment, arbitrary power, and demotivates the very ones who need our help to succeed.

Since God is our Model Teacher, we might want to look at how he deals with wrong behavior.[4] The writer of Hebrews records, "And you have forgotten that word of encouragement that addresses you as sons: 'My son, do not make light of the Lord's discipline, and do not lose heart when he rebukes you, because the Lord disciplines those he loves, and he punishes everyone he accepts as a son.' Endure hardship as discipline; God is treating you as sons. For what son is not disciplined by his father? If you are not disciplined (and everyone undergoes discipline), then you are illegitimate children and not true sons" (Heb. 12:5–8).

We see three levels in God's reaction to his beloved children's wrong behavior: discipline, rebuke, and punishment. The term *discipline* (NIV, NAS) or *chastening* (NKJV) refers to corrective instruction, tutorage, education, or training. God explains, teaches, and corrects verbally. The term *rebuke* (NIV, NKJV) or *reprove* (NAS) refers to admonishing, convicting, or convincing of wrong. The term *punish* (NIV) or *scourge* (NKJV, NAS) refers to flogging or whipping literally or figuratively.

What is God's intent in these levels of correction? "God disciplines us for our good, that we may share in his holiness. No discipline seems pleasant at the time, but painful. Later on, however, it produces a harvest of righteousness and peace for those who have been trained by it" (Heb. 12:10b–11).

In the classroom we will operate on the first level most often: explaining, correcting, training. At times we may have to call a student in for a conference to discuss his or her problems in the class. Once circumstances have been weighed and student wrongdoing established, we may need to move to level two: admonishing or convicting. In extreme cases, we may have to move to level three and speak strongly and pointedly to a student who is behaving in self-destructive ways. (See chapter 7.)

76

It is essential always to remember God's motivation for discipline is not His anger but His love. It is not the arbitrary demonstration of God's power, but the extreme need of the one gone astray— ". . . for our good, a harvest of righteousness and peace." It is love that motivates God's discipline; it should be love for our students that motivates ours. Eli failed to teach, to correct, to admonish, to discipline Hophni and Phineas, his sons. And though they were priests before God, they lived and died tragically (see 1 Sam. 1–4).

Read over the list of student responses prayerfully. Do you reflect any of these behaviors or attitudes in the way you teach? Prayerfully consider what adjustments you may need to make to discipline your students without quenching their spirit to learn.

The Limited Effects of Direct Reinforcement. Direct reinforcement strategies were most popular in the 1960s. Educational theory and practice have moved away from excessive use of behavior-shaping strategies for several reasons. First, direct reinforcement decreases intrinsic motivation in students.[5] Providing rewards to students already interested in a subject actually decreases interest. Students given rewards for correct solutions to problems subsequently chose less difficult problems than students who received no rewards at all. When rewards are given simply for completing an assignment, rather than meeting performance standards, motivation suffers.

Second, direct reinforcement narrows student focus in the learning process. Meaningful class discussions are short-circuited by questions such as "Will this be on the test?" and "Do we need to know all this?" Learning itself is reduced to memorizing essentials for tests. Rewards gained through "passing a test" become more important than learning itself.

Third, the management problems associated with selecting, using, and tracking reinforcers for each student can become tedious and time-consuming. Most teachers prefer interacting with students instead of administrating reinforcement schedules.

Fourth, and most important, is that direct reinforcement ignores the perceptions and beliefs of students—vital aspects of learning— in favor of specific behaviors.

While behavior shaping is important, particularly in specific instances of learning difficulties (such as low intrinsic motivation, lack of interest, lack of required skills, or limited general experience), the use of direct reinforcement is limited in its general effectiveness in the classroom. There is one major exception: teacher praise.

The Liberating Effects of Teacher Praise. The most effective reinforcer in education is the praise of a teacher. "Praise" means more than objective feedback on performance. It includes positive feedback on the student's personal worth, which, in itself, is a powerful motivator.[6]

Praising students effectively is a complex skill. Praise should be contingent on specific tasks[7] because random or indiscriminate praise is ineffective.[8] Praise should be given in moderation because too little is ineffective and too much is meaningless.[9] Praise should be perceived as credible, believable, and sincere. Praise should provide informative feedback and not simply be warm and fuzzy positive reactions. Praise should focus on student performance and not teacher perceptions.[10] Praise should be given for student performance and not mere participation.[11] Praise should be individual— that is, not given to everyone all the time.[12] Use prior performances as a benchmark for a student's improvement rather than the performance of peers.[13]

Complex reinforcement schedules and token economies popularized in the 1960s have given way to other approaches to motivation. Teacher praise, however, remains a powerful reinforcer. What other behavioral suggestions remain effective for shaping student success?

Suggestions for Using Shaping Principles. By clearly explaining course requirements and expectations, you set up specific targets for students to hit. Using frequent, consistent, specific, and immediate reinforcement will direct students toward achieving course skills.[14] Praising student achievements appropriately increases their level of effort.[15] Encouraging student efforts for completing course tasks increases their expectation of success.[16] By engaging student attention on specific course tasks and providing successful class experiences through the semester, not only will many of your students master the required skills, but they will also develop positive feelings about you, the subject, and themselves.

Be sure to focus on student actions, not personal qualities. A common problem with teacher praise is that it goes to the "best students"[17] rather than to the best answers.[18] Remember, too, that direct reinforcement is most effective in motivating behavior in disadvantaged learners and students who are not intrinsically interested in the subject.

Dangers of Shaping

What is the difference between behavioral shaping and manipulation? Direct reinforcement and bribery? Reward and payoff? The difference lies in the teacher's motivation for using these techniques. Am I using a behavioral approach in order to help students learn better, or am I merely shaping them to my own demands? Teaching involves beliefs and rational thought and is more than conditioning, which focuses only on performance.[19] The rational processes of students must be engaged. Behavior changes must have student cooperation.[20] The goal must be the progress of the student, not the power of the teacher.

Too much emphasis on behavioral outcomes can lead to learning that feels confined, predictable, and mechanical. Soften the assembly line model with some well-planned, relevant spontaneity. In the midst of a multisession unit on essential principles of teaching, I spend a class hour teaching the first verse of the hymn "I Surrender All" in American Sign Language. It takes about fifteen minutes to teach students the signs. Then I share an experience of personal surrender to the Lord, and invite them to do the same. Most do not realize I'm "doing a demonstration" on affective teaching. We conclude by signing (singing) "I Surrender All," closing with a prayer of surrender, and leaving in silence. It is always a deeply moving time of sharing what the Lord has done in our lives. I find this much more effective than spending the class time drilling them over ten principles of affective teaching.

One other danger sometimes associated with overuse of behavioral methods is its lack of challenge. When I completed Dr. Ford's class, I *felt* that I had not learned much, because each step along the way had been a small, incremental one. I hadn't felt challenged! In some of my other classes, I was challenged out of my mind—and earning an A was quite an accomplishment. Dr. Ford had helped me master the course—I had learned a great deal—without pain. Still, there was part of me that missed the pain. Part of the explanation for this reaction has already been stated: Direct reinforcement is effective in motivating behavior in disadvantaged learners as well as in students who are not intrinsically interested in the subject at hand. I was not a disadvantaged learner, and I was intrinsically motivated. Other, more cognitive, approaches revved my academic engine. But there is no doubt that Dr. Ford shaped me for the better during that semester, and continues to shape me today through conversations, letters, and occasional articles he sends me.

The Teacher as Social Model

The term *social model* derives from the work of Albert Bandura in observational learning.[21] Building on the behavioral ideas of Thorndike and Skinner, Bandura extended his theory beyond direct reinforcement to *vicarious reinforcement:* we often behave as we do because we (the observers) see someone we respect (the model) rewarded for their behavior. The strength of this vicarious reinforcement increases with the degree of respect an observer has for the model: child for parent, gang wannabe for gang leader,[22] student for teacher.

Rev. Neal Jones[23] was my pastor from 1970 to 1973, and my pastor-supervisor from 1976 to 1981. But far more than a pastor or boss, he played Paul to my Timothy. He was a mentor and role model. Though I am not a pastor, he modeled ministry excellence in his preaching, his love for people, and his ability to resolve conflicts. For three years, as volunteer director of deaf program services at Columbia, I observed him in the pulpit, in church council meetings, and in small group planning meetings. While I was a rather blunt, hard-hitting, get-the-job-done type of person, "Mr." (a Virginia title of respect) Jones was a gracious, soft-spoken, people person. Relationships were more important than task efficiency. The living organism of church life was more important than an organization chart. The spiritual substance of our ministry programs were more important to him than the specific form they took. His focus was on others, not himself. His sermons were practical but not shallow, profound but not academic, relevant but not sensationalistic. I observed his ministry for three years, which culminated in my decision in 1973 to attend seminary and enter vocational ministry myself.

In late 1976 the door opened for me to return to Columbia Baptist as minister of education. Stepping out of seminary studies into leadership of an educational program of nearly a thousand is a big step. But it also allowed me to observe Rev. Jones much more closely and in many more settings. I suppose his leadership in staff meetings was my greatest source of observational learning. There were endless discussions on programs and budgets and schedules and conflicts and visions. We had a variety of personality dynamics on the staff: quiet and timid, thoughtful and questioning, confrontive, happy-go-lucky, and sometimes confused. He worked with all of us to build a team, a family, a cohesive whole. Much of the skill I have today in resolving conflicts in classes and faculty discussions I learned watching him. He remains my model for ministry, though he has retired from full-time pastoring. I have not worked with him in eighteen years, nor have I seen him in twelve, but I still find myself asking, "What would Neal do in this situation?" He was my teacher, my model, demonstrating in real-world terms how to minister.

Elements of Modeling

What, then, are the specific implications for teaching that flow out of Bandura's work? Let's look at improving our status with students, modeling preferred attitudes and skills, and using guest speakers as models to be imitated.

Improving Status with Students. For observational learning to occur, an observer must attend to, focus on, a model's behavior. Essential to this attention is the perceived superiority of the model. As teachers, experts in the course's subject, we have such a superior position—at least until we dismantle it with toxic teaching. If students have a choice in their courses, why do they take ours? Why do they take us as professors? Or attend our Sunday School class? Or participate in our leadership training course? They see something in us, or in what we teach, that they want to learn. So we step into class the first day on high ground.

But we must build on this inherent position, or we'll quickly lose it. The previous chapter provides a rich resource for the triad of status-building or status-busting behaviors. Do we clearly present and explain course material, answer questions with clarity, use illustrations effectively, and communicate both meaning and relevance of the subject? Then our status will increase among thinkers. Do we handle questions and personal experiences with grace and acceptance, nurture students personally, show sincere interest in their points of view, welcome their questions, and empathize with their difficulties in learning our subject? Then our status with feelers will grow. Do we demonstrate skill in the way we handle the subject, practice what we teach as we teach it, and share experiences of mistakes we've made and how skills were developed? Then our status with doers will increase. Confusion, coldness, and inefficiency will quickly lower our status.

I'm writing this after having had breakfast with my dad this morning. After I shared with him some of these ideas, he told me of a student he once had in a training seminar: a Muslim. One day they began discussing, tentatively, the differences between American and Muslim culture. Early in the discussion my dad said, "There was once a time when Arab culture reached out and contributed to the world at large. The development of algebra and the use of the zero are two examples that come to mind. These inventions were revelations to the Western world. But then Arab nations turned inward and became isolated from the West, and so we know very little about you now." The Muslim looked intently into my dad's eyes and said, "You are an educated man." A new friendship, as well as an effective teaching/learning relationship, had begun. Dad's status jumped immediately in this Muslim's view because Dad knew and appreciated something from Arab culture. How well do you know your students? How willing are you to learn from them? How are you growing to include cultural distinctives in your own way of thinking? Your answers reveal the degree to which you can build status among a diverse student or congregational population.

Modeling Preferred Attitudes and Skills. When I use the term *modeling*, I do not mean putting on the day's lesson-fashion to parade before students. Our teaching lifestyle should not be a put-on conceived to strengthen the words we speak. Look at Jesus. He simply lived what he taught. What he taught flowed out of who he was. One day Jesus was praying. One of the disciples noticed something about Jesus' praying that intrigued him. So when Jesus had finished, the disciple asked to be taught on the subject (Luke 11:1–2). Educators call this kind of event a *teachable moment*. Creating a climate of teachable moments, particularly in a formal class setting, is difficult. But when they come, there is no greater impetus for learning. Jesus wasted no time responding to the request of the disciple, and neither should we.

Jesus lived, and out of his life flowed teaching. The Model existed in him first. Then his words and actions, reflecting the Model, reinforced each other with an authority that amazed his hearers. Observational learning is "caught from," not "taught by," a teacher. Some thirty years after Jesus had ascended to heaven, Peter wrote to pastors: "Be shepherds of God's flock that is under your care . . . not lording it over those entrusted to you, but being *examples to the flock*" (1 Pet. 5:2, 3, italics mine). Jesus was the Example—the Exemplar, the Model—to Peter and to the Twelve and to all who would follow him. If we pattern our teaching after Jesus, we too will strive to be the proper kind of example.

Easily said. Not so easily done. How do I grow as a model, as an exemplar, as an example to my students? Here's an exercise in self-analysis. I want my students to be on time. Am I? I want my students to be prepared when they come to class. Am I? I want my students to treat me with courtesy and respect. Do I treat them this way? I want them to give me the benefit of the doubt when I say something they perceive to be arrogant or self-serving. Do I give them the same latitude? I want students to be specific and focused in their written work. Am I? What expectations for students would you include? Do you fulfill them? We must integrate the expectations and goals for our students into our own behavior if we want them to grow sincerely in these areas. Otherwise, we lift ourselves above the expectations of "mere students" and take on an air of hypocrisy: "You (students) must submit complete lesson plans for your presentations, but I (teacher) don't need to write them for my classes." Why? "Because . . . uh, well, because I'm the teacher! I've been there, done that, bought the T-shirt." Wrong answer. A prime status-crashing response. "But I'm the teacher" doesn't excuse us from practicing what we teach.

What do you want your students to understand? To appreciate? To do skillfully? Write out your responses. Now, how do you live out these very goals and expectations in your own teaching? Your answers reflect the status-enhancing mountain you need to climb.

Using Others as Models to Be Imitated. Try as we might, we will fail to be all things to all people. Art Herron,[24] our forty-something youth minister at Columbia Baptist in the 1970s, was wise enough to know that he could not be all things to the youth who attended our church. During the summer, he brought in youth ministry teams from B.S.U. organizations[25] from around the country. One team carried out ministry for junior high students, and another for senior high students. Art met weekly with the teams for prayer, Bible study, leadership development, and coordinated planning. He was the coordinator, but our young people were surrounded by a dozen college-aged Christian role models.

In June 1997, I taught "Introduction to Christian Education" at Moscow Seminary. A fifty-something Russian pastor sat in on some of my sessions. He was not really a spy, but neither was he a bonafide student. Whether he was there to observe me, or my students, I never found out. Regardless, I was glad to have him. He came sporadically at first, one hour out of three, one day but not the next. He sat quietly during the first few days of class, but he was slowly drawn into our class discussions. He came more often and stayed longer. He began to smile. He began to ask questions. And then something wonderful happened: he began to expound—briefly, concisely, respectfully—on my material. As I listened to the translations of his comments to his younger "classmates," it was amazing to see how his perceptions were being changed, how he adapted and applied my lectures and cases into Russian cultural terms. But most gratifying for me was the way the students leaned into his explanations. For an American to say these things was one thing. But for an older Russian brother-pastor to illustrate them in their context was quite another. Perhaps some teachers would be jealous of the attention he received. I could only applaud the triple level of learning, the life-changing learning, that was happening in my classroom—in the students, in and through this Russian pastor, in me. The very fact that I allowed him the freedom to "translate" my ideas culturally, to use his expertise as a pastor, elevated my status in his eyes, even though he was older than I was. We became model-partners in the teaching, and all of us benefited. What a memory!

God has never called me to be a youth minister, but if he did call me, there is one thing I would initiate: I would make selected high school seniors assistant teachers in youth classes. Think of the motivational gold mine in this. Selected students work alongside an experienced adult in actually teaching (instead of sitting and listening). Younger students are motivated to be more serious and involved because the status of "assistant teacher" is theirs to earn. Since seniors are still "youth," their comments may be more relevant and meaningful to younger youth. High school seniors would more easily relate to youth than older married adults.

Improving status, modeling, and using others as models provides diverse resources for vicarious reinforcement and observational learning.

Dangers of Modeling

We cannot depend on modeling alone to motivate students. We may have students in our courses—particularly required courses—who are less than interested in us, our understanding, attitudes, or skills. We have no status to them because what they want to become has nothing to do with who we are or what we represent. They took our course because the scheduled time of classes fit their schedule, not because they were interested in the content or us. Or perhaps they are interested in the content, but are completely ambivalent towards us. Wise teachers patiently bide their time, motivate in other ways, avoid toxic actions, and work toward building status. It helps to remember that there are some students who may never consider us their example. Jesus had his Judas, and so will we. It did not change his love for Judas or the disciples; it should not change the love and commitment we have for our students.

There is also a danger in using guest speakers. In our Teaching Ministry of the Church class, we deal with Bible study literature for four major age groups: preschool, children, youth, and adult. Several years ago I believed my students would be better served if I brought in guest speakers—preschool and children's ministers—to discuss the literature and teaching principles. I taught the sessions on youth and adults. What I found, however, is that some of my students took this to mean that I did not consider teaching preschoolers and children "as important" as teaching youth and adults. If I did, their reasoning went, I would master these areas and teach them myself. So I did just that. I do not think my presentations are as complete or personal as the guest speakers' presentations are. But the *students,* particularly the theology students, consider teaching preschoolers and children more important than they did when I simply handed it over to someone else.

Do what you can to model what you teach. Involve others, including experienced students, as examples of how the subject makes a real difference. Motivation will improve over time.

The Teacher as Curiousiteur

The term *curiousiteur* is one of my own making, and flows out of the work of cognitive learning theorists like Jean Piaget and Jerome Bruner.[26] Piaget used the term *disequilibrium* to describe the mental tension between a life experience and one's perception. One can reduce disequilibrium two ways. The first is by changing the experience to fit one's perception, which Piaget called *assimilation*.[27] The second is by changing one's perception to fit the experience, which Piaget called *accommodation*.[28] The teacher's role in motivating learning, then, is to present problems or ask questions. If done right, problems can create disequilibrium, or curiosity, which stimulates the students' desire to find or devise solutions. The one-who-creates-curiosity, or teacher, is a "curiositeur."

It was my last semester of college, summer, 1973. I was already planning what courses I was going to take in seminary in the fall. The last thing I wanted to do was sit through Twentieth-Century American History. But it was required for graduation and I was stuck.

Dr. Synthesis[29] set the stage for the course early in our first session together. Five paperback books. One research paper in two parts. Part one: an integrated narrative of the events between the bombing of Pearl Harbor and the Berlin Airlift. Part two: An analysis of the political perspectives, from conservative to liberal, of the five authors. I didn't have the first idea of how to write such a paper, but the assignment intrigued me.

In less than an hour, I was led from disinterested complacency to focused attention. As I developed my strategy, motivation grew. As the paper took shape, curiosity deepened. Six weeks later, when the paper was finished, I had learned a great deal about this period of American history. More than discrete bits of dates and names and events, I had developed a multidimensional view of the period through reading the five authors. But beyond this, I had developed skills in synthetic[30] writing that proved invaluable in writing the mountains of required seminary research papers and two doctoral dissertations. Dr. Synthesis not only made American history come alive for me; he succeeded in making the process of synthetic writing itself come alive.[31]

Elements of Curiosity

Cognitive motivation centers in arousing the curiosity of students. Let's look at the advantages of using principles of optimal discrepancy, direct experience, social interaction, thought-provoking questions, learner responses, problem-solving, meaningfulness, and elaboration to stimulate student learning.

Optimal Discrepancy. If a teacher presents an idea that is well understood and accepted by learners, there will be no disequilibrium between the idea and student perception. Some learners will be bored. Little learning, if any, will happen. If a teacher presents an idea that is foreign or threatening to learners, there will be too much disequilibrium. Some learners will be anxious, others angry. Still others may dismiss the teacher's ideas as dangerous.

Optimal (the best, most effective) *discrepancy* (difference) between learner perception and teaching content refers to presenting ideas that challenge the thinking of learners and yet are meaningful to learners. Therefore, we should provide moderate levels of difficulty in our teaching.[32]

In order to do this we must know our learners. Optimal discrepancy is different for a preschooler and a teenager, for a day laborer and a professor. Know your learners. Frame your questions and explanations in a way that challenges their thinking without raising their blood pressure. Rock their boats, but don't sink them.

Direct Experience. Students discover new relationships among ideas when they interact with their environment.[33] Therefore, learning proceeds best through direct experiences with objects and events—experiences that are appropriate for the age of the learners. Direct experiences include activities[34] such as structured play, arts and music, and nature experiences for preschoolers; the use of visual aids and concrete props, projects, and learning centers for children; drama and role-play, hypothetical situations, and small-group studies for youth; and real-life experiences and testimonies for adults. Much of what we do in Christian teaching is verbal—teachers telling learners about the Bible. But real understanding occurs when we engage learners, not as passive listeners, but as active thinkers.[35]

Social Interaction. Learners may have self-centered thought patterns. They may think that things *really are* the way they see them. Social interaction helps them become aware of the ideas and opinions of others. This process reduces self-centeredness and helps individuals become more objective in their thinking.[36] Provide age-appropriate experiences that encourage learner-to-learner interaction as well as teacher-learner interaction. For example, group projects and role-play scenarios are excellent ways to intervene into the thinking of older children and youth.

Small groups of learners overcome individual differences in thinking better than large classes. Learners will more likely admit their confusion and lack of understanding in a small group than in a large class. More knowledgeable learners are better able to explain ideas in small groups than in large classes. This interaction motivates both knowledgeable and unknowledgeable students in ways that a large lecture class cannot.

Thought-Provoking Questions. Thought-provoking questions drive learners more deeply into the subject. Responders consider what they know (reflection), decide what is relevant (discrimination), and form an appropriate response (application). The quality of responses tells us how well learners understand the material.

When learners parrot memorized answers to set questions, they do not demonstrate meaningful mastery of the material. Memorized answers may hold no meaning to the learner at all, and therefore will not motivate future learning. This leads to distorted memory, as in one child's recollection of her Sunday school study: "We talked about the Father, Son, and Holy Smoke."

Learner Responses. Correct answers do not necessarily indicate understanding. Focus on the process of forming an answer, not just the answer itself.[37] Ask learners to explain how they arrive at their answers. Ask them why they answer the way they do. Focus on word meanings[38]—just what does the learner mean by the words he's chosen?

Give as much attention to incorrect answers as to correct ones.[39] These incorrect responses clarify learner mistakes in thinking. Also consider the common mistakes your learners make in answering questions. Anticipate these and prepare explanations that emphasize these problem areas.[40]

Problem-Solving. Create problem-solving situations where learners can make discoveries. Problems confront learners with unfamiliar situations and create disequilibrium. Solving the problem, based on available resources, brings about equilibration and a higher level of understanding.

The methodology of problem-solving centers on interaction among learners and teacher, hypotheses, opinions, research, and teamwork. In a seminary class in educational philosophy, teams of students might choose a particular problem in church educational programming, and develop and present a solution to that problem based on a specific philosophy. In a class in staff relationships, teams of students might gather information from leadership literature and live staff interviews to develop suggestions for solving specified interpersonal problems in church staffs. In a Sunday school class, teenagers can be teamed to find Bible verses relevant to the problem: How can we determine God's view of right and wrong? The curiosity engendered in these problem situations motivates students to stretch for answers.

Meaningfulness. The next two elements, meaningfulness and elaboration, come from information processing theory, a subset of cognitive learning theory. Rather than motivating students by increasing curiosity, meaningfulness and elaboration motivate students by satisfying curiosity.[41]

To enhance meaningfulness of study materials, connect new material to prior learnings. Begin with principles and ideas that students have already mastered. Then introduce the new material by linking it to previous learnings. Building bridges between established ideas and new material increases meaningfulness.

Elaboration. Elaboration[42] (or "elaborative rehearsal") is the process of increasing the number of mental links, or interconnections, among elements to be learned. We achieve this either by helping students see the elements in different ways, or by providing them new information.[43] Our goal is to help them create logically interconnected information, so that any part can be used to retrieve the other parts.

At the end of each chapter of my research text, I provide students with several sample test questions. I do this first to focus their attention on key ideas in the text. Many of my master's level students would like to simply memorize these questions—with the correct answer, of course—and consider this sufficient preparation for course examinations. If they do this, they will do poorly on the exam because I never ask these questions exactly the same way. The goal is not to memorize answers to objective questions but to understand fundamental connections in the language of research and statistics. So I suggest that they take each question and dissect it: "Use each stem to create other questions. Focus on the terms, the related concepts, the underlying principles contained in each sample question. If you elaborate your understanding in this way, you will have little difficulty answering questions on the examination." I picture the result of this kind of study as a multidimensional network of interwoven concepts, much like the American history research paper I mentioned earlier. Such a network provides a much richer resource for problem-solving and test-taking than discrete bits of memorized trivia, forgotten as soon as students move on to other studies.[44]

Dangers of Curiosity

Students will be motived by problems or questions only if they have some initial desire to solve them. If students do not "own the problem" as personally meaningful, the problem possesses no motivational power in itself.

Teachers in formal educational settings have an advantage, since students are motivated to do well on tests—whether they actually understand the material or not, whether they care to understand or not. Poor understanding means a poor test score, and poor test scores mean a poor course grade, and a poor course grade has long-term consequences. Wise teachers focus tests on material that will prove most beneficial to the students themselves, and go beyond "good test scores" to motivate real learning.

Teachers in informal settings have no artificial system to cover up lack of motivation. Wise teachers focus their efforts on the felt needs and personal concerns of the people in their classes. They present problems and ask questions that have high probability of touching real-life concerns of learners.

Still, we cannot expect every learner to care about our learning activities, however hard we try to make them relevant. "I'm just here for my required two-hours of ed. psyc., Coach. Don't expect me to care about it." We will need to use some other approach to draw such students into our learning circle.

The Teacher as Friend

The term *friend* comes from the work of humanistic learning theorists such as Abraham Maslow and Carl Rogers.[45] Humanists believe that learners are, first and foremost, human beings. Learners bring to the classroom their own experiences, views, and values that are powerful motivators when integrated into the educational process. Humanistic theorists advocated a learning process that they said was more humane, more personally meaningful, more experiential than their behavioral and cognitive counterparts. Open classrooms, group sharing, self-directed learning, and pass-fail grading quickly overtook programmed instruction in the late 1960s and 1970s. But humanistic learning peaked in the late 1970s because of significant drops in standardized test scores. Educators discovered that American students were definitely learning less and enjoying it more. Educational psychology textbooks began to be redesigned. New texts focused more on cognitive and cooperative learning strategies and moved "humanistic principles of learning" away from learning theory sections to units dealing with motivation.[46]

Still, our students are human beings. Their fears, past experiences, and academic skills do affect their motivation to succeed in our courses. Anyone can stand behind a podium and read course notes to students, who write them madly into their own. But the nature of good teaching is that which looks beyond course notes to the human beings sitting before us—to their deficiencies, to their abilities, to their uniqueness.

Mr. Begley was my Royal Ambassador[47] leader for nearly four years. A steady stream of leaders moved through the R.A. program of our small church, but Mr. Begley anchored the program—perhaps as a way to teach his own sons. We met on Wednesday nights to work on our steps and plan mission events. From time to time, Mr. Begley took us on outings. I can remember mountain climbing treks, bike trips, and an occasional all-night fishing trip. My first experience with shrimp was as bait for catfish, and Mr. Begley showed me how to load the hook. We sat around a campfire, read the Bible, discussed our mission studies, and sometimes our own struggles.[48] It was not until I grew older that I realized how much difficulty Mr. Begley and his family had. He worked hard as a painter but did not earn a great deal of money. His children sported home-grown haircuts, and they dressed up in jeans and T-shirts to attend church. Yet Mr. Begley taught me some very strong lessons about tithing. By his example and by his consistent support, he taught us many things about living the Christian life in a real world—even as he helped me learn lessons about missions.

Elements of Friendship

Abraham Maslow and other humanistic writers used the term *learner-centered* to focus educators' attention on the importance of the humanity of students for the learning process. Let's look at the principles of availability, educational nurture, warmth, enthusiasm, flexibility, and emotional maturity.

Availability. The professor enters the room as the bell rings, takes the roll, and then opens his course notebook to the post-it note he positioned at the end of the last class period. "Let us take up where we left off." He then proceeds to expound through his notes until the bells rings. He repositions his post-it note, bids the class farewell, and walks from the classroom. Why couldn't a well-produced videotape do at least as well—if not better if it included the ideas of other specialists, on-site interviews, pictorial illustrations and the like—as this dehumanized robot who comes to class only to read through the next fifty-minute slice of course notes? Or an absentee pastor who delivers three forty-minute devotions a week to gathered listeners who never ask a question or have a chance to? Or a Sunday school teacher who "teaches lessons" but never visits or socializes with members outside of class?

Being a friend means being available. Spending time. Learning from each other. Can students find us when they need us? The answer to their question just may be the most important thing they learn all semester. Providing times when students can conveniently make appointments—convenient for them—is a step in the right direction. E-mail reduces the distance between computer-savvy students and professors to a mere millisecond.

Educational Nurture. If students are tired or hungry or abused, their desire to learn is diminished. If they are embarrassed or humiliated in the classroom, their achievement suffers.[49] Avoid frequent competition among students[50]—it produces more losers than winners. Intentionally watch for self-esteem deficiencies among students.[51] When appropriate, use student interests to illustrate teaching points.[52] Promote feelings of success by making appropriate assignments and providing positive feedback and credible rewards.[53] Care about your students and their well-being. Personalize the content so that students can integrate it into their own experience.[54] Help students set their own goals for learning.[55] Provide alternative learning activities from which students can choose.[56] Make sure that you provide a safe, supportive classroom climate and set high, but attainable, standards.[57] By doing these things, we help students satisfy deficiency needs that hinder their motivation to learn.

Warmth. Teachers who are warm, caring, and friendly set a positive emotional tone in the classroom. In fact, this characteristic is the one most strongly linked to positive student attitudes.[58] Contrast this with teachers who are cold, uncaring, and aloof. The former concentrates on students as persons; the latter, on lessons to be taught. The former concentrates on thinking and sharing and learning; the latter, on deadlines and punctuality and performance. The former engages all students in an effort to help them learn; the latter confronts students in an effort to combat ignorance. It is clear which kind of classroom produces openness and safety.

Jesus chose twelve men to "be with him" (Mark 3:14). Jesus did not think of these learners as servants, but friends (John 15:15). These students were loved by their Teacher, and encouraged, commanded, to love each other (John 13:34). What a classroom climate!

Enthusiasm. Enthusiasm, as defined by the *American Heritage Dictionary,* refers to "great excitement for or interest in a subject or cause." Teacher enthusiasm brings life and energy into the classroom. Enthusiasm manifests itself as intensity, vigor, movement, joy, surprise, frustration, and delight.[59] Such elements reflect an intense interest in the subject as well as zeal for communicating that subject to others. Contrast this with teachers who move through their material methodically and monotonously, with little change of pace. Their focus is on their own notes, often yellow with age, rather than the newness of the material as it stirs their students' thinking. Students have difficulty generating excitement for subjects that seem boring to their teachers. Such was the contrast between the teaching of the scribes and Pharisees, who quoted prominent rabbis, and the teaching of Jesus, who spoke with authority: "You have heard that it was said to the people long ago . . . but *I tell you* that . . ." (Matt. 5:21–22, italics mine). Jesus' teaching had such intensity that "the crowds were amazed at his teaching" (Matt. 7:28–29).

Flexibility. As we saw in chapter 2, flexibility is a mark of a mature teacher and softens the structure of a course, a unit, or a class session. Here we define the motivational aspect of flexibility as using appropriate methods, whether direct or indirect, according to classroom needs. Direct methods include lecturing, explaining, and correcting. Indirect methods include questioning, listening, and accepting students' opinions and feelings.[60] Flexibility is the most repeated adjective used by students to describe good teachers.[61] Such teachers are more positive and more democratic than rigid teachers. Rigid teachers tend to use the same procedures in the same way, regardless of student outcomes.[62] They hold stereotypical views of students and tend to have low expectations of student ability. They are more authoritarian and prone to bias and prejudice. They depend more on first impressions and past records than flexible teachers.[63] In short, research has found that students in all subjects were motivated to learn more with flexible teachers.[64]

Matthew 23 reflects the distinctive difference between the flexibility of Jesus' understanding of the Law and the rigidity of the Pharisee's religion. Jesus understood Kingdom principles and used them appropriately to teach and minister. The Pharisees held rigid traditions and religious formulas and burdened their followers with them (Matt. 23:4). Flexible teachers focus on their students as persons and befriend them by employing whatever means are necessary to help them learn.

Emotional Maturity. We again revisit chapter 2 briefly to reemphasize the importance of emotional maturity in motivating student performance. Emotionally mature teachers display a sense of humor, have a pleasant manner, and are fair and disciplined.[65] Such teachers work well with others, manage their impulses, express good feelings without embarrassment, refrain from worry, and can accept constructive criticism.[66] All these characteristics are marks of a friend.

Contrast this with immature teachers, who tend to be unpleasant, impulsive, irritable, rash, anxious, and short of temper[67]—not friendly attributes. College and seminary students may be able to avoid such teachers by choosing others, but for elementary and secondary students, required by law to attend school with little or no choice in their teachers or subjects, immature teachers can make school an unbearable experience, and motivation soon dies.

Dangers of Friendship

Mr. Begley was a friend to us boys in a time and way that was safe. He and his family were members of long-standing in our church. His sons were members of the group. But things are not as clear-cut today. Particularly in adult education situations, there can be a confusion of roles if teachers become too friendly or too personal with students. There remains a power imbalance between teacher and student: teachers give the grades; students receive them. Wise teachers befriend students to help them learn and grow, not to be "buds."

A colleague of mine who teaches at a secular university shared such a problem encounter. One day, near the midterm of a semester, a pretty young coed came to his office. She was failing his course and wanted to discuss her options. She smiled and lowered her eyes, then said, "Oh, I'd do anything to earn an A in your class." "Anything?" the professor asked. "Yes, *anything*." He leaned over toward her and whispered in her ear, "Would you . . . study?" Fortunately for them both, he was a professional and maintained his role of teacher in spite of her pointed attempt to buy a grade through "friendliness." He demonstrated true educational friendship.

Then there is the problem of emotional exhaustion. Building relationships consumes time and emotional energy. Learning the names, needs, and interests of each student in a class of thirty is draining. Multiply this drain by the number of such classes, and personal involvement can become quite a burden. By the end of the semester, when the class has become "family" and the teaching-learning relationships have been established, the course ends and the process begins again with a new set of students. Church staffs can be drained by meeting the personal, marital, and program needs of the congregation. Jesus periodically left the crowds to be alone to pray and to rest with his disciples. Too much giving in a world of needs can lead to mental exhaustion and physical illness. The caution is this: meter out your emotional investments wisely.

The Teacher as Success Agent

The term *success agent* reflects the work of Bernard Weiner in attribution theory.[68] Attribution theory attempts to systematically describe student explanations for their successes and failures in classroom situations. Motivation for future achievement is affected by the attributions students give, or how they explain, their successes and failures. Over time, high achievers and low achievers tend toward stable, though different, perceptions of success and failure. High achievers link success with hard work and ability, failure with laziness. Low achievers link success with luck, failure with lack of ability. When teachers help low achievers succeed, they are accomplishing more than helping students learn a subject. They affect their very psyche, changing the way these students perceive themselves as learners. Just as theatrical agents intervene to change the persona of their clients to make them more "marketable"—to succeed in acting—so teachers intervene to change the thinking of students to make them more "educatable"—to succeed in learning.

Dr. Leon Marsh[69] was my major professor in seminary. I found myself in his educational psychology class the first semester of my seminary career. After the fourth class session, Dr. Marsh stopped me at the front of the class. He looked at me with a small smile and asked, "What did I say today?" I thought back over the lecture and the notes I'd taken and ticked off four or five ideas I thought were worth mentioning. "See me in my office after chapel." Not knowing what to expect, I approached the meeting with a great deal of foreboding. But he asked me to be one of his graders, which I naturally accepted. That one event changed the rest of my seminary career. We spent hours talking about teaching. I was given opportunities to teach his classes. Whenever I faced a new challenge, he would smile at me and say, "Well now, Rick, you can do this thing." Over the five years I studied with him, I discovered many things that I could do. He was certainly a friend to me, but we were never "buddies." To this day, I call him "Dr. Marsh." He is more like a second father to me. But much of my success in seminary and beyond I attribute to the intervention of one Leon Marsh in my life. He continues to motivate me by way of letters, and maintains greater faith in my potential than I do. But I'm far from the only one who has felt the motivational whoosh of his encouragement. There are hundreds of others who have been influenced the same way.

Elements of Fostering Success

How do we help students make the appropriate attributions for their successes and failures? Let's look at linking effort to success, reviewing past successes, promoting future success, challenging high- and supporting low-achievers, and encouraging a mastery orientation.

Linking Effort to Success. Low-achievers attribute their success to luck. When they succeed, they gain no residual motivation for future effort since they believe their success is not based on effort. The goal of success agents is to teach students to recognize that their success in learning is directly related to the personal effort they make.[70]

The most difficult course I teach is research and statistics. It is a required course for counseling and social work students, so many students begin the class with fear, sometimes anger. It is difficult material—complex, foreign to most ministerial students. Further, we move through the many facets of design and analysis quickly. I have spent more time dealing with motivational issues in that one course than in any other course I teach. I provide guidelines for study, sample questions for self-testing, a computer tutorial for interactive practice, periodic quizzes to help them establish a pattern of success, and examinations that have been validated by item analysis[71] to be clear and unambiguous. I provide time at the beginning of every session for questions on the reading. Students are free to ask questions for clarification at any time during each period. I remain after class to answer the questions of more timid students. I give out my E-mail address so that students can contact me electronically when they have a question. Over the course of the semester, the link between personal effort and course success is underscored again and again. As students discover the reality of this link, the harder they study, and the more they succeed.

Promoting Success. The link between personal effort and success means little if the efforts students make are misdirected. Help them develop learning skills and strategies[72] that will produce success.

In the research class, I make suggestions for how to take notes in class, how to read the text, and how to form questions about confusing concepts. I allow students to develop a legalized "crib sheet" for use during their first two examinations. By sifting the material for major concepts and principles to incorporate into their sheet, most master the structure of the material. Few students actually use the crib sheets during the exam because they find during the test that they understand the material. The crib sheets also lower test anxiety, which is a major block to learning. I don't allow them to use their crib sheets for the final comprehensive examination, but by then they no longer need the help. My grader corrects calculation errors and makes constructive suggestions to improve the students' work in statistical analysis.

In my educational psychology class, I spend a full class period prior to the first exam showing students samples of the test questions they will see. Since test items are tied directly to course objectives, students can focus their study on essential elements in the course. Such methods infuse hope into the process of testing and grading. Effort, and especially extended effort, results in better grades. Previous low-achievers come out of these two difficult classes not only understanding the material better than they ever thought they would but they have much more confidence in themselves as students.

Reviewing Past Successes. Help students see their progress in the course by reviewing previous material to show how "easy" it was. In my educational psychology class, I use terms studied in unit 1 to explain theories covered in unit 2. When students hear, as part of the normal context of class, terms learned just a few weeks before, they are subliminally encouraged at the progress they've made.

We can also encourage students to redo projects when they have learned more.[73] A "test retake option" allows students in educational psychology to take an alternate exam if they did poorly on the first try. Their final test score is the average of the two attempts. Comprehensive questions on the final examination are not as discriminating or difficult as on the unit exams. The relative ease of the test questions reinforces how much students have learned over the course of a semester.

If we spend too much time helping low-achievers get started, we may overlook high-achievers. Challenge high-achievers with assignments and problems that offer a mix of potential success and failure. The possibility of failure motivates high-achievers to work harder.[74]

On the other hand, teachers are often high-achievers themselves. They secured their teaching positions by mastering their subjects and demonstrating credentials. Because of this, teachers may have a tendency to encourage high-achievers in the class. Therefore, we must intentionally encourage and support low-achievers.

We can handle both of these demands by providing a mix of basic and advanced projects for learners to choose from: fewer points for shorter, safer assignments; more points for longer, more risky assignments.

Encouraging a Mastery Orientation. Students who have a mastery orientation value achievement for its own sake, believe they have the ability to improve, do not fear failure, take risks, exude self-confidence and energy, and welcome feedback.[75] By a variety of approaches found in this text—behavioral, cognitive, humanistic, spiritual—students may be helped to move toward a mastery orientation.

Dangers of Fostering Success

The settled self-perceptions of low-achievers are hard to change. "I can't do that" can become an integral part of one's self-image. When we tell such a person "you can," they may simply think we don't really know them. If success is seen as the result of luck, even an unconscious part, then occasional successes will not motivate a low-achiever to work more. There are limits to what we can do. If we do not accept this, we will be frustrated with students who refuse to succeed. We will be disappointed that our second-mile efforts result in substandard performance. We may even grow angry when students dismiss our help and reject our concern. Jesus gave the rich young ruler a choice. Sadly, the young man chose the wrong option and went away. Jesus allowed him his wrong choice and let him go (Luke 18:18–27). We must be willing to do the same. But not without pain.

In Conclusion

In nearly every Sunday school conference I lead, there is at least one teacher who will say something like this: "Well, that may have worked for your classes, but you don't know my class. They . . . ." The teacher then proceeds to tell me why this or that suggestion won't work with his or her class. It's as if these teachers take snapshots of their classes in all their unteachableness. They carry the snapshots to remind them that their classes don't want any more than they already receive. Such teachers ignore new ideas because none of them fit their snapshots.

What if others did this? What if a football coach took a snapshot of the team at the beginning of training camp and then bemoaned the fact that new plays simply didn't fit the picture? A business executive and his employees? A drill sergeant and his new recruits?

No! These leaders know where they want to go. They know what kind of results they want to see. And they take steps to move their learners toward that goal. Frame by frame, like a movie, the players move and change and become what the leader sees. Sometimes changes come fast. Sometimes changes take longer. But step by step, leader and led move toward a common goal.

Frame by frame, step by step, as in a motion picture, move your students from where they are to where they ought to be. Take the long look. Plant seeds in Jesus' name. He will bring the increase, in his way and in his timing.

Steve eventually became sick of the off-white wall in our Sunday school room. He began to sneak quick glances around the room and at me. His first comments were angry attacks at others. He asked venomous questions, worked to derail discussions, and generally caused trouble. As the class continued to accept him and "put up with him,"[76] his questions slowly turned from attack to request. He spent less time looking at the wall and more time watching his classmates. He began to listen to my explanations and ask good questions. He had become a learner instead of a hater.

One morning after class Steve asked to talk with me privately: "I went to the doctor last week because I don't feel very good. You know I drink a lot, right? He told me that if I continued to drink like I was, I would not live two more years—and I'm only eighteen!" Then, painfully, as if he were climbing the face of a rugged cliff, he edged toward me, looked me deeply in the eyes, and asked, "Do . . . you . . . think . . . Jesus can help me?"

I assured him the Lord would and could help him, if he would place his life in his hands. I told him how. We prayed together and Steve asked Jesus to come into his life, save him from alcohol, and make him whole. I looked into Steve's face, only moments before drawn and sad, to see a bright, shining face with alive and hopeful eyes. He was baptized that night.

Then on Tuesday, Steve went with friends and got drunk. He went back to his eighth-floor room, and alone, in his drunken stupor, realized that he had failed the Lord. He had broken his promise. He had squandered his last hope. So he walked out of his room to the railing and looked down eight floors to the granite floor of the lobby. He began to climb over the railing to end his misery. Just then two of our Sunday school class members turned the corner and saw what Steve was about to do. They grabbed him and literally dragged him to our apartment. We gave him a cold shower and some hot coffee. When he was able to think, he told us what he had done. We were able to tell him all was not lost. He had just begun a new life with Christ. He could be forgiven. He would continue to grow. This joyful, incredulous realization completely burst open his heart to the Lord, and his life was never the same. His manner of dress changed. His hygiene changed. His attitudes changed. His goals changed. He studied his Bible. Established a prayer time. Participated in class. And in six months, was elected president of the class. I watched him move from angry rebel to vulnerable convert to enthusiastic leader in the course of a school year. Proper reinforcement, good models, helpful questions, sincere friendship, and successful experiences all contributed to opening Steve to the Truth, and to his being set free.

May we give ourselves to caring more for people than mere content. May we learn how to shape positively, model encouragingly, query intriguingly, befriend appropriately, and promote success consistently as we go about the daily tasks of teaching.

Meaningful content and learner motivation are powerful driving forces in the learning process. In the center of it stands the teacher. Like an actor on a stage, teachers use voice, body language, facial expression, and presence to infuse their subjects with life. It is to this aspect of teaching that we now turn our attention.

Chapter 5

The Teacher as Dramatic Performer

*The people were amazed at his teaching,
because he taught them as one who had authority,
not as the teachers of the law.*

Mark 1:22

*Everyone who heard him was amazed
at his understanding and his answers.*

Luke 2:47

*All the people in the synagogue were furious
when they heard this. They got up, drove him out of the town,
and took him to the brow of the hill on which the town was built,
in order to throw him down the cliff.
But he walked right through the crowd and went on his way.*

Then he went down to Capernaum, a town in Galilee,
and on the Sabbath began to teach the people.
They were amazed at his teaching,
because his message had authority.

Luke 4:28–32

And when the centurion, who stood there in front of Jesus,
heard his cry and saw how he died,
he said, "Surely this man was the Son of God!"

Mark 15:39

*T*eaching that electrifies learners is by its very nature a dramatic performance. Haddon Robinson, professor of Preaching at Gordon-Conwell Seminary, writes that communication

> . . . isn't what it used to be. Any effort to foist dull, tired, jargon-filled material on readers or listeners meets with irritation or, worse, disdain. . . . In modern culture, people distinguish quickly between the interesting and the tedious. They scan the newspaper for stories that catch their minds. They flip through magazines and read the first sentence or the opening paragraph to decide whether it "sounds interesting." They vote in the first thirty seconds whether to tune in or turn off the channel. . . . That lonely figure in the pulpit [or *teaching podium*] may have what the folks in front of him need, but they won't listen unless he knows how to say it.[1]

Jesus knew how to say it. And how to live it. With energy and drama and focus. His persona drew people of all kinds to him. He amazed the religious elite as well as the common people with his teaching. He walked and people followed. He taught and people listened and learned. He died with dignity, despite his agony, such that even a hardened centurion marveled.

Our mission is less demanding. But as we move from his cross to our classrooms, we can still see the place of energy, drama, and focus in teaching that electrifies learners. Without these qualities, learners will tune us out before they're able to discern whether our message is worth hearing. I have chosen the term *dramatic performer* to refer to this intangible aspect of teaching—not that we put on a show or play a fictitious role. Jesus certainly didn't do this. But our platform skills play a crucial role in conveying the vitality of our message.

God's recipe for greatness, writes Calvin Miller, consists of three ingredients: inward substance, magnetic motivation, and outward daring.[2] We dealt with a teacher's inward substance in chapters 1 and 2. We dealt with a teacher's magnetic motivation in chapter 4. We deal with a teacher's outward daring here, as we look at the teacher as personal presence, speaker, storyteller, and enchanter.

The Teacher as Personal Presence

He came into the classroom in a monotone shuffle, notes in hand, looking like he was lost. He mumbled something to himself as he put his disorganized papers on the podium. An overhead cel dropped off the stack and floated to the floor. He awkwardly stooped to pick it up. He made no eye contact with the class, but focused on sorting out the pile of papers now sitting before him, as if he were alone in the room. He finished composing his papers, and then himself—checking his tie and brushing from his jacket some lingering chalk dust from a previous class—and then looked nervously around the class for a moment. The class slowly sank into a cold, uncomfortable silence as he looked down his class roll. "Stephen," he said. "It is Stephen, right? Lead us in prayer, please." When the student finished praying, there was a pregnant pause. Dr. Boar looked at his notebook and began reading. "We . . . come today . . . ahh . . . to point . . . number . . . ahhh . . . three." He then staggered through an awkward forty-something minutes of painful, irrelevant detail. This was not a single incident, an uncommon bad day. His teaching style reeked of irritating distractions and fumbling methods. The only sense of direction in the class was his yellowed notebook. As a result, his teaching lacked any semblance of "presence."

You know persons who have presence as soon as they enter a room or stand to speak. It's as if they are marching to the accompaniment of drums and trumpets in the distance. You can sense that their adrenaline is pumping. There is an incandescence about them that you can actually see and feel. People with presence walk briskly and exude an air of purpose. They are focused outward, on their surroundings, rather than inward, on their own problems. They are sure of themselves because they are decisively prepared. They don't fuss with things. They focus on their mission, stepping up to issues, moving into their audience. They project an attitude of positive anticipation—they know what they're doing and are anxious to get started. They like the responsibility of presentation and create an expectation of leadership.[3]

But Dr. Boar entered the room just as the bell rang, leaving his class preparations to be done "on the platform." He shuffled into class, as if teaching were a chore. Neither he nor his class seemed sure of any purpose for the day other than walking through several more pages of long-cold notes. He fussed with his papers and transparencies, paying more attention to his disorganized stack than to the students who sat in front of him. He rarely made eye contact with them and seemed intimidated when they, on occasion, asked questions. He remained behind his podium, as if it were a shield protecting him from classroom danger.

For me, the key to avoiding the agony of Dr. Boar's approach to teaching is to find energizing points that will ignite the drama in *me*. Some call these energizing points "soapboxes." Here are just a few of my favorites.

Kohlberg and Taverns: When my educational psychology class moves into the chapter on Kohlberg's Theory of Moral Reasoning, I begin with the following case:

> A fourteen-year-old boy, handing out Gospels of Mark on a Sunday afternoon, finds himself standing before a tavern. Should he go in and distribute the Gospel booklets? Or should he pass on by?

Students generally agree that he should not go in. When asked why, answers range from "He could be caught and punished" (which is a Stage One response) to "His parents would not approve!" (a Stage Three response) or "He's breaking the drinking age law!" (a Stage Four response). Then we define and discuss each of Kohlberg's stages. I intentionally include moral dilemmas faced by seminary students. It is usually the end of the second class period before we return to the fourteen-year-old. Only then do I tell them that the fourteen-year-old was me. I explain why I went in (a Stage Six response) despite the concerns they listed, and the positive results that came from doing so.[4]

· *Relationships and Garments:* Two chapters in *The Teaching Ministry of the Church* deal with the relational dimension of Christian education: the church and the family.[5] My soapbox for introducing this material is a conversational exegesis of Paul's "social garments" in Colossians 3:8–12.

Principles of Teaching: Gold, Straw, and Surrender: When explaining how to teach for understanding, I use Paul's "gold, silver, costly stones" passage (1 Cor. 3:11–15). Throughout the demonstration I use selected verses and pointed examples of gold and straw in church work. This double-layer approach emphasizes course content while personalizing biblical ministry standards.

During the unit on teaching for "affective response" I teach a verse of the hymn "I Surrender All" in American Sign Language. I share an experience of surrender to the Lord and invite students to do the same. The shared experiences of surrender reflected around that classroom make for one of the most meaningful spiritual experiences of the semester. We close by signing "I Surrender All" and leaving in silence.

I have at least one "soapbox" for every session of every class I teach. They grip me, energize me, excite me. I can't wait to step into the classroom—and I find teacher enthusiasm is highly contagious. These soapboxes give me purpose beyond getting my notes into student notebooks. They help me reach into the class to touch hearts in a personally meaningful way. To remain effective, old soapboxes must give way to newer ones. New experiences that draw students into the material should be added; those that don't, discarded. I've certainly not arrived. But the memory of Dr. Boar, and others like him, compels me to avoid anything resembling the numbness of nonpresence.

If Dr. Boar were to improve his presence quotient, we might be able to rewrite the scenario like this: "He strides into the classroom a few minutes early, notes in hand, looking like a man on mission.

He greets several students who have already gathered, walking over to them, smiling, shaking hands. He sets his papers on the podium and begins erasing the chalkboard. An overhead cel drops off the stack and floats to the floor. He picks it up without a fuss. As he sorts out the stack of papers on the podium, he greets students and answers questions. He focuses more on their issues than his preparation. He steps to the chalkboard and draws the first part of a diagram that will structure the class. A key word or two. The class, which has been engaged in the quiet murmuring of settling in, grows more quiet as Dr. Boar steps back to the podium. 'Steve,' he says, 'would you mind leading us in prayer, please? Thanks.' When the student finishes praying, Dr. Boar looks at his notebook, then steps to the board and begins. Adding to the incomplete drawing, he draws a line to it from one of the key words. 'We finished our last session with this element. Today, we look at its counterpart.' He walks toward the class, pushing the podium to one side. He looks his students in the eyes, smiles, and says, 'Based on your reading for today, how would you answer this question?' He confidently moves through the session, asking questions, explaining terms, sharing experiences. He knows where he is going and wants to get there. But more than this, his students want to get there too. There just never seems to be enough class time!"

Listen for the drums and trumpets. Look for soapboxes. Be decisively prepared. Know your material fluently and your students personally. Believe in your material and its benefits for your students. And personal presence will become part of your classroom atmosphere—energizing your learners!

The Teacher as Speaker

We communicate both cognitively and effectively, rationally and emotionally, as we teach. The cognitive component focuses on the structured content of our course or sermon. The affective component focuses on the emotional message, conveyed by the voice quality and body language.

The Voice of the Speaker

Dr. Boar moved on through his notes. With a monotone drone, he read from his notebook in measured phrases, neither speeding up nor slowing down, neither raising nor lowering his voice. Standing firmly behind his podium, head down, eyes focused intently on his notes, he staggered from word to word, phrase to phrase, paragraph to agonizing paragraph. His colorless words, lifeless stories, and anemic illustrations fell out of his mouth and seemed to lie on the floor about his feet.

Degrees of calmness, enthusiasm, conviction, and humor are reflected in the characteristics of our voice.[6] The quality of our vocal delivery rests on pitch, volume, rate, pausing,[7] and articulation.[8]

Pitch refers to the highness or lowness of the voice. The optimum pitch is the median level from which higher and lower pitch levels are developed by the speaker. Pitch range is the distance between the speaker's lowest and highest pitch levels. When there is little variation in pitch—a small pitch range—all words sound alike. Listeners miss transitions from one idea to another. Such a Johnny-one-note delivery weakens the structure, and therefore the meaningfulness, of the presentation.[9] More variation in pitch—a larger pitch range—gives the speaker greater flexibility and enhances the appeal of the presentation.

Pitch interval is the distance between two consecutive pitch levels.[10] Consider a teacher responding to a student's correct answer with an "o-kay." A small pitch interval between the "o-" and "-kay" produces a lifeless, unenthusiastic response. But if the teacher raises the pitch on the second syllable—"o-KAY!"—she communicates enthusiasm over the correct answer. The larger the pitch interval, the more emphasis one generates.

Volume refers to the amount of force needed for the message to be heard and the emotional message to be conveyed.[11] Too much volume strains the voice and drives an audience away, psychologically, if not physically. No one enjoys being yelled at. Too little volume renders the message inaudible for some listeners, unclear for others. Little variation in volume level creates a monotonous drone. Volume higher than average generates an emphasis. Volume lower than average secures attention, even suspense. By varying volume levels, speakers boldface and italicize their remarks, create structure, inscribing a mental outline of major and minor points, emphasizing key ideas.

Rate refers to the speed at which a person speaks. A fast rate of speech communicates vitality and aliveness, but speaking too fast impairs pronunciation. A slow rate of speech communicates emphasis and clarity, but speaking too slowly makes the presentation drag. A deliberate, constant rate of speech produces strong emphasis, but too much consistency produces monotony. The best course, as with pitch and volume, is to use a variable rate of speech. Aim for valleys and peaks in speech rate, never a plateau.[12] The proper rate depends on the type of material to be presented. Use a faster rate of speech when presenting less important details.[13] One can also use a faster rate when conveying action, imagination, emotion, personal interest—the vernacular of the heart. Such communiqués are specific, concrete, visual, and vivid.[14] A slower rate of speech should be used when presenting key points.[15] One should also use a slower rate when describing and defining new concepts, giving examples, illustrating principles—the vernacular of the mind. Such language is abstract, general, and factual.[16]

Closely related to rate of speech is the use of silent pauses.[17] Pauses give varying degrees of emphasis to your presentation.[18] A brief pause, about one second, between phrases allows listeners to absorb what has been said. An intermediate pause, from two to three seconds, emphasizes transitions from one idea to another. Longer pauses, from three to five seconds, can be used to emphasize a change of direction in the presentation. Such a long pause calls attention to itself, and therefore to the words that follow it.[19] Proper use of pauses increases the meaningfulness of the message.[20] Avoid vocalized pause—"uh," "er," "yuh know." These filler sounds convey uncertainty.[21] Moreover, they destroy the power that silence gives a pause.

Let's take a passage of Scripture and apply principles of pitch, volume, and rate of speech. "Saul, Saul, why do you persecute me?" "Who are you, Lord?" Saul asked. "I am Jesus, whom you are persecuting" (Acts 9:4–5). Now let's convert this narrative into a vocal presentation. Boldface represents increased volume. Line height represents pitch. Periods (..) represent lengths of pauses.

Use a tape recorder to record several ten-minute sections of your teaching or preaching. You will discover that the voice you hear from a tape recorder differs from the voice you hear when you speak. Do not let the strangeness of your own voice disturb you. What you hear from the recorder is what others hear. Get used to

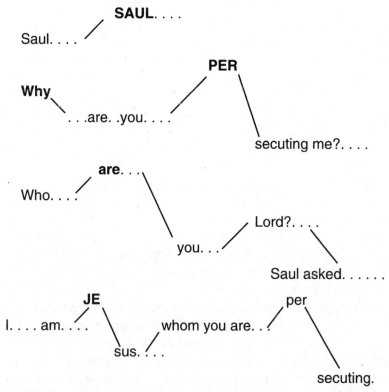

the sound of your voice by listening to the segments several times. Then begin analyzing each recorded segment in terms of pitch, volume, and rate. Are important points, words, and transitions accompanied with increased pitch and volume as well as decreased rate of speech? Are the pitch and volume ranges large enough to reflect emotional rhythms in your speech? Do you speak at a rate of about 180 words per minute? Practice slowing down fast speech by saying aloud "1-2" between phrases. Practice speeding up slow speech by reducing the number and length of pauses. Pick up the momentum of speech by condensing wordiness, using fewer words to convey essential thoughts. Spend less time choosing "just the right words."[22]

Body Language of the Speaker

Dr. Boar's monotone style did not end with his voice. His whole body, from an expressionless face to shuffling feet, exuded a sense of pervasive malaise, apprehension, and insecurity. His eyes followed the words in his notebook, and when he did look up, he riveted the back wall. He held his elbows tight against his sides, white-knuckled hands gripping the sides of the podium. The gestures he used were mostly nervous ones—putting his hands in his pockets, jingling change, shaking a piece of chalk, tugging at his clothing. When he did use his hands to make a point, his timing was usually off, so that his physical emphasis never seemed to quite match his understated vocal emphasis.

The level of empathy for the class or congregation and the dramatic intensity in our presentation are conveyed by our use of body language. Using body language incorrectly calls attention to itself and away from the message[23]—think of it as emotional static degrading the cognitive signal. Using body language correctly goes unnoticed, but enhances the message[24]—like an emotional carrier wave on which the cognitive signal is superimposed.[25] The quality of body language rests on our appearance, posture, facial expressions, eye contact, and gesturing.[26]

Proper appearance calls for sensitivity for one's audience. We should dress neither too formally nor too casually. Whatever the occasion, we do not want to distract the audience by our appearance.[27] As individuals, we may have the right to dress as we please; but when we step before a group to speak, we should be more concerned about their expectations than our rights—or we might throw away the opportunity to influence them with our message. Our clothing should be checked and adjusted—men: shirttail tucked, zipper zipped, tie tied; women: make-up freshened, slip not showing, hair fixed—before entering the classroom.

Eye contact may be the most important aspect of body language.[28] From the moment you step before the group, move your eyes from person to person. When you find someone who responds, lock in. Let the eye contact register. Let that person know he's important. Then move on to another face and read the reaction. Some may smile, others may nod, but in each case you are building relationships in the audience. Sooner or later you'll hit someone who's not with you. They look away, arms folded, leaning back. Look back to a known "supporter" and confirm your relationship while you gain strength to continue making contact with individuals in the room.[29] Such individual attention is imperative if you hope to make emotional contact with your message.[30] It is always a mistake to gaze at a spot on the back wall or at your notes.[31] Speakers who fail to establish eye contact with listeners remain emotionally detached and aloof, and so reduce the impact of their message.

Proper use of *facial expressions* is the most neglected area of body language.[32] We assume we know what we look like when we smile or frown or put on a sad face. In reality, we know how our expressions feel to us, but unless we've spent some serious time in front of a mirror, we may be quite mistaken in how we think we look. In my work in deaf ministry, I've seen just how powerfully facial expressions aid or hinder communication. Vivid expressions on faces of the deaf reflect joy or pain, discovery or puzzlement, happiness or sadness, surprise or grief, which colors the telling of experiences and stories. Then I've seen some hearing interpreters, translating a sermon or speech into sign language, who make little change in facial expression from one emotion to another. They may sign "angry" or "happy" or "brokenhearted," but you'd never know the difference by the expression on their faces. Good interpreters express emotions on their faces even as they express the emotions with their hands. Teachers should link verbal and facial emotions in the same way.

Exaggerated expressions are just as bad, if not worse. Melodramatic histrionics will drive an audience away faster than an expressionless presentation. As with the voice characteristics of pitch and volume, we need to develop a range of appropriate facial expressions. The key to effective use of facial expressions is to link what you do with your face to how it feels.[33] Look in a mirror and smile. Produce various sizes of smiles and notice how each "look" feels. Now try making a questioning face, one you might use when asking a question. Try displaying various emotions with your face, studying how changes *look* in the mirror and *feel* from inside. The best facial expressions come from within, naturally.[34] So do not put on a false face as you teach. Sensing the link between what we do with our faces and how it looks helps focus our "natural" expressions.

Posture differs from person to person, and a wide range of postures are effective in supporting the message. The posture, neither too rigid nor too slack, should be comfortable for the speaker. A stance that leans into the audience lends a sense of urgency to the presentation, while standing back on one's heels communicates withdrawal.[35] Standing with chest high and chin up exudes confidence, while slouching oozes weakness and insecurity. An appropriate posture allows the smooth movement of arms and torso.[36]

Gestures are the impulsive physical reflections of a speaker's feelings.[37] The index finger indicates location and mild emphasis. A clenched fist is dramatic and indicates a strong emphasis. Holding hands out, palms up, communicates affirmation or pleading, while palms down communicates rejection or contempt.[38] Take care not to lock elbows at your sides, gesturing with half-arm movements. Such gestures appear tentative. Practice making full-arm gestures.[39] Sign language interpreters talk about their "body box," an imaginary square in front of the signer. When one signs inside a small body box, the signs are constricted and convey less power. Increase the size of the body box, and you increase the power of the signed message. The same holds true for the range of movement of gestures.

Timing is essential to effective use of gestures.[40] One's gesture should precede a point of emphasis by a split second.[41] Take the sentence "Now this is an important point." One might expect a rap on the podium just before "this," "-por-" and "point":

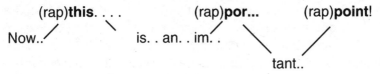

Dr. Boar might express it this way:

this
Now.. is an important (rap) point.

Nervous gestures, as we saw with Dr. Boar, take away from the message by calling attention to themselves. In addition to those mentioned earlier, we can list the following: removing and replacing glasses, folding hands in front of or behind the body, leaning on the podium, pacing about without meaning,[42] fiddling with one's hands, or clasping hands over the lower body.[43] If you have difficulty with nervous gestures, practice speaking in front of a mirror with a heavy book in each hand. At times you'll raise one hand or the other, despite the heavy books. These are real gestures. Save them. The others are nervous movements and need to be eliminated.[44]

Various components of body language work together to provide a nonverbal emphasis to the verbal message. The chart below differentiates between emphatic, questioning, and sarcastic messages.

	Emphatic	**Questioning**	**Sarcastic**
Facial Expression	*concerned*	*perplexed*	*smirk*
Posture	*forward*	*back, as if defensive*	*relaxed*
Gestures	*sharp, decisive pointing hands*	*slow palms up*	*Shrug Who cares?*

Just as a tape recorder is the best tool for improving one's vocal quality, so the video recorder is the best tool for improving body language. By videotaping yourself in teaching or preaching situations, you can objectively analyze your appearance, eye contact, posture, gestures, and timing. Improving body language increases the dramatic effect of presentations and the empathetic attention of our audiences.

The Teacher as Storyteller

So I decided to go into the tavern . . . with my Gospels of Mark . . . after all, these people needed God's Word as much as or more than the people who lived in the neat row houses I'd been visiting. I climbed a steep set of concrete steps, took a breath, and pushed through the double doors. Much to my surprise, I found myself facing a second set of double doors as the first doors closed behind me. Standing in darkness, I paused to consider what I might find on the other side. But I had already determined to go in, so I pushed on through. When the second set of doors closed behind me, I found myself in a room of midnight darkness. I couldn't see a thing—except for a small red neon "Schlitz" sign hanging on the back wall. By the sign's dim reflection on the tavern floor I saw that the space between me and the back wall was open, so I headed for the sign. My eyes were screaming for enough light to set my bearings, but all I could see was the sign. By the time I reached it, the pupils of my eyes were full open, so that as I turned around to face the entrance, I was able to see, on my left, a row of booths containing ten or twelve people. On my right was a long bar, with high stools (several occupied), and on the wall behind the bar, row upon row of bottles of every shape and color. Part of me knew I was where I shouldn't be, but another part knew why. And so I began handing Gospels of Mark to individuals in the booths on the left and then to those at the bar on the right. I could see in front of me a tiny line of light squeezing between the doors I'd just come through. The closer I moved toward that light, the more I wanted to be done with the task and out of the place. I handed a Gospel of Mark to the last patron at the bar and made for the door. Panic was beginning to set in. Time slowed, so that I moved as through molasses. Suddenly, a sharp, deep voice struck out at me, "Hey! . . . You!"

It was the bartender. I was terrified. I was caught! Would he call the police? Would he cuss me? Physically throw me out of the place? I turned toward him, "Yes, sir?"

"Well, now . . . where's mine?" he asked with the same deep, but softer, voice. "Here you are, sir," I said as I handed him a booklet, "and . . . God bless you!"

I turned and headed back to the doors. "And you too, son!" Out the doors I went . . . out into the blazing afternoon sun. It took several minutes for my eyes and soul to adjust to the light. But I still wonder—nearly forty years later—what God did with his Word, delivered by a small boy, to folks in that tiny little tavern. Perhaps one day I'll know, but for now, it's enough to know that I did the right thing. . . .

This is the true story, introduced earlier, that I tell my educational psychology classes as we finish studying Kohlberg's theory of moral reasoning. There is power in the story itself because it tells people about people. Hearing a story, we enter into the experience of others, feel what they feel, learn firsthand.[45]

The traditional format of presentation, whether it be in a conference or a sermon or a class, is: principles first, then illustrations. The story format differs, however, in that it paints an image, moving from known to unknown, concrete to abstract. This image provides the listener with a solid box for storing wispy principles.[46] The story-question of the fourteen-year-old boy and the tavern, along with other moral dilemmas, introduces Kohlberg's six stages of moral reasoning. The concluding story drives home the importance of intent and motive behind the moral choices we make.

Did you notice the direct quotes in the tavern story? Using direct quotes allows the learner to actually hear what was said, to eavesdrop on the conversation, to be there. Description separates the events from the listeners and robs the story of its immediacy. Compare the description "Jesus told Nicodemus that unless he was born again. . . . " to: "Then Jesus said to him, 'Nicodemus, I tell you the truth, unless a man is born again. . . .'"[47] Translate descriptions, like "Goliath had a heavy sword," into action: "David strained to lift Goliath's sword over his head."[48]

The story line is fixed. We are not free to embellish or change a story simply to make it more dramatic. Unlike an entertainer who invents stories, we are bound by truth. But then, so is a musical score fixed. Though the conductor is bound by the "truth" of the score, still he looks for varying intensities in the notes in order to enhance its presentation. Likewise we can look for the crescendos in a story,[49] varying the intensity of the story elements, saving the greatest intensity for the climax.

Stories involve conflict, which enhances the listeners' interest. Since the climax resolves the conflict, don't hurry through the conflict in order to quickly get to the solution.[50] Take the time to tell the story correctly, intensely. Let the conflict build. Use pauses and silence. Build suspense as you go along. A slower pace says, "Feel this—live this with me." Don't rush the story to "get to the point." The story gets to the point better than any explanation can.[51]

Use depictions of the senses—sight, sound, taste, touch, smell— to heighten the reality of the story. Sight is the most vivid,[52] so paint visual images[53] with your words: David whirling a sling, Abraham raising a knife over his son, Moses striking the rock.

Focus stories on people, not things or organizations. Listeners can identify more easily with the experiences of other people. The story should heighten curiosity ("What's behind the doors?") and contain a surprise ("Hey! . . . Where's mine?"). Use enough facts to establish the story, but don't get bogged down or sidetracked into describing irrelevant detail. Tell the story with appropriate excitement, puzzlement, or concern.[54]

Personal experiences make excellent stories, so long as they are relevant to the subject.[55] Hearing stories may be more entertaining than listening to a lecture or sermon, but detached stories, ones not germane to the topic at hand, merely fill (read, "waste") time. Relevant personal experiences increase our credibility level with students.[56] "This is something I've learned, not from a book, but from first-hand experience." Also, because personal experiences belong to us, they are more real.[57] It's easier to infuse our telling with an inherent, natural enthusiasm not available to borrowed stories. We were there!

Use humorous stories to make a point, ease tension, or lighten a heavy subject, but do not use them simply to be funny.[58] Unlike comedians who use humor to entertain and make a living, we have a more serious function: to teach, to motivate, to grow. Still, there are times in the classroom or in the pulpit where humor is helpful. Here are some guidelines:

- Do not announce a story as funny. If it is funny, people will know it without being told. If it isn't, don't try to salvage it. Just move on to the next point.

- The climax of the funny story should be the last thing you say about it. You shouldn't have to explain anything afterwards. Just move on to the next point.

- Know stories well enough to casually tell them in your own words.

- If you tell a joke on someone, it's best to tell it on yourself.[59]

There are many resources for stories other than personal experience or joke books. Many of the stories I use in class concern people in the Bible. They reinforce principles under study, are usually familiar to my students, and encourage spiritual formation as well. I highly recommend Marlene LeFever's *Creative Teaching Methods*[60] and Galli and Larson's *Preaching That Connects*[61] for their suggestions for dramatizing Bible stories.

A good story, carried emotionally from speaker to listener by presence, voice, and body language, can connect with listeners in a way that literally alters thought patterns, reorders value systems, and changes behavior. Only one step remains, and—shh! we must say this with hushed tones—that step is to enter the realm of enchantment.

The Teacher as Enchanter

> For no one can lay any foundation other than the one already laid, which is Jesus Christ. If any man builds on this foundation using gold, silver, costly stones, wood, hay or straw, his work will be shown for what it is, because the Day will bring it to light. It will be revealed with fire, and the fire will test the quality of each man's work. If what he has built survives, he will receive his reward. If it is burned up, he will suffer loss; he himself will be saved, but only as one escaping through the flames (1 Cor. 3:11–15).

"Gold . . . silver . . . precious stones. Wood . . . hay . . . straw. It must have been a powerful sermon I heard that night.
[Shrug]

Not that I remember it at all, 'cause I don't. I was only twelve or so.
[Un-shrug; softer, slower voice]

But I'll never forget the dream I had as a result of it.
[Quicken pace, remembering the dream]

I found myself standing
[hands face palms out, toward the class, belt level and slowly begin to move upward, showing the wall]

before a roaring wall of fire . . . extending up into the darkness
[full-arm stretch upward]

and

[begin moving hands down, pivoting at shoulders, keeping arms straight; look left and right]

as far as I could see to the left and right
[full-arm stretch left and right].

I sensed the fact that I had lived a long life—perhaps to 55, the age of my grandfather at the time—and had died. And now it was Judgment Day.
[Lift slightly bent arms upward from shoulders as if holding a 12-foot ball]

In my outstretched arms I held a
[look up and scan this massive ball]

huge ball of indefinable stuff,
[look back at class]

looking like ragged burlap as much as anything. As I
[look up]

looked up at this bloated mass—it must have been twelve to fifteen feet across—I sensed that it represented the total of my life's work
[pause; arms still in place].
[Lower arms to sides]
And a Voice called out of the flames to me.
[Make a beckoning motion with right hand]
'Come forward!'
[Lower arms, palms out]
Without fear of the Voice or of the fire, I
[take one step forward]
stepped forward. As I stepped into the flames, the burlap ball
[raise hands as if holding the ball; look up at the ball]

exploded into a roiling inferno, as if it had been soaked in kerosene.
[Lower hands slowly to sides]

Still, I felt no pain or discomfort, and I kept walking into the flames.

Eventually I stepped out of the flames. There,
[open right palm up, in front, pushing forward, pointing to the One before me]

in front of me, was Jesus. He was facing me, and smiling
[look at the class, slightly to one side and then the other, nod and smile]

—I remember feeling relief when I saw him smiling! He
[beckoning motion again]

motioned me forward.

As I
[take a half-step forward and hold the position]

stepped toward him, I
[open right palm, facing up, in front of stomach; look down at the open palm]
looked down at my hand, and saw some . . .
[play with the pieces]
Fool's gold
[look up at the class]
—we found a lot of fool's gold in the El Paso mountains—
[look back at the palm]
. . . and a
[point to another place on the palm]
nickel
[look up at class]
. . . silver . . . and a
[look back to palm, tapping with left index finger]
dull . . . red . . . ruby
[look up at class]
—my birthstone. As I
[extend palm forward toward the "Lord," standing in front of you]
extended my hand out to the Lord, offering to him the residuals of
    my life, the thought of how much of my life I'd spent building
    with wood and straw seized me with cold, stark reality. And
[snap fingers]
—snap!—I woke up. . . .
[question mark on face; arms down, palms forward in questioning posture]
What makes the difference?
[hands down]
I don't want to wait until I . . .
[index finger jab]
die . . . to find out.
[Serious face]
    I want to know
[index finger jab]
    <u>now</u> how to avoid wasting my life building with straw.
[Stern face]
    I want to know
[index finger jab]
    <u>now</u> how to make my life count for something in the
    Lord, how to build with gold.
[Punch left palm with fist]
    What . . .
[again]
        makes . . .

[again]
    the difference? . . .
[Relax body, open palms toward class, softer voice]
That's what we'll discover today . . . as we look for biblical principles for ministry."

Enchantment is storytelling pushed to a higher intensity. The colors are deeper; the tones, more hushed. Nouns are grittier; verbs, more resonant. Words, more forceful; sentences, shorter.[62]

A story conveys the inner feelings of a teller in a way that touches listeners' hearts. But when the teller gets inside listeners' hearts and allows them to ventilate their own feelings, their own confusion, their own desperate hope for a solution—that's enchantment. It is an experience of exquisite rapport, of emotional connection, when both teller and listener give, as Hoff describes it, their "complete commitment to the immediacy of the moment."[63] Such stories grab hold of storytellers in such a way that they actually relive the experience as they tell it. There is no need for notes or scripts when we speak of life and death matters—especially when they are our own, and when they apply to everyone.[64] Like the haunting melody of a bagpiped Celtic tune, or the melancholy of a violin, or the resonance of a Gregorian chant, the passion of a personally engrossing story transports those caught up in it to a higher plane of experience.

Enchantment is like a bubble made with a child's bubble blower—light and dainty, it floats in the air, a wonder to behold. But at any moment the magical bubble can burst and we're left with nothing more than a splatter of suds. Don't burst the bubble by apologizing for telling a personal story. If you think you need to make an apology for the story, then don't tell it. Don't introduce the story: "Let me tell you an exciting story" or "Let me conclude with this poignant tale." Simply tell the story. Your listeners will know whether it's enchanting or poignant. Avoid using superlatives: "This is the most important point in the passage." It is up to the listener to decide what is important and what is not. Say it well, say it briefly, and leave them wanting more.[65]

It is only in the telling of stories that you can develop elements that raise the experience to the level of enchantment. Too little effort, and emotion never ignites. Too much effort, and excessive emotion drives your listeners away. It takes keen awareness of self and audience to control intense feelings, like heady chariot steeds, now letting them run, now holding them back, as the race is run. Now holding back passion, now letting it out, never letting it burst into flames.

Seldom do we enchant the whole of a class or congregation. There will always be a listener or two who sneer and roll their eyes as if to say, "Wooo! Cheesy!" Ignore them. Seek out the enchanted ones, the ones who are with you. Pour your heart into them, because it is for them that you tell your story.

When I was a seminary student, I heard Dr. John Drakeford[66] speak in chapel one morning. His sermon focused on Jesus' "Ask, seek, knock" passage (Luke 11:5–10). He took Jesus' parable of a man seeking bread from a neighbor at midnight for a visitor. He pictured Jesus as having been the persistent one, who kept on asking, kept on seeking, kept on knocking, until the neighbor got up and, stepping over his children asleep on the floor, opened the door and provided the needed bread. "We are surrounded by hungry people who need the Bread of Life . . . people who are asking for our help . . . seeking the Bread we have . . . knocking on our doors of complacency." He had been building the intensity of his presentation steadily, punctuating his points with gestures and voice. The crescendo was moving to climax. I was already anticipating his close, but then, he broke the pace. Silence tangibly hung in the air. Slowly, ever so slowly, he leaned forward. Over the pulpit. Lips close to the microphone. And, in a hushed voice he said, "Get *uuup* . . . (softer) go *ouuut* . . . (whispered) and *give It* to them." And he was gone. Chapel was over. I sat in my seat, transfixed by the truth of it. By the impact of it. My heart was pounding, my head spinning. I had a class scheduled to begin in a few minutes, but all I could do was bow my head and pray: "Lord, teach me how to be available." I had been enchanted. I had been changed.

Enchantment is an experience of exquisite rapport, of emotional connection, when both teller and listener give their complete commitment to the immediacy of the moment.

The Flawed Dramatic Performer

We are pastor-teachers (see Eph. 4:11), not entertainers. The chemistry that generates the power we've been discussing through this chapter is dangerous. If we grow more interested in producing the emotional than conveying the rational, we sacrifice the treasures of presence, delivery, and enchantment for their flawed substitutes. Let's look briefly at the dark side.

Glamor Rather than Presence

Soapboxes, I said, should "draw students into the material." Soapboxes generate vitality, but when they push learning aside, the class experience turns frivolous, empty. The old adage "Sell the sizzle, not the steak" may be popular among snake-oil salesmen, but teachers—and particularly Christian teachers—need to deal in the educational equivalent of filet mignon.

Jesus was not glamorous. "He had no beauty or majesty to attract us to him, nothing in his appearance that we should desire him. He was despised and rejected by men, a man of sorrows, and familiar with suffering. Like one from whom men hide their faces he was despised, and we esteemed him not" (Isa. 53:2–3). Not glamorous, but he definitely had presence. He secured attention, but he used the attention he gained to deliver his message. With his help, we can cultivate a presence that attracts appropriate attention for the message he's given us to share.

Demagogue Rather than Speaker

A demagogue, as defined by the *American Heritage Dictionary*, is a "leader who obtains power by means of impassioned appeals to the emotions and prejudices of the populace." Synonyms include ranter, haranguer, and agitator.

We can use voice techniques (pitch, volume, pace) and body language (gestures, eye contact, movement) to psychologically manipulate listeners to do as we wish. Such behavior is nothing short of brainwashing.

Remember Jesus' warning: "But if anyone causes one of these little ones who believe in me to sin, it would be better for him to have a large millstone hung around his neck and to be drowned in the depths of the sea" (Matt. 18:6). The truth is paramount. To the extent we use voice and body techniques to enhance the conveyance of truth, we do well. If we lose the truth in style, we sin—and worse, we cause others to sin. That may be why James warned, "Not many of you should presume to be teachers, my brothers, because you know that we who teach will be judged more strictly" (James 3:1).

Yarn-Spinner Rather than Storyteller

A good story invites us to the edge of a precipice of fear, or joy, or conflict, or crisis, or release. A good story never bores us. But balancing on the edge of a precipice so brands the memory that the story may be the only part of our presentation our listeners remember. They remember the illustration but forget the point illustrated.[67] If this happens, we've become nothing more than a yarn-spinner.

I love to listen to Garrison Keillor's stories about his hometown of Lake Wobegone. He spins his stories out of childhood memories of growing up in the Midwest, in Minnesota. Through his stories we are introduced to people just like ones we knew as children. People who, despite their complexities and problems, idiosyncrasies and foibles, lived and loved and worked in community with each other. But as much as I enjoy the yarns, I recognize his stories are told for their entertainment value.

As pastor-teachers, we are called to the serious business of "rightly dividing the word of truth" (2 Tim. 2:15 NKJV). If we're more effective in doing this by the use of story, we do well. If we lose the truth in the midst of telling stories, we become nothing more than a yarn-spinner.

Charlatan Rather than Enchanter

The *American Heritage Dictionary* defines a charlatan as "a person who makes elaborate, fraudulent, and often voluble claims to skill or knowledge; a quack or fraud." There is power in enchantment. Since power corrupts, the one who would develop skills in enchantment must work much more at keeping grounded in truth. If our abilities and ambitions carry us higher than our character can support, we will fall. Satan will infuse our enchanting abilities with himself and turn our efforts into a type of witchcraft. Maintaining spiritual sensitivity through prayer, holding fast to the proper use of stories ("to help students learn"), and refusing to use story power to enhance one's own personal power are essential safeguards.

In Conclusion

Dr. Boar's style was an emotional black hole, literally sucking energy out of his students into his own vacuum. He de-energized classes, leaving them exhausted at semester's end, vowing never to take another class with him. Some changed majors, not wanting to study his field anymore. In his wake, he left the broken remnants of an obliterated learning process—a negative presence, an unappealing delivery, an agonizing absence of story and enchantment.

May the Lord help all of us to raise the level of personal chemistry in our teaching—to cultivate a confident presence, to foster an emphatic delivery, to nourish the art of storytelling, to evoke an aura of enchantment—in order to "demolish arguments and every pretension that sets itself up against the knowledge of God, and . . . [to] take captive every thought to make it obedient to Christ" (2 Cor. 10:4–5), whatever our field of service.

Jesus was not a theologian.
He was God who told stories.

Madeleine L'Engle[68]

For Further Reading

I highly recommend the following books:

Fasol, Al. *A Complete Guide to Sermon Delivery*. Nashville: Broadman & Holman, 1996.

Galli, Mark, and Craig Brian Larson. *Preaching that Connects: Using the Techniques of Journalists to Add Impact to Your Sermons*. Grand Rapids: Zondervan Publishing House, 1994.

Grant, Reg, and John Reed. *The Power Sermon: Countdown to Quality Messages for Maximum Impact*. Grand Rapids: Baker Books, 1993.

Hoff, Ron. *I Can See You Naked: A Fearless Guide to Making Presentations*. Kansas City: Andrews and McNeel, 1988.

LeFever, Marlene D. *Creative Teaching Methods: Be An Effective Christian Teacher*. Elgin, Ill.: David C. Cook Publishing Company, 1990.

Miller, Calvin. *The Empowered Leader: Ten Keys to Servant Leadership*. Nashville: Broadman & Holman Publishers, 1995.

Nash, Tom. *The Christian Communicator's Handbook: A Guide to Help You Make the Message Plain.* Wheaton, Ill.: Victor Books, 1984.

Schloff, Laurie, and Marcia Yudkin. *Smart Speaking: Sixty-Second Strategies.* New York: Henry Holt and Company, 1991.

The Teacher as Manager

Chapter 9. The Teacher as Evaluator

The Teacher as Test Writer

The Teacher as Test Item Analyst

The Teacher as Observer

The Teacher as Scribe

The Teacher as Grader

Chapter 6

The Teacher as Creative Designer

*In the beginning
God created the heavens and the earth.*

Genesis 1:1

*So God created man in his own image, in the image of God he
created him; male and female he created them.*

Genesis 1:27

*G*od created (Gen. 1:1) and brought order (Gen. 1:31) out of
chaos (Gen. 1:2). We are created in the image of God. Our chaos
is a jumble of facts, dates, persons, concepts, principles, and
resources related to a particular subject we teach. Part of our teaching task is to create out of this jumble an order, a plan, a design for
learning.

We judge the quality of the design by two basic criteria. Does it properly handle the essentials of the subject? Does it provide meaningful learning opportunities for students who must live through it? Without these two criteria, teaching is nothing more than an empty stage routine, a platform from which teachers entertain. The essence of teaching is conveying the essentials of a subject in a manner commensurate with the abilities of students to learn. Generating such a design calls for our best creativity.

As a doctoral student in 1976 I was given the opportunity to teach my very own section of educational psychology. I selected one of the texts we had used in a seminar and began developing my course. The text contained fourteen chapters, so we could cover a chapter a week, twenty-eight sessions. The final exam took up the final two-hour block. The introductory session and midterm exam took up two more sessions. Thirty-two sessions in all. Perfect.

I found out as the course progressed, however, that I was not as prepared as I had thought. I suffered from the shallow "one book" preparation mentioned early on in chapter 2. I was reading the same material as my students, sometimes just moments before heading into class to discuss it. I had no depth in my presentation because I wasn't prepared to go beyond what students had already read. I was unable to explain to my students *why* the authors emphasized the ideas they did.

My course goal was little more than "get through the book." Test items were arbitrary questions drawn out of the text. I began to fear every raised hand, much as a tightrope walker fears wind gusts. Raised hands meant questions, and every question held the prospect of slipping off my thin wire and falling to my death as a teacher.

Halfway through the course, I began to doubt my calling as a teacher. By the end of the course, I was as much in shock as one of Skinner's rats, forced to run a maze over an electrified grid. My major professor wanted me to stay on at the school and join the faculty upon graduation. The dean thought it best if I served on church staff for "four or five years first." My teaching experience made it easier to postpone my dream of faculty status and follow the dean's suggestion. So in late 1976, I was called by Columbia Baptist Church in Falls Church, Virginia, to be their minister of education. Five years later, March 1981, I was elected to the faculty. In August, we moved to Fort Worth and I began my preparation to teach. The focus of my preparation this time around was very different.

The Teacher as Researcher

All of the courses I was assigned to teach, save one, were already developed. I taught three sections of Principles of Teaching (one of them off-campus) and used Dr. Leon Marsh's syllabus. I taught three sections of Philosophy of Education (one of them off-campus) and used Dr. Jack Terry's syllabus and text. The seventh course I taught was Research and Statistics for Advanced Studies. It had not been taught in several years, and I was asked to develop a new course under this title. The first step was to develop a sense of the scope of the subject.

Develop the Scope of the Subject

I went to the seminary's library and checked out all the books I could find on the two subjects: research design and statistical analysis.[1] Each book had its own focus—business, psychology, education—but, as I scanned the books, commonalities began to appear: "hypothesis," "problem statement," "definitions," "Pearson's r," "t-test," "limitations," "analysis of variance," and so on. When I finished the stack of books, I had isolated over 350 items—some referred to many times; others, only once. This was my course scope.

Concepts and Principles

Research books emphasized research design, types of research, the scientific method, components and subcomponents of a research plan, measurement types, sampling, validity, reliability, objectivity, and the like. Statistics books emphasized statistical concepts and mathematical procedures: the normal curve and the z-test, power, error rates, t-tests, ANOVA, ANCOVA, factorial designs, multiple comparisons, correlation coefficients, chi-square tests, and regression analysis. What a chaos of terms and principles it was! How was I ever to bring order and structure from it?

Though it was obvious that research design and statistical analysis were interdependent, textbooks said little about the marriage. Here was my first challenge: to develop a course that focused not

~

only on research design and statistical analysis separately, but one that emphasized the marriage of the two disciplines.

Concept Clusters

Chapter titles in the various textbooks provided structure for the 350 separate items by clustering individual elements under larger umbrella concepts. *Correlation* provided an umbrella cluster for Pearson's r, Spearman's rho, Kendall's tau and W, the Phi coefficient, and Cramer's phi. The term *normal curve* provided an umbrella cluster for the mean, deviation score, sum of squares, variance, standard deviation, and standard score.

The 350 elements were clustered under umbrellas that in turn were clustered under the "design" or "analysis" parts of the course-to-be. During this initial organization phase, elements that were seldom mentioned in the texts were set to one side. As I developed the course, I discarded or reintroduced these elements as course time allowed.

Sequence

Clusters were arranged in logical sequence. Again, I used the sequences of material found in reference textbooks to help sequence my own clusters of concepts.

Then, concepts were logically sequenced within each umbrella cluster. For example, discussion of writing problem statements had to precede the discussion of writing hypotheses. The normal curve and z-test had to precede t-test, which in turn preceded analysis of variance. Correlation had to precede linear regression, which preceded multiple regression.

At the end of this phase of organization, I possessed a structured flow of material drawn from many sources. This universe of sequenced concept clusters provided the raw material from which I constructed the course. The development of any course requires attention to these phases of content scope, concepts, clusters, and sequencing.

The Teacher as Course Architect

An architect designs in broad strokes, taking into consideration the parameters of space, cost, function, and surrounding environment. A teacher designs a course from the broad strokes of course credit, content, and student needs.

Course Credit

Course credit usually determines the number of hours a class meets per week. A two-hour course meets two hours per week; a three-hour course, three. My research class was a two-hour course, running sixteen weeks. So, I had thirty-two hours of class time to provide for introduction, instruction, and testing. Testing is an important part of the instructional process, since it drives classroom instruction and out-of-class study.

Content—Structure

The content of my research class fell into five natural divisions: introduction to research, research fundamentals, research methods, statistical fundamentals, and statistical procedures. The introduction would analyze ways we develop our knowledge of the world and relate these ways of knowing to the scientific method. The introduction would also demonstrate the symbiotic relationship between research design and statistical analysis. The research fundamentals section would cover such items as an overview of the process of writing a research proposal, choosing and defining variables to study, writing problem and hypothesis statements, and developing a synthesis of current research. Research methods would cover ways to gather data to be analyzed: historical analysis, survey (interview and questionnaire), testing, attitude scaling, and experimentation. The statistical fundamentals would introduce my students to simple statistical concepts: mean, deviation, variance, and the normal curve. Statistical procedures would cover the most popular formulas for analyzing numerical data: z-test, t-test, analysis of variance, correlation, chi-square, and regression.

I determined to give four examinations: one over research design fundamentals, one over statistical fundamentals, a take-home examination covering use of statistical procedures, and a comprehensive final.

Student Needs

An effective course is more than content. This may surprise some who consider content to be the sole factor in designing a course. These are the same people who define teaching as "nothing more than telling what I know." The purpose of teaching is far more than talking through one's notes—it is helping students learn. Two questions must be answered in planning to meet student needs. First, what are our assumptions about the students coming into our classes? Second, what are our expectations for what they can achieve during the course?

If our assumptions and expectations are too high, we will confuse and frustrate students. If they are too low, we will bore them. My assumption concerning the research class was that my students would be novices in design and analysis. Those who had an introductory course in college would have a slight advantage, but most of my students carefully chose their courses in order to stay as far away from math as possible. So I assumed no previous preparation. If this led to boredom for a few of my students, it would be short-lived, since most college introductory courses introduce students to either research or statistical terminology, not both. Those with better than average statistical skills would quickly become tutors to others, and this merely enhances their own motivation to achieve.

My expectations for students were these: they would master the basic terminology of research and statistics, about 350 terms; develop an understanding of the six most popular statistical procedures, including their function and meaning; and develop skills in writing clear and concise proposals for research studies. My primary purpose was to produce credible consumers of research, graduates who would be able to read research articles with understanding and discernment. My secondary purpose was to encourage more ministers to engage in credible research related to Christian ministry.

Your assumptions and expectations will vary depending on whom you are teaching, what you are teaching, and the outcomes you seek to produce as a result. Assumptions and expectations must be regularly evaluated and courses changed as students change from year to year. Otherwise you will find yourself teaching a "saber tooth" curriculum, an expression referring to "out-of-date" course material.

The Teacher as Unit Strategist

I had established the five units for the course. It was now my task to develop a clear structure within each unit. This structure should provide for comprehension, direction, and motivation, all from the perspective of the students.

Leveling

The first unit, the introduction, provides a time for student leveling. Students come into class the first day with a wide assortment of fears, hopes, and perspectives. They are a collection of individuals, not a class; strangers, not a family. Before we can begin serious study, we need first to find common ground and then to discover where we are going together.

The research class was first designed to be a preparatory class on the master's level for future doctoral level work. Students viewed this course as essential to their own success in the doctoral program in general and in the writing of their dissertations in particular. Intrinsic motivation was high. Class size was small, usually twelve to fifteen students. I was seen as a helper. This was advantageous as I developed the course since students were grateful for the help I gave them and forgiving of my mistakes.

Several years later two departments in our school, liking what they saw in the course, made it mandatory for master's level study. Immediately the students' intrinsic motivation evaporated. Class size was large, usually fifty to seventy students. I was seen as an enemy to be conquered or a disaster to be survived.

Still, in both cases, leveling was required. A course syllabus detailed requirements, examination objectives, purpose, and rationale. I provided a historical overview of why the course had been developed and what skills students could expect to have at the end of the course. As we've already noted, the introduction subsumed scientific knowing into six major ways we come to know our world. These first two class sessions were to lay a foundation for the building of the semester, unit by unit.

The Unit Triad

Within each unit, give attention to how you will address issues of head, heart, and hand. As we discussed in chapter 1, this triad of thinking, feeling, and doing reflects the preferred learning mode of every student in your class. Thinkers are looking for meat to chew—new ideas and new ways of looking at the world. Feelers are looking for gifts to receive and share—relationships with new friends and personal relevance. Doers are looking for a project to finish—let's get the job done, done right, and in the quickest way possible. Each of these areas must be addressed within each unit if you are to maintain living contact with all your students.[2] Dealing with head, heart, and hand issues must be intentional because we naturally teach out of our own preference.

For the head, determine major and minor concepts that must be mastered through the unit. What conceptual questions should you ask? What misconceptions are most common? What diagrams can you use to illustrate meaning? What vocabulary do students need?

For the heart, how can you develop a sense of openness in the class? How will you help students overcome the fear of asking questions? How can you help students get to know each other and rely on each other through the course? How will you use humor to reduce tension? What personal testimonies can you share of your own difficulties with the subject? How will you demonstrate your willingness to help students learn?

For the hand, what skills will students need to master? How will you demonstrate your own skill level? In what ways will you show your willingness to help students become experts as well? What exercises will you use in class to evaluate student learning? What assignments will you make to hone study skills? How will you use this student work to enhance learning in the classroom?

Giving attention to all three of these areas will help make each unit meaningful to every student. One of the most helpful means I've found to accomplish this derives from Kolb's learning styles grid. Kolb uses four basic elements—illustrated as axes in a polar

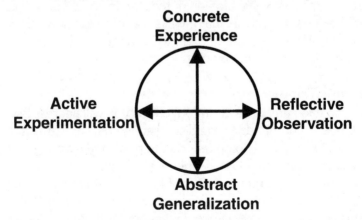

coordinate system: north, south, east, and west—to construct a test of four complex learning styles. I prefer to focus on the basic elements. Kolb calls them concrete experience (north pole), reflective observation (east pole), abstract generalization (south pole), and active experimentation (west pole). I see them in a cycle of teaching: personal experience (feeling), meaningful explanation (thinking), thoughtful reflection (thinking/valuing), practical action (doing).

Begin where students are (personal experience). What do they already know? What positive or negative experiences with the subject have they had? Personal experience can involve both testimonies of out-of-class events or review of a previous class session. Connect with students through previous learnings before moving ahead to new learnings, keeping Dr. Statistics ever in mind. For example, when I introduce the study of Jean Piaget, I begin by writing the term "television evangelist" on the board. Then I ask students to describe the term. The first responses are usually along the lines of "crook," "manipulator," "charlatan." But others will disagree and, invoking Billy Graham's name, suggest "effective communicator," "electronic missionary," and other similar terms. Then I say, "The differences we see on the board are not inherent in the term, but rather in your own minds, in your own experiences with television evangelists. Piaget explains how we develop these kinds of cognitive filters."

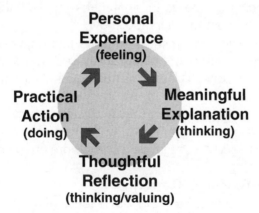

**Personal
Experience**
(feeling)

**Practical
Action**
(doing)

**Meaningful
Explanation**
(thinking)

**Thoughtful
Reflection**
(thinking/valuing)

Having made the personal connection, go directly to the heart of the unit by explaining the most important concepts and principles (meaningful explanation). Using the Piaget example begun above, I focus on the central concepts of Piaget's theory: organization, scheme, accommodation, assimilation, disequilibrium, equilibration, decentration, and conservation. Such terms provide the rich underpinning for the varied implications for teaching infants, preschoolers, children, youth, and adults.

I use both subjective and objective questions to pull learners into the material (thoughtful reflection). Subjective questions drive learners into themselves, into their own perceptions and experiences. For example, "If you had been Nicodemus, what would you have asked Jesus? (see John 3)." Or, "When has your 'shield of faith' protected you from Satan's 'fiery darts' (see Eph. 6)?" Or, "Who do you remember from your high school years that exhibited characteristics of identity confusion? (James Marcia)." Students look within their own experiences for these answers.

Objective questions drive learners deeper into the subject matter. For example, "What did Nicodemus ask Jesus? (John 3)." Or, "Explain Paul's use of Roman armor to describe the spiritual defenses we have at our disposal (Eph. 6)." Or, "Define Marcia's term 'identity confusion' in your own words." Students look to their learning, their understanding of concepts, for these answers.

The use of small groups to answer questions, solve problems, or analyze cases is an excellent way to help learners reflect on the meanings of concepts and principles. The purpose of this phase is to help learners personalize the material, to make it their own, to integrate it into what they already know.

I finish the cycle with practical exercises that require the specific application of principles in creative ways (practical doing). These exercises can be done in class or as homework. Here the emphasis is on skilled use of concepts in the "real world."

In this way all three areas of thinking, feeling, and doing are addressed in a logical sequence within the unit. Every student is addressed by the course, regardless of their preferred learning style.

Setting Up Teaching Targets

Your units should already possess a sense of direction because of the way the concept clusters are logically sequenced. But to focus attention on outcomes you desire for each unit, set up teaching targets, or unit objectives. These objectives can be written for all three areas of learning. Thinking and doing objectives provide the best support for development of examinations. Feeling objectives provide the best support for personalizing the classroom. Unit objectives are more inclusive and general than specific session objectives. Continuing with the Piaget example, we might write a session objective like this: "Learners will demonstrate understanding of Piaget's theory of cognitive development by explaining in their own words the terms 'adaptation,' 'accommodation,' and 'assimilation.'" We will discuss session objectives later on in the chapter.

A unit objective might be written like this: "Learners will demonstrate understanding of Piaget's theory of cognitive development by . . .

. . . explaining any of eight terms in their own words.

. . . describing implications for teaching children ages 7–12."

Providing lists of unit objectives at the beginning of the course provides a tangible framework for study, another structure for the chaos of unknowns confronting the student. These objectives may be even more helpful in keeping us honest in our efforts to write reliable and valid tests. Such objectives should prevent us from impulsively adding arbitrary and trivial test questions.

Hitting Teaching Targets: Unit Testing

We secure tangible evidence of student learning through the use of tests. The logical flow of material and the direction given by objectives find their fulfillment in the unit examination. In our age of hyperhumanism, many teachers are opting to forego formal examinations in lieu of "creative" work, such as portfolios, writing, and term papers. Such subjectivity reduces an academic course to a compulsory group therapy exercise in which each student finds "his or her own meaning within the context of the subject." Why do we then wonder why more and more education produces less and less learning?

Perhaps another reason for the demise of the examination is that there are so many poorly written ones. Nothing sabotages student attitudes faster than poorly written tests. But poor quality is no reason to abandon an essential part of the educational process. Well-written examinations focus on course learnings, create a level grading field, and present a just and equitable way to assign grades. Chapter 9 discusses how to develop and write such examinations.

The Teacher as Lesson Plan Tactician

Sooner or later we must come to the day-to-day activities in class. I had used my own broad-brush thinking and general planning, but I knew this meant little unless I planned how I was going to specifically teach on a day-to-day basis.

I had built structure and direction into my units, but I knew that the tangible process of unfolding the structure and moving students in the proper direction would flow out of the sequence of lesson plans that make up each unit. Like links in a chain, each lesson plan had to tie into those before and after, moving students toward unit goals. The general content of lesson plans can be designated by the concept clusters each must convey.

But looking at plans only as links in a unit chain leaves us with too vague a notion of teaching. Teachers can have general plans for their sessions, yet still arrive in class with no concrete starting point, direction, or ending point for the hour. I knew I had to give individual attention to each and every class hour. Generals can devise flawless strategies, but without skilled tacticians to execute coordinated maneuvers, deliver effective firepower, and maintain a steady flow of supplies, strategy remains an empty dream. Teachers really earn their pay as lesson plan tacticians. Creating coordinated blueprints for teaching is the beginning of consistently successful sessions.

A general lesson plan consists of one or more instructional objectives, learning readiness, instruction and learning, evaluation of outcome(s), conclusion, and (optional) assignment.

Writing Session Objectives

We've already introduced the concept of setting up teaching targets in the context of unit outcomes. Session objectives follow the same guidelines, but can be more specific. There is not space in this text to fully develop the art and science of writing clear instructional objectives,[3] but we can suggest some general guidelines.

While there are many perspectives on what objectives should be and do, I have found it most helpful for course design and student preparation to write simple statements of demonstrable outcome. First, write objectives from the learner's point of view. What will the *learner* specifically do to demonstrate achievement of the objective? Second, write the test or indicator in measurable, observable terms. What will the learner *specifically do* to demonstrate achievement of the objective?

If my target is knowledge, measurable outcomes include such things as writing or reciting from memory, identifying from a list, matching, and supplying a missing term in a statement. These suggestions are from the lowest level of learning in the cognitive domain: knowledge.

If my target is understanding, measurable outcomes include such things as explaining correctly "in one's own words,"[4] paraphrasing definitions, drawing illustrations or diagrams of terms, solving problems or cases, comparing and contrasting concepts, outlining passages of a text, synthesizing definitions from several sources, and making appraisals or objective judgments using synthesized standards. These suggestions flow out of the five "understanding" levels of the cognitive domain: comprehension, application, analysis, synthesis, and evaluation.

If my target is personal response, measurable outcomes include listening or watching attentively, sharing personal opinions or testimonies regarding the subject, making a commitment or acting in ways that demonstrate a commitment to the subject, reordering priorities or behaving in ways that indicate priorities have changed in response to the study, and making the subject a natural part of one's lifestyle. These suggestions flow out of the five levels of learning in the affective domain: receiving, responding, valuing, organizing, and characterizing.

If my target is skillful doing, measurable outcomes focus on the level of competence demonstrated by students as they prepare exercises, written assignments, term papers, or as they solve problems.

The format of the objective can be a single, simple statement, such as "Learners will demonstrate (1) of (2) by (3)," where (1) can be "knowledge," "understanding," "appreciation," or "skill." The symbol (2) represents the concept (and biblical reference, if appropriate) such as "the armor of God (Eph. 6)," or "statistical power," or "Piaget's concepts of assimilation and accommodation," or "instructional objectives." The symbol (3) represents the specific action, taken by learners, that provides tangible evidence they have achieved knowledge, understanding, personal response, or skill.

Here are a couple of examples of these single-statement type objectives:

- "Learners will demonstrate knowledge of the armor of God (Eph. 6) by listing the pieces of armor and their spiritual counterparts from memory."
- "Learners will demonstrate understanding of the concept *statistical power* by explaining the meaning of the term in their own words."
- "Learners will demonstrate appreciation for Piaget's concepts of *assimilation* and *accommodation* by sharing experiences they've had related to the terms."
- "Learners will demonstrate skill in writing instructional objectives by properly writing statements for specified levels of learning according to the models given in class."

Objectives can be more complex than this, but these fundamental, simple, direct statements are a good place to begin in targeting your teaching. Complexity can be increased easily by adding indicator statements to a common goal stem. This is often seen in terms of unit objectives. My unit objective for "instructional objectives" in Principles of Teaching looks like this:

"Learners will demonstrate understanding of instructional objectives by doing such things as . . .

. . . defining in their own words the levels of learning in Bloom and Krathwohl's taxonomies.

. . . defining in their own words the terms *goal, objective,* and *indicator*, as they relate to instructional objectives.

. . . analyzing indicator statements in relation to their appropriate level of learning.

. . . writing instructional objectives for assigned passages of Scripture and levels of learning.

. . . evaluating selected instructional objectives written by class members."

Learning Readiness

Not so very long ago, folks used manual pumps to draw water. A pitcher of water was poured into the pump to secure the seal. This would provide enough suction to lift the water out of the ground and into whatever container they had. Without "priming," the manual pump could not draw water.

The teacher who walks into a classroom thinking his class is ready to learn is making a dangerous assumption. The individuals seated before him have their minds on their own agendas. Their hearts may or may not be ready to focus on the class. Their pumps need priming. And this is what the learning readiness section of a lesson plan does.

Remember your objective when designing learning readiness activities. It does not help the learning process to begin your session with a class discussion of last week's football game or the morning's headlines (unless that discussion can lead directly into what is studied). Discussion for discussion's sake is *not* helpful. The intention of pump priming should be to focus hearts and minds on a central issue that will prepare the way for the learning activities that follow. I've provided some examples of learning readiness activities in the accompanying boxes, which are built on the objectives we stated above.

Objective: Learners will demonstrate their knowledge of the armor of God (Eph. 6) by listing the pieces of Roman armor and their spiritual counterparts by memory.

Suggested Learning Readiness: Hang a large picture of a Roman soldier on the front wall. This can be hand drawn on several sheets of newspaper. List the pieces of armor mentioned by Paul on the chalkboard or posterboard. Have the names of the spiritual counterparts printed on pieces of posterboard and randomly placed next to the drawing. Have the class identify which piece of armor goes with each component in the drawing. (The Bible study will analyze each piece of armor and its matching spiritual counterpart, creating a memorized matched list.)

Avoid gimmicks in the learning readiness that might shock, frighten, or offend learners. You will certainly get attention by using sudden loud noises (firecrackers, air horns), rude comments, abusive remarks, or embarrassing skits. But shock will do more to disrupt learning than enhance it.

Instruction and Learning

Objectives provide direction and learning readiness provides motivation, but the meat of the lesson plan is found in providing instruction and learning. I once had a friend who babied his '47 candy-apple red Ford pickup truck, but it was all for show. He never used it for anything practical, yet spent hours every week polishing it. Give me a truck that can haul serious freight. We can polish our teaching techniques, but the real question is whether we're hauling freight as we teach.

Are we establishing knowledge, or merely playing Trivial Pursuit? Are we conveying meaningful understanding, or merely talking about terms? Are we engaging students in heartfelt, subject-reinforcing sharing, or merely conducting an amateur group therapy session? Are we honing skills, or simply talking about it?

It is here, in the instruction portion of the lesson plan, that the educational process burns brightest. It is here that every pedagogical ability must be brought to bear. *What* must be done to secure triadic learning has been discussed in other places.[5] But *that* it is done we emphasize here, as part of the planning process.

The instructional target(s) that have been determined and written provide the parameters, the guidelines, for what is actually done during this instruction phase. The teacher's purpose is to select instructional methods and activities that help students achieve the objectives that have been set.

Evaluating Outcomes

The instruction section ends when your learners (or at least some of them) hit the target(s) you've set up. If your target is knowledge, can they identify or recall what you've said they would? If your target is understanding, can they explain or give examples of the concepts you've taught? If personal response, have they engaged in sharing their experiences related to the study? If skillful action, have they demonstrated skill in the ways they can use the material?

Objective: Learners will demonstrate understanding of the concept *statistical power* by explaining the meaning of the term in their own words.

Suggested Learning Readiness: Draw two overlapping normal curve diagrams on the chalkboard, labeled "1" and "2." Draw a vertical line representing the critical value on the right tail of curve "1." Label the area of the right tail of curve "1" cut off by this line as "Type I error." Label the area of the left tail of curve "2" cut off by this line as "Type II error." Then label the remaining part of curve "2" as "Power." Identify the elements of this diagram at the beginning of class, and then say, "The ability to discover real differences that exist between groups of scores is directly related to the level of power that exists in our research design. Insufficient power means we will fail to detect real differences that exist between learning methodologies, or counseling techniques, or management styles. So today we will analyze error rates inherent in statistical analysis and learn how to maximize power in our designs." (The session will focus on explaining the relationships of error rate and power, using the normal curve diagrams, and conclude with practical ways to increase statistical power in research designs.)

If not, why not? Was the target too small? Did you fail to plan your time correctly? Did you use inappropriate methods? Did something unexpected happen in class? Each time you evaluate a session, whether you succeeded or failed, you gain wisdom for writing your next teaching plan.

Conclusion

A friend of mine is a wonder at wrapping gifts. He takes such care with how he cuts the paper to fit, how he makes each fold. He uses different kinds of ribbon to make intricate patterns on the package. Then, as a final touch, he designs a special bow that sets the whole effect. His packages are so beautiful that I hate to unwrap them.

The objective for the session has been accomplished. Now, in the closing minutes of the hour, conclude the session by summarizing, or leading the class to summarize, what has happened. What have they discovered? What are they carrying away from the class? How will they use what they've learned?

The way you draw your session to a close is as important as Bill's gift wrap is to his packages. It is your last chance to "redeem the time" for your learners. Here are some suggestions for "tying it up in a bow."

Avoid total closure. People want to close discussions and end learning activities in a satisfactory way. They want to find solutions to problems you've raised. Educators call this tendency *closure.* It is frustrating for learners to leave the class wondering what the point of the study was. On the other hand, you create a sense of finality or ending to the session when you bring the class to total closure. This is not good, because you want the learning and experiences to follow your learners into the week. Therefore, draw the session to a close without coming to total closure. Here's how to do it.

Review major points. Briefly review the key discoveries of the session. You can do this passively (teacher review) if time is short, or lead the class to review actively what they've learned (learner review).

Involve learners. Ask learners to share their discoveries, feelings, and reactions to what they've learned from the session. If you listen carefully, you will pick up on the kinds of things that interest and satisfy your learners.

Objective: Learners will demonstrate appreciation for Piaget's concepts of *assimilation* and *accommodation* by sharing experiences they've had related to the terms.

Suggested Learning Readiness: Draw the profile outline of a head facing to the right and, inside it, a circle representing the mind. Draw several symbols, such as "#" and "*" and "@" inside the circle. To the right, write the word *world* and, around it, the symbols "#" and "&" and "a." Draw an upward arching arrow from head to world and label *assimilation.* Draw a downward arching arrow from world to head and label *accommodation.* Say the following: "Yesterday we defined Piaget's terms *assimilation* and *accommodation.* We noted the distortion of assimilation—that is, changing an event to fit what we know—using the example of (pointing to the symbols) the 'at' symbol and 'a.' We also noted the mind-changing nature of accommodation— changing perceptions (schemes) to fit new events—using the example of (point to '&,' follow the arrow with your finger to the mind, and write in a new '&') the ampersand.

"I remember a time in my life when I thought that all Baptists were saved and all Catholics were not. Until I met a devout born-again Catholic and an unbelieving Baptist . . ." (I proceed to tell these experiences, and how they relate to assimilation and accommodation). When have you experienced assimilation or accommodation in your own life? (The core of the day's session will be sharing experiences, reinforcing the meaning of assimilation and accommodation while learning about each other. I am prepared to move into the next part of Piaget's theory if "personal sharing" runs short.)

Tying Sessions Together

Most teachers believe they are finished when they've made their conclusion. But if you end the session with the conclusion and a closing prayer, you effectively disconnect this class hour from the others and isolate your class hour from the rest of the students' week. Do not end with the conclusion!

Open your learners to things they can do during the week that will solidify their study. Have them use what they've learned by raising a question, posing a problem, or providing a situation for students to analyze during the week. This practicing of course material reinforces their learning and integrates course learnings with other parts of student lives. For example, "Use at least one of Piaget's experiments we've discussed with your own children. Come next time ready to share some of the discoveries you made with your own children." One student had a three-year-old daughter who had one cookie, but wanted two. Momma said no, so she went to Daddy. Daddy, having studied Piaget's concept of conservation (and the fact that three-year-olds can't) simply took the cookie and broke it in half—voila! Two cookies! He'll never forget that portion of the course!

Have students prepare for future class sessions and new material by reading the text or studying a handout prepared to introduce a new subject. Give them a work-ahead assignment, as simple as a question to ponder, or as complex as a project to be done. By making an assignment, we preview the next session's activities and provide for natural review in that session. For example, "A fourteen-year-old boy is handing out Gospels of Mark in his neighborhood one Sunday afternoon. He comes to a tavern. Should he go in and distribute the booklets? Consider the implications of this for our class next time." We can also present learners an outline of key terms or an objective ("advance organizers"), or emphasize the kinds of questions that will be addressed. By building on "today's session" we both reinforce the material today and prepare for next time. These preview activities can create personal experiences, which form a perceptual framework for course material.

We need to use these assignments in the next class period. Have students share what they discovered and experienced. Use these experiences to review the key thoughts from previous sessions. By actively reviewing[6] key ideas, or using students' assigned work in

Objective: Learners will demonstrate skill in writing instructional objectives by properly writing statements for specified levels of learning according to the models given in class.

Suggested Learning Readiness: Divide chalkboard space into four sections and write "knowledge," "comprehension," "analysis," and "responding" on the chalkboard. Say: "Yesterday we defined each of these terms and provided you a handout explaining how to properly write instructional objectives. You were also given an assignment to write objectives targeting several different levels of learning. Let's have three volunteers write objectives for each of the levels listed here (point to chalkboard)." If students hesitate to volunteer, suggest that the first ones to volunteer have the luxury of choosing which objective to write. (The session will provide the opportunity for students to evaluate objective statements written by their peers. Such practice not only enhances understanding [evaluation level] but also hones skills in proper objective writing—essential for the development of a lesson plan later on in the course.)

class, or by showing how "today's session" builds on previous work, this review time can provide for a natural introduction for learning readiness. Review ties the present session to its predecessors, reinforces key ideas, and integrates the subject with personal experience.

The gaps between sessions can increase the chaos level of a course unless measures are taken to reduce them. Hard as it is for us to imagine, students have lives to live outside our classes, and they are not necessarily thinking about us or our subjects as they do. By planning ways to preview future sessions and review previous sessions, we link session to session in a meaningful way.

The Teacher as Creative Designer, Revisited

Did Jesus have lesson plans? Did he write objectives? Did the apostle Paul prepare learning readiness activities for his teaching? Or hand out assignments to be done for the following sessions? The answer to all of these questions is a confident "no."

Yet Jesus did know his purpose in teaching. He taught with direction. He knew what kinds of outcomes he sought and how to secure them. Paul taught with structure. His curriculum centered in our living union with Christ, and his learning outcomes touched on practical lifestyle implications. Jesus was God in the flesh, the greatest Teacher who ever lived. Paul was transformed and filled by the Spirit of Christ, the greatest teaching missionary who ever lived. Both knew their subjects intimately, and both knew how to communicate them.

I doubt that many of my best teachers had detailed lesson plans for every session they taught. Knowing their subject and their students, they provided effective instruction based on years of trial and error.

Having said all that, I still believe that the discipline of developing and using detailed lesson plans would improve the quality of instruction by any teacher. Further, such discipline would eliminate years of classroom trial and error, instructional dead ends, and outright mistakes.

So just how detailed should our lesson plans be? I suppose it depends on how critical a session is. In my Principles of Teaching classes, I demonstrate teaching for knowledge, understanding, and personal response outcomes. I have lesson plans for these sessions every bit as detailed as I have described in this chapter. It is imperative that those demos go well. Having taught them for over fifteen years now, I can do these sessions without the first note. But they were planned in detail. Other sessions have skeleton plans, such as the "three uses of chi-square," which is little more three words: "equal expected," "proportional expected," and "test of independence."

The order of priority in planning moves from the most essential components to the least. The most essential ingredient is the set of fundamental concept clusters to be learned in a given session. Next is the instructional target: what do you expect your learners to be able to do with these clusters at the end of the session or unit? Next in importance is the learning readiness procedure, necessary to secure the meaningful attention of learners. Varied learning activities are next, helpful in engaging all students (thinkers, feelers, doers) in the session. Finally, the "niceties" of a lesson plan—the conclusion, the assignment, and the detailed structure of command language.[7]

Any degree of intentional preparation for teaching is better than none. Any level of creative order is better than classroom chaos. The question is, How much chaos do you wish to eliminate?

In Conclusion

Unless our curriculum has been designed for us, we have the daunting task of creating order out of chaos. This was my task as I first prepared to teach Research and Statistics for Advanced Studies. Though my plans have been revised—some assignments dropped and others added, emphases shifted—the core of the course remains much as it was designed seventeen years ago.

By balancing the needs of the subject (their inherent competencies, mastery) and the needs of the students (their deficiencies, required skills, previous learning), we set a long-term destination. By structuring the subject into concept clusters and units, we develop structure. By writing session and unit goals, we generate direction for learning and testing. By blueprinting individual sessions, we secure meaningful learning experiences each time the class meets. Chapter 5 dealt with the "feel" of a course, the art of presentation. This chapter has emphasized the integrity of a course, the structure of presentation.

God has called us to teach, not merely talk or emote. He has created us to be creative. God bless you as you carry out his purposes in your own life as a teacher, as you bring instructional order out of classroom chaos.

A View Ahead

I might have an airline schedule in hand, but it does not guarantee that I'll have a timely flight, or that I'll have a flight at all! Managing the schedule in real time does that.

In the same way, having a detailed course plan does not guarantee the plan will work. Managing classroom structure and behavior in real time with real students does that. In the next chapter we move inside the classroom to discuss ways we actually manage the learning environment.

For Further Reading

The principles addressed in this chapter have been extended to the development of a complete school curricula by Dr. Leroy Ford in *Developing Curriculum: An Outcome-Based Approach* (Nashville: Broadman & Holman Publishers, 1995).

See also Robert A. Reiser and Walter Dick, *Instructional Planning*, 2nd ed. (Boston: Allyn and Bacon, 1996) for a more detailed discussion of lesson planning.

I would also recommend George J. Posner and Alan N. Rudnitsky, *Course Design: A Guide to Curriculum Development for Teachers* (New York: Longman, 1986).

Chapter 7

The Teacher as Classroom Manager

If it is possible, as far as it depends on you,
live at peace with everyone.

Romans 12:18

No discipline seems pleasant at the time, but painful.
Later on, however, it produces a harvest of righteousness
and peace for those who have been trained by it.

Hebrews 12:11

I am sitting in a twelfth-floor apartment in Moscow at the end of six weeks in Ukraine and Russia. During this time I have taught two courses. The first was Introduction to Christian Education, taught at Odessa Theological Seminary. The second was Principles of Teaching, taught at Moscow Theological Seminary.

I fought battles in classroom management in both. End of the term. Intensive courses tacked on to the end of the regular semester. The smell of summer break in the air. Thoughts of home and family, wives and children miles and months away. Courses in education, of questionable value to those steeped in systematic theology, Greek, and hermeneutics. An American professor, with strange ideas, who speaks just enough Russian to make mistakes. Temperatures near 100° with no air conditioning and blizzards of tree spores filling the air. It was a volatile mix, a challenge to orderly learning. I was not victorious in all of my battles, but, judging from the performances and attitudes of the students at the end of the courses, I think I might have won the war. But I'll save that for later in the chapter.

It underscored an important principle for me: having a detailed course plan does not guarantee the plan will work. Managing the classroom environment in real time with real students allows us to work the plan. So let's consider the teacher as environmentalist, as disciplinarian, and as self-manager.

The Teacher as Environmentalist

The *American Heritage Dictionary* says an environmentalist works "toward protecting the natural environment from destruction or pollution." Teachers operate as environmentalists when they protect the learning environment in their classrooms from behaviors and attitudes that pollute or destroy learning. We've already discussed ways immature teachers pollute the class environment with their own *toxic teaching* (chap. 2). But here we focus on the toxic influences of our learners. How do we create a healthy climate for learning among students?

We've looked at the motivational behaviors of teachers: shaping, modeling, creating curiosity, befriending, and orchestrating successful experiences (chap. 4). We've discussed aspects of teacher personality (flexibility, creativity, humor, grace) and instructional behaviors (planning skills, platform skills, social skills). But even the best classrooms, managed by the most effective teachers, experience behavior problems from time to time. Learners are people too. Their enthusiasm for learning may not be as self-motivated as our own. When that enthusiasm wanes, or their attention lapses, learning suffers. I remind myself periodically that my students have lives beyond my classes. If this out-of-class reality is toxic, it may break into the classroom, polluting the learning environment for all of us. How do we maintain a healthy climate for learning when it is threatened by the very ones we work so hard to teach?

This focus on climate control and maintenance falls under the heading of "classroom management," the process of anticipating, planning for, and handling behavior problems in the classroom. Consistent use of management principles produces a positive, well-ordered learning environment. These principles emphasize prevention more than reaction (it is easier to prevent behavior problems than recover from them), learner self-control more than teacher control (the learner ultimately chooses to behave or misbehave), and a positive rather than a negative atmosphere.[1]

How can we plan ahead to minimize problem behaviors in our classrooms? Remember Dr. Boar, and be confidently prepared to teach from the first day of class.[2] Establish class rules early, and clearly communicate them so that students know what is expected.[3] Call attention to class rules consistently.[4] Plan and define how routine procedures (attendance, collecting or returning papers, group time, seat work) will be handled in the class.[5] Determine how you will reward compliance to rules[6] and procedures.[7] Have a specific plan to insure student accountability, provide meaningful feedback,[8] and render appropriate praise.[9] Still, problem behaviors will arise. When they do, how should we handle them?

The Teacher as Disciplinarian

Perhaps *disciplinarian* sounds harsh in a Christian context, evoking images of domineering tyrants demanding submission. I use the term here to mean the maintenance of a healthy learning environment by reducing bad (disruptive) behaviors and enhancing good (learning) behaviors. I exclude from this term any form of ridicule, corporeal punishment, or harshness. Such bad behavior on the part of teachers is, in itself, disruptive to the learning process. Levin provides a helpful hierarchy of proactive and remedial intervention techniques for handling classroom misbehavior. The principle employed throughout the hierarchy is that, when faced with student misbehavior, teachers should use the least intrusive, most subtle and student-centered interventions first. Only as students continue to misbehave should interventions become increasingly intrusive and overt, until the issue is resolved and learning resumed. Levin labels the three major levels of coping skills as proactive, remedial, and logical consequences.

Proactive Coping Skills

The least disruptive of student misbehaviors are called "surface behaviors" because they result from the "normal developmental behavior of children." They are not a result of deep-seated personality problems.[10] Surface behaviors include verbal interruptions (talking, humming, laughing, calling out, whispering), off-task behaviors (daydreaming, sleeping, combing hair, doodling), physical movement intended to disrupt (passing notes, throwing paper), and disrespect to teachers and students (arguing, teasing, vulgarity, talking back).

Surface behaviors are symptoms of disengagement and boredom. Generally, you can handle these kinds of problems in the following ways. Consistently *demonstrate your competence* in the subject.[11] Use a *variety of methods* (conversational lecture, questions, case studies, small group work) to suppress boredom. Demonstrate "withitness"[12]—the ability of teachers to prove to students they are tuned in to what happens in the classroom. New classes often test teachers to see if they are "with it." Misbehavior that goes unnoticed will only grow. Keep the class *involved* in learning activities.[13] In younger classrooms, this may mean coordination of "overlapping" activities—requiring teachers to deal with more than one activity at a time.[14] Maintain a *professional but pleasant demeanor.*[15] Use *positive* rather than negative language (see following table).[16]

Positive Language	Negative Language
Close the door quietly.	Don't slam the door.
Try to work these out on your own without help.	Don't cheat by copying from your neighbor.
Quiet down—you're getting too loud.	Don't make so much noise.
Carry your chair like this (demonstration).	Don't make so much noise with your chair.

Positive Language	Negative Language
Sit up straight.	Don't slouch in your chair.
Raise your hand if you think you know the answer.	Don't shout out your answer.
Use your own words. When you do borrow ideas from another author, be sure to acknowledge them.	Don't plagiarize.
Speak naturally, as you would when talking to a friend.	Don't just read your report to us.
Be ready to explain your answer—why you think it's correct.	Don't just guess.[17]

Levin also suggests specific ways to reduce surface behaviors. When you notice several students yawning, stretching, rubbing their eyes, or staring out of the window, you know that interest is waning. *Change the pace* (which means "increase the pace" or "pick up the pace") by actively engaging students in a different activity.[18] Younger children might play a game. Ask older children a question that ties the subject to their own experiences. Have adults share a personal experience or discuss a question related to the topic. If learners have been sitting a long time, allow them to do the activity standing up. Reduce the need for emergency activities (giving the class an on-the-spot adrenaline rush), by providing for these activities in your lesson plans. *Plan time* for board work, small group seat work (diads, triads, quads), question-and-answer sessions, problem-solving, and personal sharing. Such planning reduces periods of boredom and disengagement.

Control seductive objects. Toys, magazines, combs, and the like can distract students. With children, take the objects away and keep them safe until after class; with youth and adults, ask them to put the objects away.

Boost interest in students who appear to be drifting away by giving attention to their work or asking them to put samples of their (correct) work on the board. *Redirect off-task behavior* to on-task behavior. If someone is daydreaming, ask them a question.

If they answer correctly, respond positively. If they can't answer, ask the question again to the whole class. Do not ridicule the student for daydreaming ("You would know where we were if you'd been paying attention!") as this merely increases resentment and the likelihood of more daydreaming.[19] *Provide cues*—standing at the podium, moving to a marker board, flashing lights—which signal times for beginning and ending activities.[20] These proactive coping skills handle many surface behaviors; but if disruptive behaviors occur, we must move to remedial coping skills.

Remedial Coping Skills

When surface behaviors continue, the intensity of intervention must increase. We should keep two principles in mind as we increase the intensity of our interventions. First, students control their own behavior, for better or worse. Our efforts to remedy problem behavior should focus on helping students control themselves. Our task is to give them opportunities for self-control. Therefore we begin interventions as subtle, nonintrusive measures that are student-centered, yet communicate disapproval. Then, if the misbehavior continues, we increase the intensity of the interventions. Interventions become more overt, more intrusive, and more teacher-centered.

Second, we should try to intervene in ways that do not, in themselves, disrupt the learning climate. Sudden bursts of frustration or anger from the teacher disrupts the learning climate for the whole class. Begin efforts as private, nonverbal cues to the misbehaving student. If the misbehavior continues, interventions become more public and verbal,[21] and may, in extreme cases, require some disruption of learning. Let's look at four nonverbal and four verbal intervention strategies.

Nonverbal Interventions. The four nonverbal interventions include planned ignoring (low nonverbal intensity), signal interference, proximity control, and touch control (high nonverbal intensity). *Planned ignoring* is based on the principle of extinction[22] in behavioral learning theory. A behavior that is not reinforced is less likely to be repeated. If a teacher reinforces misbehavior by giving more attention to the misbehaving student, then removing the reinforcement of teacher attention will eventually cause a decrease in the misbehavior.[23] I say "eventually" because removing attention could increase misbehavior over the short term, as the misbehaver seeks to regain the attention. Also realize that ignoring misbehavior may simply not work. Students may be reinforced by the attention they receive from friends in the class. This type of reinforcement increases with age, since older students desire peer approval, while younger learners desire teacher approval. Finally, be aware of the ripple effect of bad behavior—students who misbehave and get away with it generate misbehavior in other students.[24] Planned ignoring is effective only with minor nuisance behaviors.

Signal interference refers to nonverbal actions that communicate disapproval.[25] Make eye contact with a business-like expression (smiling sends a mixed message to the misbehaver).[26] Slightly shake your head or finger "no." Hold up your hand to stop a student calling out. Increase the intensity of signal interference by making eye contact with a disapproving look.[27]

Proximity control involves teachers moving toward (lower intensity) or positioning themselves near (higher intensity) the disruptive student.[28] This movement or positioning is done without comment and without any break in instruction. Intensity can range from a nonchalant movement toward a student to obviously standing behind the student's chair.[29]

Touch control involves light, nonaggressive physical contact,[30] such as taking a child's hand, escorting a child to a seat, or placing your hand on a child's shoulder. Remember that to some children, touch signals aggression ("Don't touch me!"), which will result in more misbehavior. Do not use touch control with visibly angry students. Further, physical touch should be used with extreme caution, if at all, with older students, especially with students of the opposite sex, as your intentions could be misinterpreted.[31] Finally, never cause physical discomfort by grabbing, pinching, or hitting.[32] If the misbehavior continues, move to verbal intervention.

Verbal Interventions. When subtle, private, student-centered interventions do not curb disruptive behavior, we must become more overt, more public, and more teacher-centered. Four verbal interventions that address misconduct openly and directly are hints (low verbal intensity), questions, demands, and explicit redirection (high verbal intensity).

Hints verbally address the misbehaving student rather than the misbehavior directly. Ask a question and call on the misbehaving student to answer. Use peer reinforcement: praise students who are behaving appropriately. This communicates your expectations to the misbehaver (hint, hint). Or defuse the situation with the use of humor[33] focused on the situation or on yourself. Avoid being sarcastic toward the student, since this will increase his or her resentment (and misconduct), as well as hurt the respect other students have for you.

If hints fail to curb the misbehavior, indirectly *confront* the student about his actions with a question.[34] "Are you aware that you are humming out loud?" Making students aware of their own disruptive actions, and how those actions affect others, is a potent resource for behavior management.

If the misbehavior continues, move to the next level of verbal interventions, which are *demands*. Directly appeal to misbehavers to change their conduct. "Billy, please work quietly." Note the use of positive language, which is less direct than the more negative, more intense "Stop humming." Include in your direct appeal the positive impact of appropriate behavior ("It is easier for everyone to concentrate when we all work quietly"). This is called positive phrasing.[35] Another form of demand is to remind the misbehaver of the classroom rules.

Explicit redirection is an order to stop the misbehavior and return to appropriate behavior. It is a teacher command, highly intrusive, public, and control-oriented. It is simple, clear, and closed. It leaves the student with only two choices: behave or defy the teacher. ("Billy, stop humming and work quietly so others can concentrate.") Such a response may not stop the misbehavior, but rather prompt argument in the form of an excuse: ("But Jimmy hums and you never tell him to stop"). If this happens, repeat your explicit redirection. Some teachers add "That's not the point" before restating the redirection. If the student continues to argue or make excuses, repeat this method two or three times and then disengage (see logical consequences below) from the misbehaver and return to the class-as-a-whole. This repetitive process is called the *broken record* method because the teacher begins to sound like one.[36]

"You are one of the most obnoxious students I have ever had the misfortune to deal with. How many times have I asked you not to call out answers? If you want to answer a question, raise your hand. It shouldn't tax your tiny brain too much to try and remember that. I'm sick and tired of your mistaken idea that the rules of this classroom apply to everyone but you. It's because of people like you that we need rules in the first place. They apply especially to you. I will not allow you to deprive other students of the chance to answer questions. Anyway, half of your answers are totally off the wall. I'm in charge here, not you. If you don't like it, you can tell your troubles to the principal. Now sit here and be quiet."

When Mr. Hensen finished his lecture and turned to walk to the front of the room, John (the subject of his tirade) discreetly [made an obscene gesture] and laughed with his friends. John spent the rest of the period drawing pictures on the corner of his desk. The other students spent the remainder of the period either in uncomfortable silence or invisible laughter. Mr. Hensen spent the rest of the class trying to calm down and get his mind back on the lesson.

Here are examples of what Mr. Hensen could have said, presented as a hierarchy of verbal interventions, to help John refrain from calling out his answers.

1. "Fred and Bob, I really appreciate your raising your hands to answer questions." (Peer reinforcement)
2. "I must be hallucinating. I hear someone talking before I called on anyone to answer." (Humor)
3. "John, are you aware that when you call out answers without raising your hand, it robs other students of the chance to answer the question?" (Questioning awareness of effect)

(continued)

4. "John, please stop calling out answers so that everyone will have a chance to answer." (Direct appeal)
5. "John, you will be called on as soon as you raise your hand." (Positive phrasing)
6. "John, the classroom rules state that students must raise their hands before speaking." (Reminder of the rules)
7. "John, stop calling out answers and raise your hand if you want to answer a question." (Explicit redirection)
8. Mr. Hensen: "John, stop calling out answers and raise your hand if you want to answer a question."
John: "But I really know the answer!"
Mr. Hensen: "That's not the point. Stop calling out answers and raise your hand if you want to answer a question."
John: "But you let Mabel call out answers yesterday!"
Mr. Hensen: "That's not the point. Stop calling out answers and raise your hand if you want to answer a question."
Return to lesson. (Broken Record)[37]

To be continued . . .

Logical Consequences

If the verbal interventions do not solve the problem, then the teacher must take action. The student must comply or face the logical consequences of his misconduct.[38] The term *logical* refers to a meaningful relationship between misconduct and disciplinary consequences. For example, if two students talk with each other at inappropriate times, a logical consequence would be to separate them. *Contrived* consequences, on the other hand, are merely punitive measures imposed by an authority that are either unrelated to the offense (write on the chalkboard one thousand times: "I will not talk in class"), or out of proportion to the offense ("two weeks detention because you talked at inappropriate times").

Use the following principle to guide the application of logical consequences: "Misbehaving students have a choice: either behave appropriately or receive the consequences." Directly state the choice to the student: "Billy, either work quietly or move your seat to the back of the room. You decide." Then disengage[39] and work with the class-as-a-whole. If Billy continues to hum, say, "Since you continue to hum, you have chosen to move your seat to the back of the room. Move there now, please." If he does not move, directly state his choice: "Either move your seat to the back of the room, or I'll need to have a conference with your parents. You decide." Then disengage. Do not argue with the student.

It is important that we remain in control *of ourselves* as we attempt to control disruptive behavior in students. The students' respect for us and our teaching will increase if we deal with misconduct with mature self-control. Respect will decrease if we lose control, humiliate the offender, or present a harsh demeanor. Even if the student refuses to comply with our directions and chooses the (negative) consequences of his own misconduct, we have not failed. Why? Because in this process we established a link between conduct quality and type of consequences. The consequences students actually receive, good or bad, depend on how they choose to behave.

The Teacher as Self-Manager

Good classroom management skills are essential for our own psychological and emotional well-being, which in turn is essential for long-term effectiveness as a teacher. Without the ability to manage the disruptions that inevitably occur in the process of teaching, teachers' stress levels climb, week by week, semester by semester, year by year. Stress gradually reduces our emotional cushion, which makes further disruptions more stressful. Chronic stress reduces classroom effectiveness (flexibility, long-range planning, care for the learners), which in turn encourages more disruptive behaviors. Chronic stress over a long period of time

Dealing with John *continued*

John continues to call out answers.

9. "John, you have a choice. Stop calling out answers immediately and begin raising your hand to answer, or move your seat to the back of the room and you and I will have a private discussion later." (Logical consequences)

If the first level of "logical consequences" does not change the behavior, move to a second level, which can involve parents and the school administration.

10. After he was given a choice to stop calling out answers or move to the back of the room, John calls out again. "John, you called out; therefore you decided to move to the back of the class. Please move."

John begins to argue and tries to sidetrack Mr. Hensen from delivering the consequence.

John: "You know Tom calls out all the time and you never do anything to him."

Mr. Hensen: "That's not the point. Please move to the back of the room."

John: "I get the right answers!"

Mr. Hensen: "That's not the point. Please move to the back of the room."

John: "This is really unfair."

Mr. Hensen: "That's not the point. Please move to the back of the room."

John: "I'm not moving and don't try to make me!"

Mr. Hensen: "John, you have a choice. Move to the back of the room now or I will be in touch with your parents. You decide." Disengage.[40]

can lead to burnout.[41] We know we're close to burnout when teaching, once so exciting and satisfying, now seems frustrating and overwhelming.

The dimensions of burnout include emotional exhaustion, depersonalization, and perceived ineffectiveness. Emotional exhaustion refers to feelings of being emotionally and physically drained, lack of energy, and the inability to get enough sleep. Depersonalization refers to distancing oneself from others, creating emotional barriers to guard against being hurt further. Depersonalization is expressed in criticism, cynicism, and putdowns. It leads to generally uncaring behavior. Perceived ineffectiveness refers to feelings of worthlessness and failure that result from continually dealing with people in need. Deep and consistent rest, meaningful relationships with students and colleagues, and acceptance of one's worthiness all battle against stress and eventual burnout.

Russian Classes Revisited

So there I was,[42] in Ukraine in May and Moscow in June, teaching, through an interpreter, students who were less than interested in what I had to say. I was there in response to the Lord's call, having studied Russian every day for a year. I had prepared my notes, designed overhead cells in Russian, and dreamed of breaking new ground in teaching and learning in these two seminaries in the former Soviet Union. By Wednesday of the first week in both classes, I questioned my ability to accomplish my goals, to speak the simplest Russian, to build relational bridges, or to engage my students in meaningful learning.

As I look back on the experience, there were several events that captured the role that classroom management played in making the experiences positive ones. First, I had an organized plan. While I was not sure exactly what Russian and Ukrainian Baptists needed to learn about the teaching ministry of the church, I knew that the basic biblical principles of teaching ministry are universal. So I focused on those fundamental principles. Practical application to Russian and Ukrainian churches came in-the-process of the class. I knew where I was going with the course, and students eventually picked up on our direction.

I had a good deal of spare time while I was in Ukraine and Moscow (no television, no radio, no newspapers) and so I was able to take time to "sit, drink tea, and talk" with my students. Most of them could speak English. I also had time to play chess, a favorite pastime for Eastern Europeans. One student in particular was quite bored with my class and was somewhat disruptive the first week. Then he heard that I play chess. "Dr. Rick, do you really like to play chess?" "Yes," I said. "Would you like to play chess . . . with me?" "I'd love to." "Oh, good! I love to beat Americans at chess!" The challenge was on. We played a total of four games. After he beat me the first time, he asked me, "Will this affect my grade?" "Of course not," I told him. "This is chess. That is Teaching Ministry. You'll get the grade you earn!" His attitude in class changed for the better after that first game.

I lost the second game as well, won the third, and lost the fourth (though Victor said I played well each time). But my greatest victory was won in the classroom. Not only did Victor's attention improve, but he became one of my advocates among the students.

Because I was a foreign guest in my students' homeland, I chose to err on the side of patience. I tended to let personal conversations go longer than I would in my American classes. I went the extra mile in answering questions. I repeated material more often than usual, and waited longer for students to respond. I knew where I wanted my students to be at the end of the course, but the specifics of how to get there were much more flexible and open-ended than in my classes back home. I taught principles and called on them to determine how best they could be applied in their churches. I found that this generated, in time, a sense of mutual respect between us. I fought to keep my own feelings of failure from interfering with my teaching.

Student behavior changed for the better, became more focused, as they began to sense the importance of the church's teaching ministry and my commitment to teach them. I was able to take a firmer stance with them on other issues. When students dragged into class late after break times, I reminded them of the importance of promptness. When private conversations disrupted classroom activities, I intervened firmly. When a few students dominated the discussions, I directed the discussions to others. Over time, disruptions and extraneous interruptions decreased. Student questions became more frequent, more serious, and more personal. Some ventured to share personal experiences related to the subject, though this appeared more difficult and risky for Russians than Americans.[43] While some students attempted to chase rabbits or disrupt the flow of the class, most tuned in, most remained engaged, most demonstrated an eagerness to learn.

The students completed their work in excellent fashion. The final exam included a question asking students to explain how they would use course material in their churches. Answers to this question revealed that the material had made its way into their hearts and minds as they considered the teaching ministry in their own churches. Several asked for my signature in their textbooks (a Russian practice of courtesy and respect), exchanged addresses with me (a Russian practice of friendship), and introduced me to their families (a Russian practice of hospitality). We had not covered all the material in either book, so some of the students formed voluntary study groups to continue their work through the texts. As I had opened my life to them, they opened their lives to me, and the connection filled me with an indescribable joy. I cannot wait to go back next year, another year of Russian study under my belt, a revised course plan in my briefcase, and a better sense of the value of good classroom management skills.

An organized plan, a love of chess, a patient manner, a firm stance: each of these had their place in defining the structure and direction for the classes in real time. Nothing in the practice of teaching is as devastating when done wrong, nor as rewarding when done right, as real time classroom management. May God grant you wisdom to manage the inevitable problems in student attitude and behavior you will face as you teach.

A View Ahead

There are times when you will face uncommon problems in the classroom: specific physical and learning disabilities that threaten the best of plans. It is to this subject we next turn our attention.

For Further Reading

Two excellent resources specially related to classroom management are: Robert H. Zabel and Mary Kay Zabel, *Classroom Management in Context: Orchestrating Positive Learning Environments* (Boston: Houghton Mifflin Company, 1996).

James Levin and James F. Nolan, *Principles of Classroom Management: A Professional Decision-Making Model*, 2nd ed. (Boston: Allyn and Bacon, 1996).

For specific psychological approaches to common classroom problems, *see*: Daniel Linden Duke and Adrienne Maravich Meckel, *Teacher's Guide to Classroom Management* (New York: Random House, 1984).

Chapter 8

The Teacher as Special Agent

Blessed is he who has regard for the weak;
the LORD delivers him in times of trouble.
The LORD will protect him and preserve his life;
he will bless him in the land and not surrender him
to the desire of his foes.

Psalm 41:1–2

Defend the cause of the weak and fatherless;
maintain the rights of the poor and oppressed.
Rescue the weak and needy;
deliver them from the hand of the wicked.

Psalm 82:3–4

$\mathscr{E}$arly in my career, our Foundations department faculty asked me to teach a four-hour Principles of Teaching class. This was uncommon since all of our courses were designed as two-credit-hour courses. When I received my class roll, I was disappointed by my enrollment of fourteen. Had I been teaching two two-hour sections, I'd have had thirty-five students in each. But my greatest shock came when I walked into class and saw Neil sitting on the front row. My shock was due to Neil's physical condition: he had severe cerebral palsy. His body swayed back and forth in his seat. His arms flopped helplessly across his desk, following his shoulders. He looked up at me and flashed a huge smile. Struggling desperately to keep his face and eyes fixed on mine, he said "Heh-hhhhhhhhh-llooooooh."

My thoughts collided as they raced around my mind. What is he doing here? In my room? In seminary? What church will ever have him on their staff? How are we going to do the course with him in the class? We do group work and class discussion. Each student also leads the class in a ten-minute MicroTeach session and is videotaped. How will Neil do that? A four-hour course! Only fourteen students! How am I going to handle this!?

"Hello," I replied with a smile. I took a step toward him and put my hand on his shoulder. "I'm glad you're here." He swung his body to the right, leaning over the chair arm, and then thrust himself back upright, looking me in the face. "Thaaaaaaaaaaaaanks!"

I greeted the other students. Their eyes silently screamed their own terror. I smiled at each one of them, and then led them in prayer. I called the roll, asking each student what name they wished me to use. We discussed the course and what was required. Just before dismissing the class for that day, I handed out the syllabus. Without thinking, I handed Neil the five-page document. He took the syllabus in his right hand and picked up his briefcase with the left. Then I watched his right hand thrust the syllabus toward the open briefcase. The syllabus crumbled as he jammed it into the side of the case. Back came the hand and again, smash! Back, and then smash! And smash! Each smash tore and disfigured the pages more. On the fifth thrust, he succeeded in placing the now-broken pages of his syllabus inside the case. All of this had taken no longer than an eye-blink. He closed the bag, looked in my direction, flashed me a wide smile, and said, "AwwwwwwwRiiiiight! Leeeht's geeeht staaaaaaarted!" Oh, Lord, I prayed under my breath, *What am I going to do?*

It is a natural, human tendency to favor some people over others. We tend to favor clean people over dirty, neat people over messy, organized to disorganized, people "like us" over people who are different. It is a natural human tendency of teachers to favor good students over poor, successful students over unsuccessful, motivated students over unmotivated, whole and healthy students over fractured and disabled. This tendency toward favoritism is clearly condemned in Scripture (see James 2:1–10), but becoming a "no respecter of persons" requires supernatural help. Many individual differences, from slight to severe, produce a rich diversity of needs that colors what we do in the classroom. In this chapter, we look at differences in learning styles, culture, learning abilities, behavior disorders, as well as intellectual and physical impairments.

The Teacher and Student Differences

In 1975 Congress passed the *Education for All Handicapped Children Act* (Public Law 94–142) which required states to provide "a free, appropriate public education for every child between the ages of 3 and 21 years of age (unless state law does not provide free public education to children 3 to 5 or 18 to 21 years of age) regardless of how, or how seriously, he may be handicapped." In 1986, Public Law 99–457 extended the requirement to all handicapped children ages 3 to 5, even if states do not have public education for children this age. In 1990, PL 94–142 was amended by the *Individuals with Disabilities Education Act* (PL 101–476) which replaced the word *handicapped* with *disabled* and expanded services for disabled students.[1]

Under these laws, states were required to develop means of educating students with disabilities in the least restrictive environment, meaning in as regular a setting as possible. States were further required to individualize education through the development and use of an individualized education program (IEP). An IEP details the student's present status, goals for the year, short-term measurable objectives that lead to those goals, services to be provided to the student, how students will participate in the regular school program, and a schedule telling how the student's progress will be evaluated. The third provision was that, whenever possible, parents would be involved in the development of the IEP for their child.[2]

These laws called for a decrease in separate "special education" classes and an increase in inclusive classrooms[3] where students with disabilities are placed in regular classrooms. But what does "regular" mean? Every group of students contains a wide variety of differences among learners. How large do differences have to be before learner needs can no longer be met in a regular classroom? Wakefield uses a normal curve ("bell-shaped curve") to illustrate.[4] In the diagram below you can see a central point that represents the average ability level of a group of students.

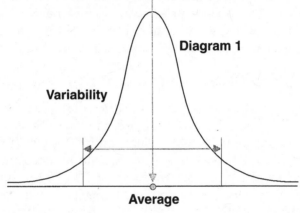

Diagram 1

Variability

Average

Ability levels spread out from this average in both directions. Some children have better than average ability; others, less than average ability for their grade level. The amount of spread, or variability, about the central point, or mean, increases with grade level. Wakefield uses the example of reading achievement to illustrate this increase. The range of reading achievement equals the grade level plus one year. So in a third grade class, one would expect a reading achievement range of four years (3+1=4). Children in a third grade class will demonstrate reading levels ranging from first (3-2 years) to fifth grades (3+2 years). Children in a seventh grade class will have a reading ability range of eight years (7+1=8), and so will demonstrate reading levels ranging from third (7-4) to eleventh (7+4) grade. So variability of ability increases with schooling, just as in an automobile race, the distance between the fastest and slowest cars increases throughout the race. So how much variability is included in normal variation among students?

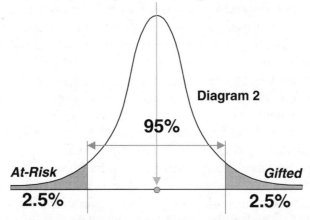

The area between the shaded "tails" of the normal curve represents 95 percent of the children in a given grade level. The shaded left tail represents approximately 2.5 percent of children who score significantly below average. These children possess risk factors, limitations, or disabilities that prevent them from achieving in the normal range. I use the terms *risk* or *limitation* or *disability* rather than *handicap*, which carries an unpleasant stigma. I'll never forget the deaf student at Gallaudet College who declared with conviction, "I am not handicapped. I just can't hear!" He was speaking of a disability, not a handicap. We should always remember that students with disabilities are students first. "Blessed is he who has regard for the weak" (Ps. 41:1a).

The shaded right tail represents approximately 2.5 percent of children who score significantly above average. These children, classified as "gifted," possess specialized abilities that allow them to achieve above the normal range. We will discuss all three segments: normal range differences, at-risk differences, and gifted differences.

The Teacher and Normal Range Differences

Within the 95 percent normal range of learners lies a myriad of individual differences. Three of the most common kinds of differences are learning styles, cognitive styles, and cultural distinctives.

Learning Styles

The focus on learning styles grew out of humanistic psychology and learning theory which places greatest emphasis on the learner as a person.[5] The essence of learning styles is that preferences for classroom conditions varies from learner to learner. These conditions may be physical (seating, lighting, temperature, noise level), social (working alone or in groups, working cooperatively or competitively), emotional (friendly or aloof, nurturing or self-reliant), instructional (lecture or discussion; direct, indirect, or self-directed; visual, tactile, or kinesthetic), and managerial (few or many rules, clear or implied consequences, leadership styles).[6] Since learning centers in the learner, proponents of learning styles advocated arranging schedules, classes, and conditions so that each and every learner achieves "most effectively" at least part of the day. Such thinking led several universities to offer "parallel sections" of courses based on preferred learning style. But this rapidly became an administrative nightmare. As Woolfolk so clearly points out, preference does not equate with effectiveness. Poor students can certainly prefer conditions that are easy and comfortable. Yet real learning is often hard and uncomfortable.[7] Studies in learning styles merely put a new face on an age-old prescription for effective learning: provide a wide variety of experiences for students. This is particularly important for children, who are required by law to be in school for hours each day. If their preferred learning modes are never addressed, then school can feel more like a prison than a place for learning. Adults can adapt their learning across preferred styles and have greater freedom in the choice of courses and professors. Still, a proper regard for all of our students and their achievement must include an awareness of their learning preferences.

Cognitive Styles

Another normal-range difference, closely related to learning style, is cognitive style. Cognitive style refers to the consistent ways in which learners respond to a wide range of intellectual tasks. While over twenty different dimensions of cognitive style have been derived, one of the most widely investigated forms is the field-independent/field-dependent dimension.[8] This dimension refers to the ability of learners to overcome the effects of distracting background elements (the field) when they attempt to differentiate the relevant aspects of a particular problem.[9] For example, when confronted with a math word problem, field-independent learners are more likely to extract and use the information relevant (or be less distracted by irrelevant elements) for solving the problem than field-dependent learners.[10]

Field-independent learners take notes that are more organized and more focused on key elements. They are better at restructuring problems to fit end goals. They prefer to work alone and do well under individualized contract systems.[11] They prefer academic disciplines, such as pure sciences, which are abstract and impersonal.[12]

Field-dependent learners attend more to context cues and solve problems more globally. They look to others in defining their own attitudes and beliefs. They reflect more social sensitivity, being drawn to people, and prefer academic disciplines, such as the social sciences, which are people oriented. They prefer cooperative and group learning experiences over competitive experiences.[13]

Such research leaves teachers wondering how we can provide class exercises that meet the preferred learning and thinking styles of each of our students—particularly in a class of thirty students. We can take comfort in recent research targeted on this very question. Increases in learning come from instruction that is better matched to goals and tests, not from attention to learning or cognitive styles alone.[14]

The two abiding principles that flow from these studies are that we need to vary our instruction (lecture, small-group work, projects, individualized instruction, learning centers). The second abiding principle is that our learners are indeed different and calls for us to be sensitive to those differences as we teach. Sound educational advice for any age!

Cultural Distinctives

American schools are, for the most part, Eurocentric. Teachers tend to emphasize whole-group (versus small-group) instruction, a competitive (versus cooperative) orientation, learning from textbooks (versus oral stories), and analytical (versus relational) problem-solving skills.[15] Such an orientation places minority learners at a disadvantage since research indicates a preference for a relational orientation (see Table).

Analytic Orientation	Relational Orientation
Details	Total picture
Learn best through reading	Learn best through hearing
Sequential processing	Simultaneous processing
Prefer impersonal information	Prefer "humanized" information
Task-oriented	People-oriented
Others' opinions less important	Others' opinions very important
Learn in spite of teacher	Learn with support of teacher
Integration to life less likely	Integration to life immediate
Individualistic behavior	Collective behavior
Independent thinking and work	Conformity in thinking and work
Identified as Anglo-American or Asian-Eurocentric preference	Identified as African-, Native- and Mexican-American preference[16]

While research demonstrates that average achievement levels in school of African-American, Hispanic-American, and Native-American learners are lower than Anglo-American learners (Asian-Americans average higher), research also shows that minority learners can do as well or better than Anglo-American students.[17] Another way of saying this is that variability of scores within a cultural group is larger than the variability across groups. The essential principle here is this: we should never judge a student's ability to succeed because of his or her cultural or ethnic group. Still, there are factors related to culture that we need to recognize. These include role models, textbooks, and language.

Role Models. The work of Albert Bandura (Social Learning Theory)[18] demonstrated that role models are more effective when observers can identify closely with them. Since 90 percent of public school teachers are Anglo, 7 percent African-American, and 3 percent "other,"[19] it is easy to see a cultural bias in available role models for minority children. I suspect that the percentages of minority teachers in Christian private schools are less than in public schools.

We cannot, as individual teachers, change the percentages of minority role models in our classrooms, but we can certainly bring role models from various culture groups into our classrooms by way of guest speakers, biographies, testimonies, books, and articles. We can champion the success stories of minority leaders and encourage students to explore the lives of minority leaders as part of their academic program.

Textbooks. Textbooks represent the most frequently used instructional tool. Up until recent years, textbooks reflected a strongly Eurocentric view of history and culture. Even as late as the 1970s, textbooks underrepresented the contributions of African-American and Hispanic men and women. Minorities were rarely depicted in higher-status or decision-making roles. There was some improvement through the 1980s, but content analysis of kindergarten through ninth grade textbooks published between 1980 and 1987 showed that Anglo culture (1) was depicted as superior to cultures of people of color, (2) received the most attention, and (3) dominated the list of achievements. Another finding was that minority groups were repeatedly discussed in relation to Anglo culture, not to other minority cultures.[20]

Analyze the textbooks you use to determine their cultural sensitivity. Where texts provide a narrow or biased perspective, supplement your subject with materials that provide alternative views.

Language. Words and facial expressions common in one culture have different connotations in others. Since 90 percent of all public school teachers are Anglo, words and expressions common to Anglo culture may inadvertently offend or miscommunicate. For example, Anglo culture may refer to the "forest" as a wild place that needs to be tamed and harnessed. But to Native Americans, a "forest" should be protected and left in its natural state. Eurocentric thought tends to refer to minority cultures as "primitive," or "undeveloped," or "backward."[21]

Nonverbal expressions can also be misunderstood. A smile can mean "rapport," or "embarrassment," or "potential hostility," depending on one's cultural group. Eye contact can show respect or disrespect. An Anglo teacher might say, "Look at me when I'm talking to you!" However, minority children may well have been taught that direct eye contact with someone in authority is inappropriate and antagonistic, so they intentionally avert their eyes as a sign of respect. Close physical proximity can communicate friendship or aggression. Slow speech can indicate interest and consideration or rudeness and indifference.[22] Awareness of these differences can help us react positively rather than negatively to these kinds of (what to "us" are inappropriate) student responses.

Culturally Responsible Teaching

What can we say, then, concerning cultural differences and teaching in the classroom? Teachers who want to be culturally responsible should check their understanding, their attitudes, and their methods (think-feel-do triad). As to understanding, how well do we understand the cultural diversity that sits before us, waiting to learn? How open are we to learn about cultural diversity? As to attitudes, how willing are we to promote the success of minority learners? How much confidence do we have that any learner can learn? How much respect do we have for children who must juggle the demands of two different cultures? As to methods, how often do we use relational means to academic ends? Are we organized (structure) with built-in openness (flexibility)? Do we provide clear overviews? Do we avoid cultural jargon? Do we use visual aids and verbal cues to emphasize main points? Do we pose questions throughout the entire period in order to test learner comprehension?[23] (Asking "Are there any questions?" during the last five minutes of class is ineffective.) Do we assign projects that demonstrate culture-specific understanding and skills? Do we encourage older students to explore cultural differences?[24]

We can help minority learners become better achievers through techniques such as peer tutoring, in which one student helps another. Such cooperation and mentoring fits well with cultural preferences of Hispanic and Native Americans. Cooperative learning, which places learners in small diverse groupings, helps relational students learn from others. Mastery learning—which uses specific objectives, sequencing, variety of methods, self-pacing, feedback, and test-until-mastery—has been shown effective for lower ability students.[25]

Multicultural awareness is simply putting Paul's standard into practice: "I have become all things to all men so that by all possible means I might save some. I do all this for the sake of the gospel, that I may share in its blessings" (1 Cor. 9:22–23.) We who teach in the name of Christ, the Lord of Love, the One who embraced everyone, should be sensitive to those different from ourselves.

The Teacher and At-Risk Differences

There are differences in student learning that go beyond personal and cultural preferences. These differences can become so severe that learners cannot function in a regular classroom environment. Still the present tendency is to do everything possible to include students with disabilities in regular classrooms. At-risk differences include intellectual disabilities (mental retardation), physical disabilities (deafness,[26] blindness, epilepsy, and cerebral palsy), behavior disorders (anxiety, aggressiveness, hypersensitivity) and learning disabilities.

Intellectual Disabilities

Mental retardation is diagnosed by means of evaluations of intellectual and adaptive "real-world" functioning. Classification as mentally retarded would include an I.Q. score of 70 or less and the inability to adequately function in communication, self-care, home living, social skills, self-direction, health and safety, functional academics, leisure, and work.[27]

Consider the following suggestions for teaching mildly retarded students in your classroom. State objectives simply. Present material in small, logical steps. Practice extensively before going on to the next step. Work on practical skills and concepts based on demands of adult life. Do not skip steps. Make connections between concepts explicit. Do not expect retarded children to "see" the connections for themselves. Be prepared to present the same idea in many different ways. Focus on a few target behaviors so you and the student can experience success. Be aware that retarded students must overlearn, repeat, and practice more than children of average intelligence. Pay attention to social relations in the classroom, so that retarded students will be accepted and will make and keep friends.[28]

Physical Disabilities

We will consider here four types of physical disabilities: deafness, blindness, epilepsy, and cerebral palsy. There are, of course, many others we could discuss, such as spina bifida, muscular dystrophy, cystic fibrosis, leukemia, asthma, diabetes, limb deficiencies, and sickle cell anemia.[29] But we will limit ourselves here to these four.

Deafness. "Deafness cuts people off from people; blindness cuts people off from things." It is hard to imagine classroom discourse without verbal communication. Hearing loss impairs the verbal communication process. Symptoms of mild hearing impairments include failing to follow directions, frequent distractions or confusion, mispronouncing names or words, reluctance to participate in class discussions, and repeatedly asking for information to be repeated. As hearing loss becomes more pronounced, speech reading ("lip reading") and manual communication in the form of sign language and fingerspelling is required. Deaf students will require the use of a sign language interpreter in an inclusive classroom.

In mild cases of hearing loss, allow students to place their seats where they can best receive classroom information. Speak clearly and distinctly, yet normally. Do not exaggerate mouth movements. Face students with hearing disabilities so they can draw clues from your facial expressions. Minimize auditory and visual distractions in the classroom. Involve students in mixed groups within the class. Teach hearing students basic skills in fingerspelling and sign language. Use clear visual aids. Emphasize two-way communication with hearing-impaired students.[30] Encourage them to ask questions and make comments—through the interpreter if necessary. Determine whether the interpreter is using American Sign Language (ASL) or some form of signed English. ASL is the language of the deaf community in America (contrary to popular opinion, sign language is not universal). ASL is the clearest mode of communication with deaf students, especially when meaningful explanation is the goal. Key vocabulary words need to be fingerspelled, however, rather than "interpreted" so that deaf students are not deprived of essential terminology. Provide deaf students with lists of important words. If teaching through an interpreter, keep in mind the time delay between your instruction and the deaf students' reception of it. Because of this inherent communication delay (present in any interpreted situation), be prepared for deaf students to lag behind the rest of the class, asking questions or making comments "late."

Do not be afraid of manual communication. Research has long shown that the use of sign language increases both academic achievement and social maturity among deaf students.[31] The battle that raged during the 1960s between "oralists," who promoted speech reading and speech for deaf students, and "manualists," who promoted the use of sign language with deaf students, is long since passed. Today the most common methodology used with deaf students is total communication, which combines elements of speech reading, fingerspelling, signed English, and ASL—"whatever it takes to communicate content."

Since "deafness cuts people off from people," the deaf community exists as a culture in its own right, centered around American Sign Language. Therefore, teaching deaf students involves some of the same multicultural issues we've already discussed. Since sign language is a bonafide language, teaching deaf students involves bilingual issues. Since deafness cuts students off from incidental learning (overhearing conversations, television and radio programs, movies), their general experience levels may be lower than their hearing classmates. Finally, we who can hear have a 24-hour-a-day unidirectional security system attuned to our environment. Familiar sounds are unconsciously screened and ignored by our auditory system. Unfamiliar sounds rouse our attention, even when we are asleep. Deaf persons compensate for the loss of this system with their eyes, which are directional and active only when we're awake. So deaf persons may act in ways completely normal for them, but that seem paranoid to hearing people.

When working with interpreters, insure that they know which terms you use are important for deaf students to know. Insure that interpreters know you encourage deaf students to participate. Insure that both you and they understand that interpreters are communication-aides, not teachers. Said another way, teachers, not interpreters, teach deaf students. Interpreters are a communication bridge between teachers and learners. Work together with students and interpreters to insure the best educational environment possible.

Blindness. Blindness cuts people off from things, but not people. Verbal communication presents no problem, but visual materials do. Look for students who rub their eyes, hold their books too close or far away, squint, frequently complain of burning eyes, misread the chalkboard, or hold their heads at an odd angle. These are indications of visual impairment.[32]

Mild cases of visual impairment can be corrected with glasses. Large-print books and materials, large-print typewriters and computers, variable-speed tape recorders (which allow lectures to be reviewed quickly), three-dimensional maps, clear copies of materials, and student guides and notetakers all help overcome visual impairment. About 1 in 2,500 students are visually impaired enough to be considered "educationally blind."[33]

Epilepsy. Epilepsy produces seizures in learners. Seizures can range from mild to severe. Mild seizures (sometimes called *petit mal*) involve only a small part of the brain and individuals exhibit a brief loss of contact with the world. Students may stare for one to thirty seconds, or drop objects. Help the class to understand what is happening. Do not let learners come out of their seizures to find the class staring, or worse, laughing, at them.

Generalized seizures (sometimes called *grand mal*) involve a large part of the brain and exhibit jerky movements for two to five minutes, followed by deep sleep. If learners go into a generalized seizure, lower them gently to the floor, away from furniture and walls. Loosen tight clothing. Turn their head to the side. Place something soft, like a clean handkerchief, between their back teeth. If learners have multiple seizures, or do not regain consciousness after a few minutes, call for medical help. Expect heavy perspiration, foaming at the mouth, and loss of bladder or bowel control.[34]

Learners are medicated for this condition, and epileptic seizures will rarely happen in class. Still, you need to be prepared for seizures so that when they happen, you can be calm and sympathetic. Your attitude and behavior provide the model for other children in the class.

Cerebral Palsy. Cerebral palsy causes a lack of muscular coordination. Mild cases may appear as clumsy behavior. More severe cases make voluntary muscle movements nearly impossible. My friend Neil, introduced at the beginning of the chapter, is an example of a more severe case of this disability.

The damage to the brain may be such that only movement is affected. While such children may require leg braces or a wheelchair, no special educational program is needed. But many children with cerebral palsy also have other disabilities, such as hearing impairment, speech problems, or mild mental retardation. Suggestions for these disabilities will prove helpful in these situations.[35]

Behavior Disorders

Behavior disorders, also known as emotional disturbances or emotional impairments, cover a variety of learning impairments. These include such characteristics as the inability to learn unexplained by intellectual, sensory, or health factors, the inability to form interpersonal relationships with fellow students or teachers, inappropriate behavior or feelings in normal circumstances, a pervasive mood of depression or unhappiness, and the tendency to develop physical symptoms or fears associated with school.[36]

While these characteristics may be found in the normal range of student abilities, the extremity and duration of these behaviors can place students at risk. Boys tend to externalize their disturbances and exhibit aggression, hyperactivity, disobedience, persistent uncooperativeness, and social maladjustment. The best approach in these cases is to use behavioral management techniques, as we discussed in the last chapter, to teach self-control. Girls tend to internalize their disturbances and exhibit anxiety, depression, shyness, withdrawal, timidity, and social incompetence. The best approach in these cases is to teach social skills.[37] Other approaches effective in handling behavior disorders include behavior modification techniques, counseling, and humanistic classroom climates.[38] In general, good classroom management procedures are essential in curtailing disruptions to learning.

Learning Disabilities

The term *learning disabilities* is a general term applied to learners who are not mentally retarded, emotionally disturbed, educationally deprived, or culturally different, with normal vision, hearing, and language capabilities, yet who still cannot learn to read, write, or compute. Conditions often associated with learning disabilities are inattention, impulsiveness, hyperactivity, difficulty in organizing information, thinking disorders, sharp emotional ups and downs, and speech and memory difficulties.

Care must be used in applying the label of "learning disability" to problem learners.[39] The diagnosis is sometimes given to slow learners in average schools, average students in high-achieving schools, second-language students, "troublemakers," or those behind in their work because of excessive absence or frequent change in schools.[40] The single condition that has received the most attention in recent years is Attention Deficit/Hyperactivity Disorder (ADHD).

ADHD is a condition recognized by excessive squirming, fidgeting, talking, and abnormally high activity levels. Such students have difficulty adjusting to the "sit-down" pace of school life. Students have difficulty remaining seated, following instructions, sustaining attention, and refraining from interrupting others' activities. Students often lose things, engage in physically dangerous behavior (such as running into a street without looking), shift from one unfinished activity to another, and blurt out answers before questions are completed.[41] Treatment ranges from medication, usually Ritalin or Dexedrine,[42] to specific behavioral and motivational programs (sometimes called "skill and will" training[43]).

An associated condition is Attention Deficit Disorder without Hyperactivity (ADD) in which learners are excessively distracted and impulsive, requiring more than normal supervision.[44] These students are unable to focus their attention on the task at hand. Characteristics include inability to finish tasks, failure to listen, difficulty in concentrating, frequent calling out in class, and difficulty in waiting turns.[45] The following suggestions will help you support ADHD learners in your classroom.

Minimize extraneous demands. The more complex and demanding the classroom, the more difficulty ADHD children have. ADHD children do best in classrooms where there are only necessary rules, where they are allowed to make frequent choices, and where the teacher does not make unnecessary demands.

Provide continuous monitoring. ADHD children have difficulty complying with instruction for a sustained period. Monitoring progress and repeating instructions will minimize difficulties.

Maintain a high rate of instructional feedback and reinforcement. ADHD learners have deficits in rule-governed behavior and are better controlled by consequences of behavior than antecedents. Where there are high rates of feedback on performance and positive reinforcement, there are large reductions in ADHD symptoms.[46]

The Teacher and Gifted Students

When the Soviet Union surprised American scientists and government leaders in 1957 by orbiting the satellite Sputnik, American educators were called on to develop talent in science, technology, and foreign language. Consequently, programs in identifying and developing gifted learners were born. The emphasis caused educators difficulty, since the goals of "equality of education for all" (help disadvantaged learners succeed) and "excellence in education for the gifted" (help talented students do better) stand at cross-purposes. Both emphases coexist uncomfortably in American education.

Learners are categorized as "gifted" when they produce I.Q. scores in excess of 130 (the top 2.5 percent of learners)[47] and exhibit characteristics of high motivation, creativity, academic ability,[48] artistic ability, and leadership capacity.[49] Most educational institutions provide expanded learning opportunities for gifted learners through enrichment programs, special interest classes,[50] accelerated classes, and allowing the gifted to skip grades.[51]

We can help gifted students in our own classes by doing such things as posing challenging problems, using group activities, including real-life problems, and using performance assessments to go beyond simple knowledge and remembering of facts. By posing challenging problems and giving students the responsibility and freedom to control their own inquiry, we allow students to take the subject beyond simple mastery and make it their own.

Group activities help the gifted pick up on others' ideas and create new and unusual variations from them. Brainstorming sessions, group discussions, panels, peer interviews, teams, and debates provide ways to involve gifted learners in the whole class.

Real-life problems allow gifted learners to transfer newly acquired information to practical considerations. Require library or laboratory research to provide an objective foundation for conclusions.

Performance assessments (we'll talk more about these in the next chapter) carry testing beyond superficial recall and comprehension items. Require gifted learners to explain the reasons behind their answers, to put together known facts into something new, and to judge the outcome of their own inquiry.[52]

The Teacher and Inclusion Strategies

Regardless of the severity of learning differences we find in our classrooms, there are several basic strategies we should follow as we help all our learners achieve to their fullest.

1. Master techniques of classroom management discussed in chapter 7 so that discipline problems do not impair learning.
2. Ask questions at the right level of difficulty for the students in your class. Questions that are too easy lead to boredom. Questions that are too difficult lead to confusion. Either state impairs learning.
3. Provide positive feedback for all learners.
4. Mix students together in a variety of ways. Do not resegregate students with disabilities within the classroom.
5. Integrate needed special education services into the class routine (such as having speech therapy sessions for one learner while others do individual seat work).
6. Insure your language and behavior toward students with disabilities provide a good model for all learners.
7. Teach about individual differences as part of the regular curriculum.
8. Make use of cooperative learning techniques or special projects so that students of various ability levels can work together.
9. Keep activities for all students as similar as possible.[53]
10. Provide supplementary materials and activities for gifted students in the class. These can be worked on when their regular work is completed.
11. Adjust the pace of teaching and the opportunity for practice and feedback according to the special needs in the class.
12. Provide structure and support for organizing course material by setting goals at the beginning of each unit, using advance organizers to focus on key elements, introducing key terms before students read the text, creating study guides with questions that focus attention on important concepts, and asking students to summarize information in the text.[54]
13. Treat students with disabilities the same as those without disabilities. Apply the same (reasonable) expectations for achievement to every student in the class.

14. Involve students with each other, encouraging interpersonal interactions, as much as possible.[55] Gifted students learn more through teaching others. At-risk students learn more from peers "like themselves" than from teachers.

15. Adjust approaches to teaching when you find exceptional learners in your classes. Learners have been designated as "exceptional" because they require more than regular classes provide. Adjust attitudes toward students, and see them as persons who need to grow socially and personally, as well as academically.[56]

16. Set challenging goals for all students, but provide an academic safety net to catch those who fall behind. The real trick is to challenge the brightest without losing the slowest, and to support the slowest without boring the brightest. The most effective way to do this is through peer tutoring and mentoring, as discussed above.

In Conclusion

It was providential that Neil came into a Principles of Teaching class that had twice the class hours (four, rather than two) and less than half the normal class size (fourteen, rather than thirty-five). We developed a sense of "family" in the class much faster than I normally experienced in larger classes.

I had worked for ten years with deaf adults, and some of them had cerebral palsy. I had developed an ability to understand slurred speech, and so was able to understand Neil's speech without a problem. My experience with cerebral palsy students at Gallaudet University allowed me to interact with Neil naturally, and I think this helped set the class at ease.

But Neil himself made the difference in our class's attitude. He demonstrated his abilities as an excellent classmate. His questions were clear and to the point. His comments were insightful and clever. He had a keen sense of humor, which he used to underscore his points or allay the fears of classmates. Within a week the class had become comfortable with him.

He did all the work in the class, including his ten-minute MicroTeach, in which he used his own physical impairment as an illustration of how God is able to overcome life's obstacles. "We all have disabilities," he said. "One of mine is more visible than yours.

But we all have hidden disabilities. Only God is able to overcome them and set us free."

Neil went on to graduate from Southwestern, rolling across the platform to have his diploma tucked into a book bag suspended from his chair. A few years later, in the mid-1980s, I saw him walking through the foyer of our school. He was wearing a western-style jacket with two-inch leather fringe running along the arms. We embraced and I asked him how he was doing. "Well, since graduation I have been serving the Lord as camp chaplain at a special camp in New Mexico for children with cerebral palsy." My own narrow-mindedness slapped me in the face. God knew all along where Neil was needed—the perfect fit between ministry and minister—and again Jesus' words echoed in my mind: "Take my yoke upon you and learn from me" (Matt. 11:29).

The last time I saw Neil was at the Southern Baptist conference center in Glorieta, New Mexico, three years ago. He told me he was getting married to his social worker. He flashed that wonderful wide grin and, with a mischievous twinkle in his eye, he said, "Yah, I'vvvve deciiided to quiiiit myyy joooob and liiive offff the wiiiife for a whiiiile!" We laughed together (since we both knew he was kidding) and then caught up on what we'd been doing. Though he could not walk without arm-braced canes, and struggled with every movement he made and every word he spoke, he had a joy of life unexplainable outside of the love of God. What a treasure he is, and how glad I am that I know him.

Whatever the limitations of our students, from minor differences in learning preferences to major differences in mental or physical abilities, we are called to help them learn, to move beyond the differences that separate to find the commonalities that bind us all together. Jesus showed us how. He taught everyone regardless of their ethnic,[57] cultural,[58] religious,[59] social,[60] or physical condition.[61] He saw beyond the superficial differences and embraced "the person." May the Lord teach us how to do the same with every individual who enters our classrooms.

For Further Reading

I heartily recommend the following text for extending the scope of your study of special concerns in teaching:

Barbara Wilkerson, ed. *Multicultural Religious Education* (Birmingham: Religious Education Press, 1997).

Additional help can be found in these texts:

Gary D. Borich and Martin L. Tombari, *Educational Psychology: A Contemporary Approach* (Boston: Addison-Wesley, 1996), chapter 13: "Teaching Exceptional Learners," chapter 14: "Teaching At-Risk and Discouraged Learners," and chapter 15: "Multicultural and Gender Fair Instruction."

Myron H. Dembo, *Applying Educational Psychology*, 5th ed., Chapter 11: "Exceptional Children" (New York: Longman, 1994).

Guy R. LeFrançois, *Psychology for Teaching*, 8th ed., Chapter 8: "Teaching Gifted and Exceptional Children" (Belmont, Calif.: Wadsworth Publishing Co., 1994).

John F. Wakefield, *Educational Psychology: Learning to Be a Problem Solver*, chapter 7: "Individual Differences: Considering Specific Learners" (Boston: Houghton-Mifflin Co., 1996).

Anita Woolfolk, *Educational Psychology*, 5th ed., chapter 4: "Learning Abilities and Exceptionalities," and chapter 5: "The Impact of Culture and Community" (Boston: Allyn and Bacon, Inc., 1993).

Chapter 9

The Teacher
as Evaluator

Do not use dishonest standards when measuring length, weight or quantity.
Use honest scales and honest weights, an honest ephah and an honest hin.
I am the LORD your God, who brought you out of Egypt.

Leviticus 19:35–36

The LORD abhors dishonest scales, but accurate weights are his delight.

Proverbs 11:1

Shall I acquit a man with dishonest scales, with a bag of false weights?

Micah 6:11

He was one of a hundred students in the class. He studied hard and earned midterm and final test scores in the upper nineties. When he received his grades in the mail, he had been assigned a grade of D. Certain his professor had made a mistake, he went

---

193

to discuss the situation. To his utter amazement he was told that no mistake had been made. He had earned a course average of 96. The students in the class had done so well that only those scoring an average of 99 and above received A's. B's were assigned to the 98 averages; C's to 97 averages. Since he had averaged 96, he received a D. Just let this professor's statement sink in—"the class did so well that a 96 average equaled a D." Here is the pinnacle of toxic grading.

Or, how about the college teacher who required a course average of 90 percent for an A, yet assigned a B to a student whose course average was 89.85 percent. Why? "Because he didn't score 90 percent." This student lost an entire grade level, 1 point on a 4-point scale, due to 15/100ths of a point on a 100-point scale (and the inability of the professor to correctly round decimal fractions). This is not only toxic grading, but bad mathematics and rather poor ethics ("Shall I acquit a man with dishonest scales, with a bag of false weights?" Mic. 6:11).

Evaluating student performance is an essential part of the educational process. Evaluating performance arbitrarily is not only an abomination to the Lord, but it is also absolutely the fastest way to pollute student attitudes and contaminate the learning environment. Most toxic grading practices flow out of ignorance of good evaluation processes, but ignorance does not excuse us from using dishonest measures. Grades have meaning beyond the class, following students throughout their academic careers. Grades should reflect the actual mastery level of each student in the class. They do so only when they are based on precise measurements.

We will spend most of our time in this chapter looking at how to write and evaluate objective tests. But the practice of assigning grades should include a wider range of evidence than examinations. Let's look at the teacher as test writer, test item analyst, observer, scribe, and grader.

The Teacher as Test Writer

We've discussed in previous chapters how to construct a series of lessons and units based on course goals. Formal tests provide a powerful way to assess how well students have achieved those goals. Let's investigate three components of tests that produce "honest weights": valid, reliable, and objective scores; clearly stated objectives; and clearly written items.

The Measurement Triad

Tests that provide systematic, unbiased information on student achievement possess three characteristics: validity, reliability, and objectivity.[1] A test is "valid" if it measures what it says it measures. A valid I.Q. test measures intelligence. A valid marital satisfaction inventory actually measures marital satisfaction. When the content of a test matches the universe of learnings the test covers, it is said to have *content validity*.[2] A test designed to cover a specific unit should contain items that reflect the major concepts and principles from that unit and no others. Including test items from previous units ("in order to test recall") or from footnotes or optional reading assignments ("the better students will have studied these") violates content validity.

Reliability refers to the precision of the test, or how accurately the test measures student achievement. Poorly written questions inject random noise into student scores and lower test reliability.

Objectivity refers to absence of personal bias in scoring answers. It is essential that test scores reflect student achievement and not the biases or poor attitudes, fatigue, or arbitrary grading practices of the grader. If grading procedures are biased, the scores are not systematic assessments of student achievement, and are "dishonest weights."

Based on Clearly Worded Objectives

If teachers can develop the skill of writing clearly worded, measurable objectives, then a wide variety of test questions can be written to test whether the objective has been achieved. A "knowledge" level objective calls for recall of facts and simple concepts. Test items can be written to evaluate the ability to recall these facts and concepts. In fact, objective test items are written so often for simple recall that objective tests and test items are criticized as trivial.

The problem is not the objective-type question, but the level of learning for which the question was written. We can write objective items to test comprehension of simple concepts and "application" of understanding and higher levels of learning.[3]

Knowledge Objective
   Learners will demonstrate knowledge of the Disciplers'
Model by (1) drawing the model and labeling each component and (2) identifying each component's counterpart
in educational psychology.

Test Item

Draw the Disciplers' Model in the space below. Identify each
component by writing its number on the component in the diagram. Write the letter for each educational psychology component in the diagram.

1. Needs of learners	A. Subject content
2. Growth in Christ	B. Humanistic theories
3. Helping learners think	C. Group dynamics
4. Helping learners value	D. Cognitive theories
5. Holy Spirit as Teacher	E. Maturation
6. Word of God	F. Individual differences
7. Helping learners relate	G.————

   Note: This item reflects the names of components of
the Disciplers' Model (major focus of unit) and their relation to areas of educational psychology (summary of
chapter). Students are simply asked to recognize the links
as they were given in the text.

Understanding Objective (Application level):
Learners will demonstrate understanding of key contributions of selected theorists to educational practice by matching the theorist to stated contributions. "Selected theorists" include Erikson, Piaget, Bruner, Kohlberg, Skinner, Bandura, Lewin, Maslow, and Rogers.

Test item:

____ 1. The struggle of adolescents to find their proper identity.	A. Bandura
____ 2. The push-pull between new experiences and what I already understand creates the motivation to learn.	B. Bruner
____ 3. The importance of structure and transfer in the learning process.	C. Erikson
____ 4. Sequence, feedback, goals.	D. Kohlberg
____ 5. We teach values better when we ask "why?" than when we "tell why."	E. Lewin
____ 6. Observation and modeling as a key to effective learning.	F. Maslow
____ 7. Learning is enhanced when learners' life spaces intersect through discussion.	G. Piaget
____ 8. Levels of personal needs as an explanation of motivation.	H. Rogers
____ 9. Trust learners. Be transparent. Embrace the feelings and experiences of your students.	I. Skinner

Note: These statements express key ideas of these theorists, but use language that has not been directly memorized by students. Therefore, students must translate these paraphrases into forms they've learned (comprehension) and choose the correct theorist (application).

Test Items Written Clearly

Objective Items. An objective test is made up of questions that can be answered with a word, short phrase, or by circling an answer. Answers to objective questions are either correct or incorrect. Graders do not need to interpret student responses,[4] so different graders will award the same score for each student.[5]

Objective tests have several advantages over essay tests. First, students can answer many objective questions in the same time that they can write answers to three or four essay questions. Using many objective items provides a much better sampling of student knowledge and understanding than the few essay items. Second, grading objective items is far easier than analyzing essay answers. Third, scores from objective items provide a more reliable measure of what the student knows than essay items.[6] However, writing good objective questions is more difficult and time-consuming than writing essay questions.[7]

The most common types of objective questions are the true-false, the multiple choice, the supply (fill-in-the-blank, or completion question), and the matching question. Let's look at how to write each of these types of questions.

THE TRUE-FALSE ITEM. The true-false item presents the student with a factual statement that is judged to be either true or false.[8] True-false test items are efficient in that a large number of items can be answered in a short period of time.[9] They are potent because they directly reveal common misconceptions and fallacies.[10] Scoring true-false items is fast and easy.[11]

However, a good true-false item is hard to write.[12] An item that makes good sense to the writer may confuse even a well-informed student. Statements require careful wording, evaluation, and revision. Also, true-false items encourage guessing[13] since students can earn 50 percent on a test by chance, simply by guessing at the right answer.[14]

The following guidelines will help you avoid major pitfalls in writing true-false test items.

Focus on one central idea.[15] Each statement should focus on one central idea in order to minimize confusion.

Poor: T F   Objective questions are more reliable and essay questions are more valid.

Better: T F   Objective questions are more reliable than essay questions.

Avoid specific determiners.[16] True-false items containing specific determiners such as *only, all, always, none, no,* or *never* are usually false. Items containing the specific determiners *might, can, may,* or *generally* are usually true. Write items without using these terms.

Poor: T F   Consistent use of instructional objectives always improves learning achievement.

Better: T F   Consistent use of instructional objectives improves learning achievement.

Call for an absolute answer.[17] Base true-false items on statements that are absolutely true or false.[18] Well-informed students will have greater difficulty answering confusing statements correctly because they have more information to process in trying to understand what the item is asking.

Poor: T F   Christians are "complete in Christ," and therefore have no need for secular theories of development.

Better: T F   Christians can learn from secular development theories without compromising their faith.

The first statement mixes spiritual truth ("complete in Christ") with human growth. Christian students would be hard pressed to respond "false" to such a statement. Yet, educational theories do help us understand the teaching-learning process better.

Minimize the use of negative statements.[19] State items in the positive rather than the negative to reduce confusion.[20] Avoid double negatives altogether.[21]

Poor: T F   It is not infrequently the case that three-year-olds play in groups.

Better: T F   Three-year-olds play in groups.

The latter item tests knowledge of three-year-olds and social development. The former requires knowledge plus an ability to wade through a double negative.

Use precise language.[22] Avoid using terms like *few, many, long, short, large, small,* or *important* in test items. These terms are ambiguous. How much is enough for a true-false answer? How big is "big"? How many is "many"?

Poor: T F   Writing clear test items is important in motivating students to study for exams.

Better: T F   Students are motivated to study for exams when teachers write clear test items.

Avoid direct quotes.[23] Do not use direct quotes from class notes or required readings. Quotes taken out of context are too ambiguous to use as test items. It is better to focus on the sense of class notes or readings rather than exact words.[24]

Poor: T F   Abraham Maslow wrote, "It is quite impossible for the student to discover for himself any substantial part of the wisdom of his culture." (false: B. F. Skinner)

Better: T F   Abraham Maslow opposed Jerome Bruner's discovery approach to education because of its focus on self-initiated learning.

Attribute opinion to a source. When asking a question about a statement of opinion, include its source. By doing this, you inform the student that you are asking whether the source, not the student, holds that opinion.[25]

Poor: T F   It is not possible for students to discover for themselves any substantial part of their culture's wisdom.

Better: T F   Skinner believed that it is not possible for students to discover for themselves any substantial part of their culture's wisdom.

Watch item length. Avoid making true statements longer than false items. True statements often require qualifications to insure they are absolutely true.[26]

Avoid complex sentences. Complex grammatical constructions and obscure language confuse students. Write items that are simple statements of truth or misconception.[27]

Use more false than true items. When developing a true-false test, make about 60 percent of the items false.[28] False items discriminate between students better than true items.

You can increase the difficulty[29] as well as improve the reliability of true-false items if you have students correct false items to make them true. I always underline the key term I want changed if the item is false to prevent trivializing the change. (Students would insert the word "not" to change false statements to true—which was not my intent!). See the accompanying box for an example.

> Here is an original item with an improper, though technically correct, response:
>
> T(F) Objective items are I more valid than essay items.
>   \not\
>
> Here is the improved item (the key term *valid* is underlined), with the improved response:
>
>
> T(F) Objective items are more ~~valid~~ than essay items.
>
>   \reliable\

THE MULTIPLE CHOICE ITEM. The multiple choice item is the most popular type of objective question.[30] It consists of a sentence or question stem and several responses. One response is correct. The others, called distractors, are incorrect but plausible. The most common form of this type is the multiple choice question with four or five responses.

Multiple choice items are less ambiguous and more structured than true-false or short-answer questions.[31] They demand more concept discrimination than other forms of objective questions. Guessing is reduced, and achievement can be tested at higher levels of learning than other question types.[32] Multiple choice items produce a better sampling of course content than short-answer essay items because they can be processed faster.[33]

Writing good multiple choice questions is both time-consuming and difficult.[34] Distractors are hard to create, particularly if you are providing a fifth or sixth alternative response.[35] Multiple choice tests are less efficient than other objective types because students can process fewer multiple choice items.[36]

The following guidelines will help you avoid major pitfalls in writing multiple choice items.

Pose a singular problem. The stem of the question should pose a clear, definite, singular problem. A common mistake in multiple choice questions is the use of an incomplete stem. Make the stem a complete sentence or a direct question rather than a sentence fragment.

Poor: Behavior modification is

a. punishment

b. classical conditioning

c. self-actualization

d. reinforcement contingencies (*)

Better: Which of the following alternatives best characterizes the modern clinical use of behavior modification?

a. punishment I and II

b. classical conditioning

c. self-actualization

d. reinforcement contingencies (*)[37]

One and only one correct answer.[38] Be sure that one and only one response is correct. Avoid using synonyms or overlapping responses.[39]

Poor: Which of the following types of research describes a current situation?

a. experimental

b. descriptive (overlaps c)

c. correlational (overlaps b)

d. ex post facto

Correlational research is descriptive research. Either b or c could be considered a correct answer.

Better: Which of the following types of research describes a current situation?

a. experimental

b. base-line design

c. correlational (*)

d. ex post facto

Minimize negative stems.[40] Avoid negative stems if possible. Negative items can confuse some students who might otherwise know the material. If you must use a negative in the stem, emphasize it by using CAPS, <u>underline</u>, **bold-face**, or *italics*.

Poor: Which of the following is not an example of an objective type item?

Better: Which of the following is **NOT** an example of an objective type item?

Make responses similar. Avoid making the correct response systematically different from the others in terms of its grammar, length, or construction. Responses should be written in parallel form so that the form of the response is not a clue to the correct answer.[41]

Poor: The boiling point of water is

a. 424°F

b. 282°F

c. 212°F at sea level, in an open container

d. 98°F

Better: The boiling point of water at sea level, in an open container, is

a. 424°F

b. 282°F

c. 212°F (*)

d. 98°F[42]

Make responses equally plausible.[43] All responses in an item set should be equally plausible and attractive to the less knowledgeable student.[44] Each response should be credible and logical.[45]

Poor: Which of the following is **NOT** an objective-type question?

a. constant alternative

b. essay

c. completion

d. large-group discussion (not credible)

Better: Which of the following is **NOT** an objective-type question?

a. constant alternative

b. essay

c. completion

d. changing alternative

Randomly order responses.[46] Teachers unwittingly place the correct answer in the middle of the set more often than in the first (a.) or last (d.) positions. Responses should be randomly ordered for each question.[47]

Avoid sources of irrelevant difficulty.[48] Avoid irrelevant sources of difficulty in the stem and responses. Some teachers confuse students by using complex vocabulary.

Eliminate extraneous material.[49] Do not include extraneous material in a question. That is, do not attempt to mislead students by including information not necessary for answering the question.

Avoid responses such as "none of the above."[50] Alternative responses such as "none of the above," "all of the above," and "both b and d" should be eliminated if possible. These responses reduce the number of possible correct choices.[51]

Test at higher cognitive levels.[52] Multiple choice items can present a complex case and then offer alternative explanations for it. Charts, maps, or graphs can be used in conjunction with a series of multiple choice questions that call for analysis, synthesis, and evaluation.

SUPPLY ITEMS. Supply (completion, fill-in-the-blank) items present a statement with one or more blanks. The student fills in the blanks in order to correctly complete the statement. This question type should be used when the correct response is a single word or brief phrase.[53]

When different graders obtain the same scores for a given test, it is said to have _____. (objectivity)

Supply items are relatively easy to construct.[54] They are efficient in that a large number of statements can be processed. Since recalling a term is more difficult than recognizing it, supply items discriminate better and offer less opportunity for guessing the right answer than true-false items.[55]

However, supply items are notorious for being ambiguous. It is difficult to write a supply item that is clear and plainly stated. Grading can be arbitrary and unfair, depending on how synonyms are handled.[56] Finally, misuse of completion items can lead to overemphasis on memorization.[57]

The following guidelines will help you avoid major pitfalls in writing supply items.

Limit blanks. Use only one or two blanks in a supply item. The greater the number of blanks, the greater the item ambiguity.[58]

Poor: Piaget wrote that _____ consists of _____ and _____.

Better: Piaget wrote that adaptation consists of _____ and _____.

Target only one correct answer. Write the item in such a way that only one explicit term or definite word will correctly complete the statement. If there are equally acceptable terms for a given concept (i.e., "true-false" and "constant alternative"), then credit should be given for either answer.

Omit important, not trivial, words.[59] Leave only important words or phrases blank. Blanking out minor words makes the item trivial.

Place blank at the end of the statement. In most cases, it is better to place the blank at the end of the sentence. This allows the entire sentence to provide the basis for the proper term.

Avoid irrelevant clues.[60] Avoid irrelevant clues to the correct answer. Make all blanks the same length. Avoid grammatical clues, such as the use of "a" or "an" instead of the more inclusive "a(n)" just before the blank.

Avoid text quotes.[61] Do not use directly quoted sentences out of required reading. Sentences taken out of context are usually ambiguous. Write the supply item based on a clear concept, not a specific quote.

MATCHING ITEMS. Matching items present students with two columns of items that relate to each other. A common version of a matching question has a numbered item list on the left and a lettered response list on the right.

Match the terms on the left with the associated theorist by writing the appropriate letter in the numbered blank.

____ 1. Programmed Instruction	a. Erikson
____ 2. Life Space	b. Kohlberg
____ 3. Equilibration	c. Levine
____ 4. Trust-Mistrust	d. Maslow
____ 5. Hierarchy of Needs	e. Piaget
	f. Skinner
	g. Thorndike

The matching item can test a large amount of factual material simply and efficiently.[62] Response pairs can be drawn from various texts, class notes, and additional readings to form a summary of facts. Grading is easy.

However, a good matching item is difficult to construct. As the number of response pairs in a given item increases, the more mental gymnastics are required to answer it. Matching items are restricted to measuring factual information and simple concepts.

The following guidelines will help you avoid major pitfalls in writing supply items.

Limit number of pairs. Do not include too many pairs to be matched in a given item. The list should contain no more than eight[63] to ten[64] pairs. Design the test so that the entire question is contained on the same page.[65]

Make the response list longer. If each response is used once and only once, then the response list should contain more responses than are needed to match all the items (see the example above). This prevents students from answering the last item simply by elimination. Opinions vary on how much longer to make the response list. Suggestions range from two to three items[66] to 50 percent[67] longer. However, if responses can be used more than once, then both lists can be the same length.[68]

Insure that there is only one correct match for each item.[69] It is important to insure that each item (left column) matches only one word or phrase in the response list (right column). Response options may be used more than once, however.

Maintain a central theme throughout the matching item.[70] A matching item should contain matched pairs that all relate to one central theme. Avoid mixing names, dates, events, and definitions in a single matching item. If the material requires it, construct several matching items, each with a central theme: dates-events, terms-definitions, authors-writings, and so forth.

Keep responses simple.[71] It is better to place longer statements in the item list (on the left) and the shorter answers in the response list (on the right). This helps subjects rapidly scan the response list for the correct match.

Systematically organize the response list.[72] Arrange the answers in the response list (right) alphabetically or chronologically.[73] This makes the task of searching the responses list more systematic.

Provide specific instructions for answering.[74] Be sure to clearly explain how the matching is to be done. Indicate whether answers can be used more than once.[75] Show an example, if necessary.

Essay Items. Essay items are open-ended questions that require students to write out their response in their own words. For example, "Discuss educational motivation from the perspective of the three major learning theory systems." Essay test items are easy to construct. They allow much greater flexibility and freedom in answering. Since grammar, structure, and content of the answer are left to students, teachers gain insight into students' ability to organize, integrate, and synthesize.[76] Essay items permit testing at higher levels of learning than objective questions.[77] Finally, answers to essay questions permits a greater range of answers than objective items. Guessing is eliminated.[78]

The greatest disadvantage of essay items is that they are difficult to score consistently.[79] The answers are more ambiguous and subjective than objective responses.[80] The reliability of scores is lower than those produced by objective tests over the same content because of the variability of response.[81] Essay items produce a smaller sample of material because of the amount of time required to analyze and understand the question, develop the answer, and write it out in complete sentences. This poses content validity problems.[82] Finally, essays are tedious and time-consuming to grade.[83]

The following guidelines will help you avoid major pitfalls in writing essay items.

Use short-answer essays.[84] It is much better to use several short-answer[85] essay items than one or two long ones. This increases sampling of material, focuses the essays sufficiently to increase reliability of grading, and produces a better measure of what students know.[86]

Write clear questions.[87] Write essay questions that give sufficient information to guide students toward your intended response.[88] A student shared with me an essay question he'd recently faced: "Explain the doctrine of God (10 points)." Scholars have devoted lifetimes to answering this question. It is much too broad and vague.

Poor: Discuss learning theory and its role in Christian education.

Better: Describe the three major learning theory systems and explain how each system can be used in a Christian teaching context.

Require all students to answer all questions.[89] A common practice, given the strong influence of "student choice" from humanistic educators, is to list six to eight essay questions and allow students to choose any four to answer. This reduces the systematic nature of the scores on the test since students are not being evaluated on the same questions. It is better to set course objectives, teach according to those objectives, and systematically test whether students achieve those objectives.

Develop a grading key. Develop a specific grading key or model answer for each essay item. Award points for each element in the key. Major elements should receive more points than minor ones. A point or two can be awarded for grammar, punctuation, or organization. A grading key provides a systematic guide for objectively grading an essay answer. Without such a key, scores are as much a reflection of the grader's perception as it is the knowledge of the student. Grade papers "blind," that is, without knowing its author.[90] Grade one question at a time across all papers.[91] Scores will then be more reliable and objective.

Consider assigning essays as homework.[92] Rather than confronting students with essay-type questions on an examination, assign essays as homework. The lack of time pressure and availability of resources will permit students to write better papers. Use objective tests to systematically evaluate student understanding in examinations.

The Teacher as Test Item Analyst

All teachers evaluate student learning in some way. But how do we know whether our evaluation tools are themselves fair and honest in their measurements? We may try to write good questions, but how do we determine if they are, indeed, "honest measures"? Every item in a test should contribute to making measurement more accurate. Those that do not should be revised or eliminated. An item analysis procedure called the "discrimination index" allows us to determine which items in an objective test differentiate between informed and uninformed subjects. After administering and grading an exam, apply the procedure as follows:[93]

Rank order students high to low by their overall grade on the exam. The rank position of each student is a reflection of their overall preparation for the examination.

Identify top and bottom proportions of students to compare. You can choose a percentage ranging from 10 to 40 percent. Twenty-five percent is common, and gives you the top and bottom quarters of the class. The number of students in *one* of the groups (NUMBER) is used to compute the discrimination index.

For each question in the exam, count how many students in the top group answered correctly (HIGH) and how many in the bottom group answered correctly (LOW). If the question is fairly separating students by their level of preparation, more of the top group should answer it correctly than in the bottom group. The discrimination index for each item is computed by subtracting LOW from HIGH and dividing by NUMBER.

Let's say you have a class of 40 students who take an exam. After grading the exam, rank the students by their overall test score. Select top and bottom quarters (25 percent) for computation of the discrimination index. In this case, you'll have the ten highest scoring students in group one and ten lowest scoring students in group two. Begin with question one and count how many students in the groups answered it correctly. Let's say that in our case, 8 of the top 10 subjects answered #1 right (HIGH=8) and 3 of the bottom 10 answered #1 right (LOW=3). The discrimination index for item one is "(8 - 3)/10," or +0.500. Repeat this for every item.[94]

A discrimination index ranges from -1.00 to +1.00. *Negative indices* indicate faulty questions. More LOW students answered the items right than HIGH students. These questions should be analyzed. Did the better-prepared students answer incorrectly because of poor teaching or poor item construction? If the former, rewrite course objectives or procedures. If the latter, rewrite or eliminate the item.

Positive indices indicate well-written questions. The more positive the index, the more discriminating the question. Questions that produce positive values close to zero are called barrier questions. These do not discriminate well between upper and lower groups, but may pinpoint important learnings that you want every student to know.

Negative indices indicate poorly written questions. These are usually ambiguous statements that are over-analyzed by better-prepared students. Rewrite or eliminate all questions that produce negative indices.

Objective examinations should mix discriminators and barrier questions. A good starting point is 40 percent discrimination and 60 percent barrier questions. Tests can be made legitimately more difficult by increasing the percentage of discriminating questions and by selecting questions with higher discrimination indices.

Using the discrimination index helps solve one of the most frustrating aspects of schooling: arbitrary testing. The index provides a way to develop examinations that yield valid measurements of student learning. Base discrimination index values on as many students as possible. Indices become less reliable in classes of less than forty students. While the discrimination index is an extremely helpful tool in evaluating test items, use it in conjunction with other forms of student feedback.

The Teacher as Observer

One of the major advantages of objective tests is the ability to efficiently test recall and thinking over a large amount of material. When test items randomly sample course material, as in diagram 1, we accurately measure student learning over the entire scope of the unit or course. But as time passes, we tend to "teach to the test," giving answers to test items as we lecture rather than securing genuine understanding of the concepts being tested. When this happens, our tests no longer measure "thinking" and "problem-solving," but simple recall, and, as shown in diagram 2, reduce the universe of learning to the information tested. Remembering right answers becomes more important than understanding, transferring, and applying course content. Remembering facts and getting right answers are good things, but real learning demands more. Educators suggest basing course grades on a wider range of evidence than objective tests.[95] These "new assessments"[96] or "authentic tests"[97] focus on standards of performance rather than objective test scores.

Diagram 1

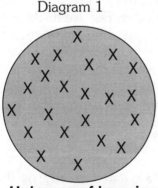

Universe of learning
sampled **by test items**

Diagram 2

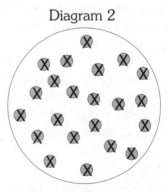

Universe of learning
defined **by test items**

Performance-based tests can range from evidence as simple as writing a theme, solving an equation, and diagramming a sentence or as complex as presenting a music recital, playing a sport, conducting a mock trial or experiment, or doing laboratory work. The major types of performance-based tests are simulations, work samples, portfolios, and exhibitions.

Simulations

Simulations allow learners to demonstrate skill in handling an "operational model of a process, mechanism, or system."[98] The advent of the computer has allowed educators to teach risky or expensive problem-solving skills in "real-world" settings. Flight simulators allow pilots to test various control combinations without risking a million-dollar plane. A computerized chemical lab allows learners to try various chemical combinations and processes without endangering the school building. Computerized artificial intelligence provides the means for ever-increasing complexity in simulations. Programs like "Where in the World Is Carmen Sandiego?" use a private eye motif to teach geography. Adventure games like "Myst" and "Riven" teach analytical skills as players collect clues and solve puzzles. Combat games like "Command and Conquer" and "Total Annihilation" confront players with objectives requiring complex management of resources, equipment, and movement.[99] Whether these computer games have any academic value remains a question. But as computers become more sophisticated, educators can use this technology to provide simulations that can demonstrate greater academic value. But, we might ask, does success in flying a computerized plane guarantee success in actual flight? Does successful computerized surgery translate to the operating room? Can students who successfully control a computerized environment make better decisions about their own neighborhoods? The solution is to follow up simulated performance with real-world evaluations.

Work Samples

A work sample is a sample of actual student performances. If the class is studying how to write instructional objectives, a work sample might be several objectives written for particular subjects and levels of learning. If the class is studying a foreign language, a work sample might be translations of sentences or paragraphs, or a rough draft of a lesson plan.

These work samples provide a broader scope of student competence, a wider range of evidence of student learning, and a clearer perspective of reflective thinking than answers to objective test items.

Portfolios

A portfolio is a purposeful, systematic collection of work samples. The name "portfolio" comes from the practice of professional photographers or graphic artists in developing a collection of their best work to show prospective clients. In an academic setting, students choose their best work samples to place in their portfolios. These samples can be revised over time, which allows the portfolio to reflect both student progress and teacher feedback. Portfolios can contain either the actual work of students (essays, math solutions, translations, computer programs, and the like) or representations of that work (such as pictures, or video or cassette tapes). The value of the portfolio is its ability to document changes over time, including self-reflections, teacher and peer comments, and improvements in performance. Assessment of the portfolio is usually done in a fifteen- to twenty-minute student conference, in which the work samples are evaluated according to stated criteria.[100]

Exhibitions

An exhibition is a portfolio with two additional characteristics. First, an exhibition is a portfolio expressly produced for presentation to an audience. Second, an exhibition represents the culmination of a study more than the progress of study.[101]

Performance-based tests require more time to develop, are more complex, and less exact than objective tests. Products from such assessments are less comparable from student to student, create a larger volume of records, and are difficult to summarize.[102] However, for some disciplines, performance-based assessment provides a much more meaningful picture of student learning.

Reliability and Validity of Authentic Tests

A serious consideration concerning the use of "authentic" tests is the reliability and validity of their scores. Since performance-based tests are less exact than objective types, special care must be taken to insure solid measurements.

Reliable scores are obtained by using objective measures such as checklists and rating scales. A *checklist* is a list of characteristics required for successful completion of a project. The grade of the assignment equals the number of characteristics demonstrated by the work.

MicroTeach Checklist
❑ Stated clear instructional objective (after session)
❑ Used an appropriate learning readiness activity
❑ Transitions were clear
❑ Used appropriate methods for meeting stated objective
❑ Instructional objective was met
❑ Conclusion was appropriate for stated objective
❑ Avoided distracting mannerisms
❑ Demonstrated good platform skills
❑ Made meaningful eye contact with learners

While a checklist records objective information about specific characteristics, it does not provide a way to measure the quality of those characteristics. What about students who state poor instructional objectives? Do they receive the same credit as those who state excellent objectives? A *rating scale* extends the checklist by adding a scale of points that can be awarded according to the quality of each characteristic.

MicroTeach Rating Scale (1=low, 4=high)
1 2 3 4   Stated clear instructional objective (after session)
1 2 3 4   Used an appropriate learning readiness activity
1 2 3 4   Transitions were clear
1 2 3 4   Used appropriate methods for meeting stated objective
1 2 3 4   Instructional objective was met
1 2 3 4   Conclusion was appropriate for stated objective
1 2 3 4   Avoided distracting mannerisms
1 2 3 4   Demonstrated good platform skills
1 2 3 4   Made meaningful eye contact with learners

The use of these instruments provides an objective basis for assigning points and comparing one student's work against another.[103]

The validity of scores is obtained by analyzing the conditions under which performances are conducted. Is the work the student's own? What kind of assistance may the student have received from outside sources? Is there evidence of cheating? To what extent is the performance a demonstration of the student's mastery of the subject? A valid grading system requires us to determine (1) what we want students to gain from a course (goals targeting concepts/values/skills), (2) how we will reliably evaluate achievement of these goals, and (3) what we will do to facilitate students in the process of achieving the goals.

The question regarding objective tests or performance-based evaluations is not an either-or proposition. Some courses require students to master technical vocabulary, specific concepts, and interrelated principles. Such goals lend themselves to objective examinations. Other courses require students to integrate terminology and principles into specific skills. These goals lend themselves to performance-based evaluations. Some courses may very well blend both kinds of evaluations. I use objective examinations (true-false, multiple choice, matching, short-answer essay items) in my educational psychology and research and statistics classes.[104] But in my principles of teaching classes, I use performance-based evaluations (written objectives, reflections on readings, formal lesson plans, and a videotaped MicroTeach experience). I believe, after eighteen years of tinkering with them, that each grading system serves the purposes of their respective courses well.

The Teacher as Scribe

The more complex a grading scheme becomes, the more teachers take on the role of a scribe, converting the work of students to record entries and notations. Several semesters ago I had my secretary add up all the reports, assignments, papers, and tests my two hundred plus students in seven classes generate, and it came to over 2,700 separate items. Each item had to be collected, tracked, graded, posted, and averaged through the semester to provide students feedback on their progress, and establish the appropriate grade level for the course.

I have used a computer spreadsheet program to track and average grades for over ten years now. Recently our school acquired the program "GradeBook," which is used by our secretaries to provide up-to-date information on assignments and grades. The program allows us to print out attendance sheets, seating charts, and a wide variety of grade reports. Assignments can be weighted by points or percentages. These computerized tools have greatly reduced the accounting burden of grading.

Note cards or notebooks can be used to keep anecdotal records on each student: prayer requests, questions asked, problems expressed with the course or "in life," special needs, and the like. Cumulative records—using dots, dashes, checks, pluses, and minuses[105]—can be maintained as part of the attendance record to indicate daily difficulties, progress, or successes.

This record-keeping is worth the effort. I can remember classes in which I was expected to demonstrate mastery of thirty hours of lecture and a thousand pages of reading by a one-hour midterm and a two-hour final. The semester's journey is too long and learning too complex to be evaluated by means as narrow as this. The scribe's accurate records of multiple indices of learning provide a solid basis for assigning grades.

The Teacher as Grader

The translation of individual assignments into a course grade is a heavier responsibility than many teachers realize. The longer we teach, the less we remember what it is like to be a student in a classroom. In fact, I recommend that any serious professional development program for faculty include provisions for every teacher to be a student in a semester-long course in another institution at least once every five years. Nothing softens the hardened hearts of teachers better than reexperiencing what it is like to be a student.

Furthermore, the more we've succeeded as teachers, the less we feel the long-term damage done by arbitrary grade categories. The professor who assigned D's to students earning a 96 percent average thought nothing of it. His students, I can assure you, have not forgotten his cavalier attitude, even after twenty years. And they continue to tell anyone who asks, with undiminished emotion, how unfair that grading system, and that professor, really was.

The professor's first problem was his use of a norm-referenced system of grading. In a norm-referenced system, students compete against each other,[106] since only a certain percentage can make A's, B's, and so forth. Individual differences are maximized. Academic competition ("dog-eat-dog survival") is encouraged; academic cooperation among students, diminished. And we wonder why graduates from schools that promote norm-referenced grading have difficulties working with each other?

Criterion-referenced grading makes comparisons student-to-standard, not student-to-student.[107] The standards for grades in a particular course are set. Any student achieving the stated standards, meeting the stated criteria, receives the associated grade. Here individual differences are minimized. Competition is not against other students, but toward the goals of the system. Cooperation with other students is not only enhanced, but encouraged. Students learn to work together, learning from each other, teaching each other, to master course goals.

Norm-referenced systems are based on a normal curve distribution of grades. The most extreme version of this system requires a distribution of grades of 10 percent A, 20 percent B, 40 percent C, 20 percent D, and 10 percent F in any given class. In such a system, 10 percent of the students in a class must fail, no matter how much they learn! What proponents miss is that the normal curve represents naturally occurring distributions. Height, weight, I.Q., and income are all naturally occurring variables that fall into a normal-curve type distribution. But education is an intervention, not a natural phenomenon. Therefore we should never expect grades to be normally distributed. To force grades into a normal curve is to do a great disservice to the teaching-learning process. A 96 percent D. Such a system must be utterly rejected by any Christian institution.

Criterion-referenced grading is not "weak" or "soft" on academics, as some advocates of norm-referencing suggest. We can set the standards as high or as low as the desired outcomes require. All of my courses are criterion-based. The course "Teaching Ministry of the Church" is a student-friendly course, affective in nature. Since both theology and educational ministry students must take this course, we have an opportunity to address pastor-staff issues in a cooperative way. We focus on reading the text, writing reflective essays, and discussing as a class or in small groups the critical issues regarding teaching ministry. There are no examinations in the course. Written assignments, lesson plans, and leading a teachers' meeting in a local church (with participant evaluations) make up the elements of the course. My research and statistics class, however, is, according to my students, the most difficult course in the school. Four examinations, problem sets, application-oriented questions, and two languages to master (research and statistics) make for a difficult semester. Any student in either class who meets the standards for an A earns an A. About three-fourths of my teaching ministry students earn A's. About one-third of my research students earn A's. These are very different courses, but both use a criterion-referenced system to establish course grades.

When considering how you will assign grades, keep the following principles in mind.[108] Explain the grading system early in the course. I hand out a syllabus to each student on the first day of class. The syllabus specifies exactly what assignments are required, when they are due, and how much they are worth toward the total grade. Violate this principle by surprising students with new assignments or a change in grading procedure during the semester.

Set reasonable standards. Evaluate the workload and the level of testing from semester to semester to insure that you are not setting the standards too low, which causes boredom, or too high, which causes confusion. Adjust the course and the tests to meet these standards. Violate this principle by expressing an attitude of "know it all, whatever the cost."

Base course grades on objective evidence. Be sure you administer reliable tests. Use grading keys to insure reliable scoring of answers. Use checklists and rating scales to evaluate performance-based tests. Violate this principle by giving grades based on subjective elements such as student personality, cooperativeness, or friendliness.

Do not change a grade, except for a clerical error. Establish a clear rationale for assigning grades from the beginning. Be able to articulate why a particular grade was assigned for the work the student submitted. Violate this principle by giving in to student pleas for a grade change on the basis of expended effort ("But I worked twelve hours on my research paper!" when it received an objective C) or personal difficulties ("I just took too many hours this semester. Gimme a break, I need to keep my GPA up").

Give the student the benefit of a doubt. No test can measure student performance exactly. There is some degree of error in every test score. Course averages are not exact indicators of performance. In borderline cases, look at records of attendance and participation, as well as instances of missing, late, or incomplete work to determine whether "close" numerical averages warrant the next higher grade. The professor who assigned the student earning an 89.85 course average a B grievously violated this principle.

In Conclusion

Test writer, item analyst, observer, scribe, and grader. There is no greater damage done to the "little ones" of the Lord in our classes than that from arbitrary, unfair, and shoddy testing and grading practices. "Woe to those who make unjust laws, to those who issue oppressive decrees, to deprive the poor of their rights and withold justice from the oppressed of my people" (Isa. 10:1–2a). Jesus warns us that we will be evaluated as we evaluate others: "With the measure you use, it will be measured to you—and even more" (Mark 4:24).

It is a matter of simple ethics that our evaluations of students be as accurate and fair as possible. Challenge students toward excellence, but measure their accomplishments with honest weights. Let us move beyond scholarly discourses to include the qualities of nurture, guidance, and support, not only in our teaching style, but in our grading practices as well.

You must have accurate and honest weights and
measures,
so that you may live long in the land
the LORD your God is giving you.
For the LORD your God detests anyone who does
these things, anyone who deals dishonestly.

(Deut. 25:15–16)

For Further Reading

I recommend the following excellent texts on testing and measurements:

Jum C. Nunnally, *Educational Testing and Measurement: Classroom Application and Practice* (Glenview, Ill.: Scott, Foresman and Company, 1987).

David A. Payne, *The Assessment of Learning: Cognitive and Affective* (Lexington, Mass.: D. C. Heath and Company, 1974).

I also recommend the suggestions and examples found in the following texts:

Gary D. Borich and Martin L. Tombari, *Educational Psychology: A Contemporary Approach*, chapter 11: "Assessing for Learning: Objective and Essay Tests," and chapter 12: "Assessing for Learning: Performance Assessment."

Myron H. Dembo, *Applying Educational Psychology*, 5th ed., Part V: (chapters 12–13) "Assessment and Evaluation" (New York: Longman, 1994).

Paul Eggen and Don Kauchak, *Educational Psychology: Classroom Connections*, chapter 13: "Classroom Assessment" (New York: Macmillan College Publishing Company, 1994).

Guy R. LeFrançois, *Psychology for Teaching*, 8th ed., chapter 13: "Measurement and Evaluation" (Belmont, Calif.: Wadsworth Publishing Company, 1994).

John F. Wakefield, *Educational Psychology: Learning to be a Problem Solver*, chapter 14: "Assessment Design" (Boston: Houghton-Mifflin Company, 1996).

Anita Woolfolk, *Educational Psychology*, 5th ed., chapter 15: "Classroom Evaluation and Grading" (Boston: Allyn and Bacon, Inc., 1993).

Part Four

The Teacher as Minister

Chapter 10. The Teacher as Minister

Chapter 10

The Teacher as Minister

For this reason, since the day we heard about you, we have not stopped praying for you and asking God to fill you with the knowledge of his will through all spiritual wisdom and understanding. And we pray this in order that you may live a life worthy of the Lord and may please him in every way: bearing fruit in every good work, growing in the knowledge of God, being strengthened with all power according to his glorious might so that you may have great endurance and patience, and joyfully giving thanks to the Father, who has qualified you to share in the inheritance of the saints in the kingdom of light.

Colossians 1:9–12

Sergei Golovin was trained as a physicist in one of the best schools of the former Soviet Union. When he came to faith in Christ several years ago, he asked himself: "Why doesn't the Lord simply take us directly to heaven when we profess faith in him? Why does he leave us in this world?" The Lord gave him two answers. He leaves us in the world to learn and to teach. Sergei now pastors a Baptist church in Simferopol, Ukraine, and heads a ministry of Christian apologetics, focusing his teaching efforts on the academic elite of the former Soviet Union. Why are we here? To learn and to teach.

In our very first chapter we described the synergistic teaching of Jesus. We defined the Christian Teachers' Triad and noted the three roles of his teaching ministry: Prophet, Priest, and King. As we near the end of our journey together, let's review our four-dimensional philosophy of time (process) and the thinking-feeling-doing, head-heart-hand, Prophet-Priest-King triadic focus of teaching.

The Teacher as Prophet

Recall that Jesus the Prophet reflected cognitive elements of teaching by proclaiming and explaining the kingdom of God through stories and illustrations (see Matt. 13:57; Matt. 21:11; Luke 24:19; John 6:14). Jesus reflected the thinking element of the triad as he emphasized the Father's eternal truths and the objective standards of Kingdom living.

Through the chapters of this text we have analyzed ways we can be effective prophets—proclaimers, communicators—to those we teach. To focus on the cerebral, logical, and rational elements of teaching. Emphasize concepts more than words, thought-provoking questions more than pat answers, problem-solving more than reason-giving, and illustrative examples more than isolated facts. We described conceptualization, decentration, and metacognition. Explicit sequences of conceptual clusters. Emphasizing, rephrasing, explaining, and synthesizing in real time. Rocking cognitive boats through disequilibrium. Stirring up curiosity and dispensing meaningfulness. Telling relevant stories. Recognizing learning impairments and prescribing the proper antidotes. In all these things, the prophet strives to convey his message so that listeners can understand and benefit from it. But then, remember that too much emphasis on the rational produces a dry and impersonal learning environment.

The Teacher as Priest

Recall that Jesus the Priest reflected affective elements of teaching (see Heb. 3:1; 4:14). He loved and cared for his disciples and followers. He healed and fed them, calming their fears, ministering to them. He nurtured them, wept over them, and prayed for them. He taught them with compassion and retaught them with patience. He forgave them when they failed. Ultimately he gave his own life for them—and us. Jesus reflected the feeling element of the triad, caring for his learners as a mother hen cares for her chicks, or a family doctor his beloved patients.

Through the chapters of this text we have shared ways we can be effective priests—shepherds, nurturers—to those we teach. To focus on the subjective, relational, supportive, and affective elements of teaching. To be personal, spontaneous, and warm, creating a classroom atmosphere of openness and love. To be the students' friend. Sensitive, flexible, and gracious. Sharing personal experiences, developing positive attitudes, establishing values, reorganizing priorities. Accepting students as they are (while helping them grow). Using humor appropriately and building trust. In all these things, the priest strives to love and care for listeners. But then, remember that too much emphasis on the affective produces a learning environment that is shallow, self-centered, and speculative.

The Teacher as King (or Leader)

Recall that Jesus the King reflected behavioral elements of teaching (see Mark 15:2; Luke 23:3; John 18:37; Acts 17:7). He chose twelve apprentices and trained them for action. He gave explicit instructions, but went beyond words to demonstrate through his own ministry the skills he taught others. He modeled the role of Kingdom ministry and sent his followers into the whole world to make disciples. He corrected mistakes and rebuked mistaken attitudes. His reality-based training and performance-based assessments were carried out in the weave and woof of daily ministry. Jesus focused on the action element of Kingdom living.

Through the chapters of this text we have presented ways we can be effective leaders—guides, coaches—to those we teach. To focus on the skillful, competent elements of teaching. To provide experiences that are hands-on, interactive, and task-oriented. To be skilled ourselves in the art and science of teaching as well as our disciplines. To conduct scholarly research. Synthesize subject content and learner needs. Compose learning sequences in units and sessions. Target learning with measurable objectives. Write and analyze evaluations that are both valid and reliable. Assign grades based on objective measurements of student performance. In all these things, the leader strives to direct listeners toward competence, skill, and excellence for the Kingdom's sake. But then, too much emphasis on doing produces a learning environment of busyness, overwork, and, eventually, exhaustion.

It is in the four-dimensional balance of time and triad that we find the greatest success, growing as prophets, priests, and king-leaders. But the ultimate end of our four-dimensional growth rests not in ourselves, but in our classrooms, which stand before us as the open door to ministry: our mission field, our congregation, and our Kingdom school.

Classroom as Mission Field: A Focus on Evangelism

Greg was well named by his parents, because he is one of the most gregarious people I ever met. The year was 1973 and we had just begun working at Gallaudet College for the Deaf in Washington, D.C. Greg was among the first students to attend Sunday school and worship at our church.

During the year, our Sunday school class grew from three to thirty-five. Only two of these thirty-five were Baptists, and Greg was one of those. Week by week, we gathered in our classroom and studied a portion of the Bible. Since there were several self-proclaimed unbelievers in the group, I made sure that every week, no matter the passage or theme, I shared in one way or another what it means to "know Christ personally." Through the year, week by week, class members would walk forward at invitation time to give their hearts to Christ. Toward the end of the year, Greg made that walk as well.

I hadn't been as concerned about Greg as I had the others. He had been a member of a Baptist church and joined our church early in the school year by "letter." He fit right into our activities. But he did not know the Lord. After he was baptized, I asked him about his decision. He said he *thought* he was a Christian because he had been baptized at the age of twelve. He was in the sixth grade, and had gone to Vacation Bible School at his church. The pastor came in on the last day and explained the plan of salvation. Several of his friends went forward to accept Christ, and, not wanting to be left out, Greg went with them. But Greg was deaf, and his church provided no interpreters, so he had never known a single word the pastor had said. His profession of faith was nothing more than a walk and a dip with his friends.

In our Sunday school class, week after week, Greg heard about characteristics exhibited by "those who know the Lord." Week after week, he increasingly realized that those characteristics did not describe him, and that, whatever "knowing the Lord" really meant, he did not. The day he walked forward was the day he realized he needed to repent of his sin and ask the Lord into his life, to walk with him and obey him, to learn from him and tell others about him. It was the beginning of a whole new life for Greg. That year, thirty-three of the thirty-five class members made professions of faith. Some had been religious; others had never been in a church before. But none of them had ever heard about the life available to them through union with Christ.

My wife teaches a course on ministry with the deaf every three years at Southwestern Seminary. Half of the course discusses deaf culture and ministry. The other half develops basic communication skills in American Sign Language (ASL). One of the assignments requires students to write out their salvation testimony, translate it into ASL, and present it to the class. In every semester but one, there has been a student or two who realize they've never experienced the reality of the words they're signing, and give their hearts to the Lord. Seminary students, preparing for ministry, yet unsaved.

From experiences in teaching deaf adults in churches and ministerial students in seminary, I've come to realize that we can never know for sure if our students truly know the Lord, or if they've just "learned the lingo." We might expect to find unbelievers in our Sunday school classes, but it's easy to assume that students in Christian schools, colleges, and seminaries already know the Lord. It may not be so. Our classrooms are mission fields.

On the other hand, I've seen teachers who, like counter-intelligence agents, obsessively sniff out the supposed unbelievers in their classes. Using guilt and scare tactics, these teachers can drive students—believers and unbelievers alike—away from themselves and their classes.

To avoid the negative, treat every learner as if they are believers, insiders, accepted and acceptable. Just as Jesus accepted and embraced Judas, even as he sought to teach him. To embrace the positive, teach so that anyone who does not know the Lord will recognize their need and come to faith in Jesus. For in our teaching, we are to evangelize our students—head, heart, and hand.

Evangelize the head. Positively, explain the gospel in easy-to-understand words and illustrations. Use the context of your subject to articulate the reasonableness of the gospel. Negatively, clarify misunderstandings that keep people from the Lord.

Evangelize the heart. Positively, accept learners—believers and unbelievers—as they are. Care about learners one at a time. Negatively, expose toxic attitudes and values of the world that contaminate learners and keep them from faith.

Evangelize the hand. Positively, model proper Christian behavior and challenge your learners toward biblical standards. Negatively, underscore the tragic consequences of self-centered behaviors that ultimately destroy.

Create a classroom climate that allows learners to ask questions, share experiences, debate issues. "Keep telling the story, be faithful and true, Let others see Jesus in you." Our classrooms are mission fields.

Classroom as Congregation: A Focus on Ministry

Paul explains to us that Christ gifted the church with "pastors and teachers, to prepare God's people for works of service" (Eph. 4:11–12). The commentators I've read refer to "pastors and teachers" as one office, not two. Pastor-teachers are shepherds who nurture their flocks, feed their flocks, protect their flocks. Pastor-teachers are also instructors who train, prepare, and equip the sheep of the Lord.

Our classrooms are not churches, per se, but they are congregations of believers. And we are their pastor-teachers. Equipping students for works of service, based in our subject field, is an essential part of our ministry. The "teacher" part of the role comes as part of our job description. But how well do we all handle the "pastor" part? For in our equipping ministry, we do more than instruct. We are to shepherd our students—head, heart, and hand.

Shepherd the head. Positively, clarify biblical truths for life and work, and build bridges between your subject and daily living. Negatively, unravel the twisted thinking of the world. Demonstrate the distortion and deception of worldly perspectives.

Shepherd the heart. Positively, be transparent. Share your own spiritual struggles as it is appropriate to do so. Deal with students with grace and humility, love and compassion. Listen. Share a burden. Or a joy. Negatively, confront toxic attitudes and values that contaminate learners as you find them.

Shepherd the hand. Positively, exhibit Christian values and model Christian behavior as best you can, "being examples to the flock" (1 Pet. 5:3) in the way you teach. Negatively, avoid any attitude or behavior that would harm or humiliate your students.

Such teaching ministry creates a climate of trust and openness, in which the old garments of selfishness can be laid aside and new garments of *koinonia*, of relationship, can be put on (see Col. 3:12–18), even in the context of an academic study. Our classrooms are congregations.

Classroom as Kingdom School: A Focus on Discipleship

Students in the seminaries of Jesus' day were called *talmid*. The talmid were scholars who attended classes, took notes, memorized passages of text, sat examinations, and earned degrees. The disciples of Jesus were called *mathetes* (from the root "to learn"[1]) which can be translated "apprentice." Apprentices would attach themselves to a master craftsman and learn his trade firsthand, through demonstration, discussion, and practice. The disciples of Jesus were not academic scholars, but apprentices of the Master Teacher. They did not take notes or memorize passages, but through attentive observation, personal experience, and pointed explanation, they learned in a laboratory setting how to be leaders and teachers in the kingdom of heaven.

Whether we teach in Sunday school, a church school, a Christian college, or seminary, our focus should be on helping our learners to "grow up into him who is the Head, that is, Christ" (Eph. 4:15). It is more difficult to do this in an academic setting, because our primary task there is to teach our assigned subject—Romans, biology, statistical analysis, or whatever. The dangerous tendency, however, is teaching subjects more than teaching students. Reproducing overhead cels more than translating cels into ministry. Recalling author names and dates more than remembering "who we are and Whose we are." Giving correct answers more than asking correct questions. Gradually turning our students into *talmid*.

Yet in the context of academic study, there is a place for Christian teachers to encourage students to be *mathetes*, apprentices, disciples. Our classrooms are Kingdom schools, for in our teaching, we disciple head, heart, and hand.

Disciple the head. Positively, tie course principles to growth in Christ. Help students evaluate new ideas objectively, so as to meaningfully integrate them into their thinking. Move students beyond the "textual meaning of Romans" to its personal relevance. Beyond the inherent "structure of living organisms" in biology to the One in whom "all things hold together" (Col. 1:17). Beyond the "natural dimensions of the normal curve" to the supernatural dimensions of the empty tomb. Negatively, lead students to analyze perceptual filters that keep them from testing new ideas. Inspire them to give up their limited two-dimensional views of truth for the richer three-dimensional realities of God's Truth.

Disciple the heart. Positively, create a climate of learning in which students accept each other as brothers and sisters, care for one another in their lives, and assist one another in their studies. Help students improve their own transparency, their own willingness to share with others. Negatively, sensitize students to toxic attitudes, in the class and in the world, that impair students' growth in the Lord.

Disciple the hand. Positively, expect students to produce good work in a responsible manner. Challenge students to excellence. Praise students who exhibit positive attitudes and behaviors. Negatively, hold students accountable for improper attitudes and poor work in the name of justice. Deal redemptively yet firmly with irresponsibility and mediocre performance.

We teach more than subjects. We teach believers who will process our subjects—head, heart, and hand—and translate them into principles, values, and skills fit for the service of Christ. Our classrooms are Kingdom schools.

In Conclusion

Let us take advantage of every opportunity to learn from the Lord and from one another, and to teach others to know him and to grow up in him. May we honor his name and his example by the way we learn and the way we teach—head, heart, and hand—

whatever our assigned teaching task. After all, Sergei Golovin would tell us it's the only reason God leaves us on this earth.

Take my yoke upon you and learn from me,
for I am gentle and humble in heart,
and you will find rest for your souls.
For my yoke is easy and my burden is light.

(Matt. 11:29–30)

Postlogue

Called to Teach

So, the book is done. Triad—head, heart and hand—and Time form the four dimensions of an effective teaching ministry. Dynamic Synergist, Mature Person, Clear Communicator, Sincere Motivator, Dramatic Performer, Creative Designer, Organized Manager, Special Agent, Honest Evaluator, Minister.

Last Sunday I began teaching a new young married adult Sunday School class at my church. I prepared. I prayed. I taught. We began a journey together. Bridges begun. Explanations made. Sharing. Life.

But nothing spectacular happened as far as I know. We covered verses and concepts, shared a few experiences. And left the room to go to worship. I was disappointed.

Once again I was reminded how much easier it is to share ideas about teaching than it is to teach. Yet I have full assurance that week by week, as the Lord blesses our gathering, as we apply the principles of this text, the class will grow, learners and teacher will be changed by his Presence and his Word. Session by session. Triad and Time.

Do not be discouraged!

If he has called you to teach, he will give you both the will and the ability to work for his good pleasure (Phil. 2:3). He himself will teach you how to teach (Matt. 11:29)—head, heart and hand.

May God bless you richly as you pull with him in his yoke of teaching.

Endnotes

Chapter 1

1. Yount, William R., *Created to Learn: A Christian Teacher's Introduction to Educational Psychology* (Nashville: Broadman and Holman, Publishers, 1996).

2. Ibid., 250.

3. The term "parallel processor" comes from the field of computers. A sequential processor executes one program instruction at a time. "Moving freely from system to system" in teaching relates to sequential processing. A parallel processor, on the other hand, provides multiple channels which can execute program instructions simultaneously. Consciously dealing with behaviors, concepts, and values simultaneously provides a richer learning environment.

4. A conceptual essay focuses on objective facts, concepts, and principles. It does not express personal experiences, reactions, feelings, or values. Conceptual essays explain, interpret, and illustrate.

5. The Holy Spirit convicts of sin (John 16:8). My role—even in Bible study and preaching—is to teach clearly.

6. Students teach for ten minutes before the class. They are videotaped and evaluated based on principles studied in the course. I call this experience a "MicroTeach" session.

7. "Chasing rabbits" is a slang term for moving away from the main subject into tangential issues. Sometimes these "rabbits" steal valuable time from the "real" subject. But often these "rabbits" are a window on student thinking and values. Dealing with student questions—even if they may seem to be "rabbits"—communicates caring. Whether or not to pursue such a tangent is a decision that is made each time a rabbit pops up—and wisdom in making the decision to chase or ignore comes with experience. (Read this last as "You've got to make a lot of mistakes, wasting time with trivial questions and/or ignoring what may be important student questions, to learn when to chase.")

Chapter 2

1. QuickVerse 2.0, a computer concordance. "2 Timothy 2:15"

2. When I was a teenager we attended an independent Baptist church in Bayside, Long Island, New York. The pastor, Dr. King, was a Scottish gentleman. I will always remember him for two things. The first was his habit of describing a verse as being "prrrrreyg-nunt" with meaning. The second was his belief that "theh ohnly cohmentahry on theh boook is theh boook." I took that to mean that if one really wanted to understand Scripture, one must study the Scripture.

3. Refer to chap. 4 of *Created to Learn* for an overview of Piaget's theory of cognitive development.

4. *Egocentrism* is the inability to see a situation from any other perspective but one's own. Young children are by nature egocentric. If adults are egocentric, it is by choice.

5. My assumption, of course, is that all the perspectives are focusing on the truth-of-the-whole. There are times when perceptions are simply wrong, not merely different.

6. See chapter 9, "Information Processing Theory" in *Created to Learn* for more information.

7. *Ignorance* is not used here as derogatory, merely a statement of "not knowing." *Ignorance* is not a synonym for *mentally deficient*.

8. He had been teaching a group on fasting when Jairus arrived, asking for help for his daughter. Jesus showed no sign of irritation at the interruption, but immediately left the "class" and made his way to Jairus's house. On the way, he was stopped ("interrupted") by the woman with an issue of blood. Again he showed no sign of irritation, but met her need and healed her. By the time he arrived at the house, Tabitha was dead. He once more showed no sign of irritation at having been delayed, but simply raised her back to life. In all this, Jesus demonstrated great patience.

9. *Learning readiness* means more than "gaining attention." It refers to learning experiences that prepare the hearts and minds of students for the day's session.

10. Peter, James, and John were the top three disciples of the Twelve. They witnessed firsthand the raising of Tabitha from death (the nine stayed outside), as well as the Transfiguration of Jesus (the nine stayed at the bottom of the mountain). In the Garden of Gethsemane, the eight (nine minus Judas) stayed back at the gate, while Peter, James, and John went farther into the garden with Jesus. Peter is listed first in the four lists of the Twelve.

Chapter 3

1. By the way, I refer to God as "he" even though I know that God is not "male." It's the way Scripture refers to "him," and if inspired writers over 1500 years all agreed, why should I begin to address "him" differently now? I find myself hoping as I write this that it isn't too provocative.

2. Lottie Moon was the first Southern Baptist woman missionary to China. She died of starvation, giving her own food to feed hungry women and children to whom she ministered. There is much to learn from Ms. Moon's commitment and sacrifice, but her ship's cabin number isn't part of her wonderful legacy.

3. The answer to this "Master's level" midterm question was "elephant."

4. We'll look more closely at conceptual clusters in chapter 6.

5. See "conceptualization" in chapter 2.

6. See "Writing Instructional Objectives" in chapter 6.

7. Make the outline or handout detailed enough to communicate clear structure, but not so detailed that it makes the class session boring. It will take practice to serve your porridge so that it's "just right!"

8. Details will be found in chapter 6.

9. In teaching analytics, the formula for computing the area of a circle [$A = \pi r^2$], you would first state the purpose for the formula (foundational). Next you would explain the symbols for a circle's area [A], the symbol pi [π], a constant that approximately equals 3.14, and the circle's radius [r]—the distance from the center to the circumference, or half the circle's diameter (conceptual). Then you would illustrate the formula by computing a circle's area by measuring its diameter, computing the radius, and applying the formula (illustrative). Finally, you would insure that students understood the use of the formula by giving them several problems to work on their own (functional).

10. In teaching globals, the formula for computing the circumference of a circle [$C = \pi d$], you might begin by having students use a 24-inch piece of string to make circles of various sizes. Have them measure both the circumference and diameter of the circles they create (functional). They will discover that, regardless of the size of the circle they make, the ratio of the circumference to the diameter of a circle is a little more than 3 (illustrative). Explain the symbols [C], [π], and [d], as well as the formula [$C = \pi d$] (conceptual). Finally, explain the purpose of the formula and its use (foundational).

11. Introduction, problem, purpose, synthesis of literature, hypothesis, population(s), sample(s), collecting data, analyzing data, testing the hypothesis, and conclusion.

12. Compare and contrast key ideas. See chapter 6.

13. Create a multidimensional concept from several disparate pieces. See chapter 6.

14. See chapter 4 of *Created to Learn* for a full description of this process.

15. Intentional learning is associated with "education." We also learn automatically, unconsciously. But without intentionality, we are unable to retrieve this information. So though we "know" every word of every lecture we've ever heard, it does us little good unless we can retrieve it. And this requires intentional learning. See Information Processing Theory in chapter 9 of *Created to Learn*.

16. Piaget called these perceptions "schemes."

17. Not to be confused with "withit-ness" which will be discussed in chapter 8.

18. See material under "Low Tech" a little later in the chapter.

19. See chapter 6 on instructional objectives.

20. Professor of Psychology and Counseling, Southwestern Baptist Theological Seminary, 1956–85.

21. Well, usually. Sometimes I find it helpful to have minimalist diagrams or words on the board. These are landmarks for the hour. Just enough detail to remind me what I need to say. But not enough so that students know what I'll say. Chalkboard structure with flexibility.

22. *New* is a relative term, especially in computer software. As I write these words, the best presentation packages are PowerPoint 97 from Microsoft, Presentations 8 from Corel, and Astound 5.0 by Gold Disk.

23. Associate Professor of Youth Education, School of Educational Ministries, Southwestern Baptist Theological Seminary.

Chapter 4

1 . For background information on behavioral learning theory, see *Created to Learn*, chapter 7, "Teaching for Behavior Change: B. F. Skinner," 159–179.

2. Dr. Leroy Ford was professor of Foundations of Education in the School of Religious Education (now Educational Ministries) at Southwestern Baptist Theological Seminary. He served from 1966 to 1984 and emphasized behavioral types of learning: programmed instruction and teaching systems. He was instrumental in leading the faculty of the school to develop a curriculum guide that lists every course in the school, including objectives, outline, teaching procedures, resources, testing, and bibliography.

3. See *Created to Learn*, "Cooperative Learning," 241.

4. There are hundreds of references to God's wrath and discipline in Scripture, responses to man's rebellion and sin. Here the focus is on the loving relationship between father and son, a caring relationship.

5. The four points made in this section come from Paul Eggen and Don Kauchak, *Educational Psychology: Classroom Connections*, 2nd ed. (New York: Macmillan College Publishing Company, 1994), 340.

6. Guy R. LeFrançois, *Psychology for Teaching*, 8th ed. (Belmont, Calif.: Wadsworth Publishing Company, 1994), 275.

7. Ibid., 275.

8. Don Hamachek, *Psychology in Teaching, Learning, and Growth*, 4th ed. (Boston: Allyn and Bacon, 1990), 271, 274; and Anita Woolfolk, *Educational Psychology*, 5th ed. (Boston: Allyn and Bacon, Inc., 1993), 377.

9. LeFrançois, 275.

10. Hamachek, 275; Woolfolk, 377.

11. LeFrançois, 275.

12. Hamachek, 271.

13. Hamachek, 275; Woolfolk, 377.

14. Richard Hamilton and Elizabeth Ghatala, *Learning and Instruction* (New York: McGraw-Hill, Inc., 1994), 331.

15. Eggen and Kauchak, 436.

16. Hamachek, 272.

17. Woolfolk, 216.

18. For other, more specific, recommendations, see *Created to Learn*, "Suggestions for Using Conditioning Principles," 177–179.

19. N. L. Gage and David C. Berliner, *Educational Psychology*, 3rd ed. (Dallas: Houghton Mifflin Company, 1984), 295.

20. Ibid., 296.

21. For background information on observation learning theory, see *Created to Learn*, chapter 7, "Teaching for Behavior Change: Albert Bandura," 179–185.

22. Essential in vicarious reinforcement is that the observer desires to become what the model is. The model may be little more than a thug, but if the observer respects that (strength, control, "freedom" from constraints), the thug will provide a "good model" for the observer to follow.

23. Neal Jones was pastor of Columbia Baptist Church, Falls Church, Virginia, from 1969 to 1992.

24. He is now a student ministry consultant with LifeWay Christian Resources of the Southern Baptist Convention.

25. B. S. U. stands for Baptist Student Union, the center of Baptist activity on many Christian and secular college campuses.

26. For background information on cognitive learning, see *Created to Learn*, chapter 8, "Teaching for Understanding."

27. Several of my colleagues and I have spent hours sorting out Piaget's meaning for "assimilation." Some define it as simply taking in information about something one already knows. I disagree, since such simple intake does not require disequilibrium. Assimilation does infer "taking in," but that which is taken in is not the life experience itself. It is an experience distorted to fit what one already knows. Think of a slice of pizza. Before it can be assimilated into my system, it is changed through biting and chewing. Pizza on a plate and pizza in a stomach are two very different things.

28. Using the pizza analogy above, one's stomach expands to accommodate the pizza being assimilated. We accommodate ourselves to new, or conflicting, experiences either by adding new cognitive schemes or by adjusting ones we already possess. This is called "learning."

29. I do not remember the real name of this professor. My mind was mostly focused on moving to Fort Worth and beginning seminary.

30. This is writing that is *synthetic* in the sense of "a whole from many parts" rather than artificial or unreal.

31. Perhaps you are interested in how I solved my problem and wrote the paper. I secured a booklet that outlined American history from the Spanish-American War to the present. I isolated the chronological events, along with important names and places ("key words") between 1941 and 1949. I organized a three-ring binder with key words written at the top of blank pages of paper—one word per page, in chronological order. I took the first book and looked up each key word in its index. Using black ink, I made bibliographical entries in the notebook. I did the same with the second book, using blue ink; the third with red; and the fourth with green. The last book had no index, so I was forced to read it sequentially, making notes in purple. By the time I finished the fifth book, I had a global view of this period of American history, with quotes and references in chronological order. Part one of the paper flowed out of my chronological notebook with ease. As I scanned each page of my notebook, differences of opinion and perspective became obvious. By the time I finished part one, I had developed a general sense of authors' varying views on Fascism, Communism, and American Democracy. Now I focused on the different colors of inks. How did blue differ from black and red? And green from purple? Five short essays, from most conservative to most liberal, summarized the political positions of the authors. Not only did I use this method in seminary classes, but also in doing my two dissertations. I teach this approach to devel-

oping the synthesis of literature to research students. I also used it effectively in synthesizing thirty recent textbooks in educational psychology in preparation for writing *Created to Learn*.

32. John A. Glover and Roger H. Bruning, *Educational Psychology: Principles and Applications*, 3rd. ed. (Glenview, Ill.: Scott, Foresman/Little, Brown Higher Education, 1990), 132.

33. Robert E. Slavin, *Educational Psychology: Theory and Practice*, 4th ed. (Boston: Allyn and Bacon, 1994), 46.

34. LeFrançois, 73.

35. Myron H. Dembo, *Applying Educational Psychology*, 5th ed. (New York: Longman, 1994), 365.

36. LeFrançois, 74.

37. Slavin, 45.

38. Woolfolk, 33.

39. Dembo, 366.

40. Glover and Bruning, 131.

41. For more information on meaningfulness and elaboration, see *Created to Learn*, chapter 9, "Information Processing Theory," 215–218.

42. See Norman A. Sprinthall, Richard C. Sprinthall, and Sharon N. Oja, *Educational Psychology: A Developmental Approach*, 6th ed. (New York: McGraw-Hill, Inc., 1994), 290.

43. Eggen and Kauchak, 334.

44. For other, more specific, recommendations, see *Created to Learn*, "Constructivism and Bible Teaching," 203–205.

45. For background information on humanistic learning theory, see *Created to Learn*, chapter 10, "Teaching for Attitude Change."

46. Of thirty such texts I've studied, only one—Biehler and Snowman—continues to subsume humanistic learning theory under the learner theory unit. The other twenty-nine discuss humanistic principles under motivation.

47. Royal Ambassadors is the Southern Baptist missions education program for elementary and high school boys. The curriculum includes study of missions and missionaries serving both in the U.S. and around the world, as well as sports and games. Learning was marked by a series of ranks, each with its accompanying insignia.

48. It occurs to me as I write this that Mr. Begley's behavior, his interest in boys, and our regular overnighters would likely raise questions about his motives today. But his motives were pure and his priority was helping boys grow in Christ and learn about missions.

49. Eggen and Kauchak, 440.

50. Glover and Bruning, 262.

51. Eggen and Kauchak, 440.

52. Glover and Bruning, 262.

53. Ibid., 261, 250.

54. Eggen and Kauchak, 436.

55. Hamilton and Ghatala, 355.

56. Eggen and Kauchak, 436.

57. Ibid., 433.

58. Hamachek, 399.

59. Hamachek, 399.

60. Ibid., 414.

61. Ibid., 417.

62. Ibid.

63. Ibid., 401.

64. Ibid., 417.

65. Ibid., 402.

66. William Yount, *The Discipler's Handbook* (Fort Worth: Southwestern Baptist Theological Seminary, 1981–1995), 28.

67. Ibid.

68. For background information, see *Created to Learn*, chapter 12, "The Teacher as Motivator," 289–291.

69. Dr. Marsh was professor of Foundations of Education, School of Religious Education, Southwestern Baptist Theological Seminary, from 1956 to 1987.

70. LeFrançois, 284.

71. *Item analysis* is a procedure for determining whether objective test questions are valid. Do they correctly discriminate between better prepared students and less prepared students? I wrote a computer program to do this for me. If interested, send a formatted IBM-compatible 3.5-inch diskette and a self-addressed stamped envelope to W. R. Yount, P.O. Box 22428, Fort Worth, TX 76122-0428.

72. LeFrançois, 285.

73. Woolfolk, 360.

74. Hamachek, 279.
75. Woolfolk, 359.
76. "Bear with each other" (Col. 3:13) has the sense of "put up with."

Chapter 5

1. Haddon Robinson, foreward to *Preaching That Connects: Using Techniques of Journalists to Add Impact to Your Sermons* by Mark Galli and Craig Larson (Grand Rapids, Mich.: Zondervan Publishing House, 1994), 9–10.
2. Calvin Miller, *The Empowered Leader: Ten Keys to Servant Leadership* (Nashville: Broadman & Holman Publishers, 1995), 7.
3. Ron Hoff, *I Can See You Naked: A Fearless Guide to Making Presentations* (Kansas City: Andrews and McNeel, 1988), 31.
4. If you're interested in studying Kohlberg's theory, see *Created to Learn*, chapter 5, "Kohlberg's Moral Development Theory."
5. *The Teaching Ministry of the Church* (Nashville: Broadman & Holman, 1995) was edited by our dean, Daryl Eldridge, and written by the members of our Foundations of Education Department: Drs. Jack Terry, Terrell Peace, Norma Hedin, and myself. These two chapters were written by Dr. William A. "Budd" Smith.
6. Herbert V. Prochnow, *1001 Ways to Improve Your Conversation and Speeches* (Grand Rapids: Baker Book House, 1952), 22. This text is a classic.
7. Al Fasol, *A Complete Guide to Sermon Delivery* (Nashville: Broadman & Holman, 1996), 66.
8. Ibid., 48–56.
9. Ibid., 57.
10. Ibid., 59.
11. Ibid., 56.
12. Mark Galli and Craig Brian Larson, *Preaching That Connects: Using the Techniques of Journalists to Add Impact to Your Sermons* (Grand Rapids: Zondervan Publishing House, 1994), 118.
13. Fasol, 63.
14. Galli and Larsen, 118.
15. Fasol, 63.
16. Galli and Larsen, 118.
17. Fasol, 66.
18. Homer K. Buerlein, *How to Preach More Powerful Sermons* (Philadelphia: Westminster Press, 1986), 176.
19. Fasol, 66.
20. Buerlein, 176.
21. Fasol, 67.
22. Laurie Schloff and Marcia Yudkin, *Smart Speaking: Sixty-Second Strategies* (New York: Henry Holt and Company, 1991), 13–14.
23. Buerlein, 179.
24. Ibid.
25. An AM or FM radio wave consists of two parts, the audio signal and the carrier wave. The audio signal holds the message; the carrier wave broadcasts this message at a given frequency.
26. Fasol, 85.
27. Ibid., 73.
28. Buerlein, 182.
29. Hoff, 34–35.
30. Buerlein, 122.
31. Fasol, 75; Buerlein, 182.
32. Buerlein, 183.
33. Fasol, 76.
34. Buerlein, 183.
35. Fasol, 76.
36. Ibid.
37. Ibid., 77.
38. Buerlein, 184.
39. Fasol, 82.
40. Ibid.
41. Buerlein, 183.
42. Buerlein, 185.
43. Schloff and Yudkin, 118.
44. Hoff, 63.
45. Galli and Larsen, 82.
46. Ibid., 88.

47. Ibid., 84.
48. Ibid., 87.
49. Ibid., 85.
50. Ibid., 86.
51. Ibid., 87.
52. Galli and Larsen, 87.
53. Tom Nash, *The Christian Communicator's Handbook: A Guide to Help You Make the Message Plain* (Wheaton, Ill.: Victor Books, 1984), 263.
54. Ibid.
55. Ibid.
56. Buerlein, 41.
57. Ibid., 42.
58. Prochnow, 27.
59. Ibid., 28.
60. Especially chapter 8, "Never Too Old for 'Tell Me a Story'" (Elgin, Ill.: David C. Cook, 1990).
61. Especially chapter 7, "How to Tell a Good Story."
62. Reg Grant and John Reed, *The Power Sermon: Countdown to Quality Messages for Maximum Impact* (Grand Rapids: Baker Books, 1993), 140.
63. Hoff, 224.
64. Ibid., 227.
65. Grant and Reed, 140.
66. Professor of Psychology and Counseling, Southwestern Baptist Theological Seminary, from 1958 to 1986.
67. Grant and Reed, 122.
68. As quoted by LeFever, 189.

Chapter 6

1. I will be using some technical terms from research and statistics. Do not let these terms throw you. I use them because they represent my own struggle to create a course in the field, but also to demonstrate that these principles of course design will help regardless of the subject matter.
2. I've actually divided other classes into thinkers, feelers, and doers by way of a simple quiz and am amazed how close the divisions fall into equal thirds, with men and women in all three groups.
3. For more information check out chapter 6 of *Created to Learn*, chapter 11 of *Teaching Ministry of the Church* (Nashville: Broadman & Holman Publishers, 1995) and Robert Mager's books on *Goal Analysis* (Fearon: Palo Alto, Calif., 1972) and *Preparing Instructional Objectives* 2nd ed. (Fearon: Palo Alto, Calif., 1976).
4. In our hyperhumanistic age, students sometimes understand the phrase "in my own words" as "defining a term any way I please." Such self-centered fluff should be avoided in establishing clear, and correct, understanding.
5. See chapter 3 of this text, as well as chapter 2 of *The Disciplers' Model* and chapters 6–11 in *Created to Learn*.
6. Active review entails prompting students to recall and discuss essentials from previous sessions; passive recall—teachers review essentials. Active recall is more effective for learning.
7. Command language refers to the practice of writing out, verbatim, what you plan to say so that anyone could teach from your lesson plan. Rather than writing "Discuss the Pharisees for five minutes," you would write out word for word a five-minute lecture on the Pharisees.

Chapter 7

1. John F. Wakefield, *Educational Psychology: Learning to Be a Problem Solver* (Boston: Houghton-Mifflin Company, 1996), 546.
2. Robert F. Biehler and Jack Snowman, *Psychology Applied to Teaching*, 7th ed. (Boston: Houghton-Mifflin Company, 1993), 632.
3. Wakefield, 548; James Levin and James F. Nolan, *Principles of Classroom Management: A Professional Decision-Making Model*, 2nd ed. (Boston: Allyn and Bacon, 1996), 136.
4. Biehler and Snowman, 633.
5. Wakefield, 548; Levin and Nolan, 128.
6. Levin and Nolan, 130.
7. Wakefield, 549.
8. Biehler and Snowman, 627.
9. Don Hamachek, *Psychology in Teaching, Learning and Growth*, 4th ed. (Boston: Allyn and Bacon, 1990), 554.
10. Levin and Nolan, 155.
11. Biehler and Snowman, 635.

12. Jacob Kounin, *Discipline and Group Management in Classrooms* (New York: Holt, Rinehart, and Winston, 1970) as used in Biehler and Snowman, 623; Hamachek, 547; Levin, 155; and Robert H. and Mary Kay Zabel, *Classroom Management in Context: Orchestrating Positive Learning Environments* (Boston: Houghton-Mifflin Company, 1996), 166.
13. Hamachek, 549.
14. Levin, 155; Zabel and Zabel, 166.
15. Biehler and Snowman, 635.
16. Hamachek, 553.
17. These examples of positive and negative speech come from T. L. Good and J. E. Brophey, *Looking in Classrooms*, 4th ed. (New York: Harper and Row, 1987).
18. Levin and Nolan, 156.
19. Ibid.
20. Levin and Nolan, 157.
21. Ibid., 158.
22. Zabel and Zabel, 195.
23. Levin and Nolan, 160.
24. Biehler and Snowman, 625.
25. Zabel and Zabel, 197.
26. Zabel and Zabel use the term *evil eye* (197).
27. Levin and Nolan, 161.
28. Zabel and Zabel, 198.
29. Levin and Nolan, 165.
30. Zabel and Zabel, 199.
31. Levin and Nolan, 168.
32. Zabel and Zabel, 199.
33. Ibid., 201.
34. Levin and Nolan, 175.
35. Ibid., 177.
36. Ibid., 178.
37. From Levin and Nolan, 168–184.
38. Ibid., 179.
39. Ibid., 180.
40. From Levin and Nolan, 168–184.
41. The term *burnout* is borrowed from research in the helping professions (nursing, social work, child-care, nursing-home work, medicine, police work) which serve clients with problems, usually under difficult conditions. Burnout is the chronic inability to cope with stress. Symptoms include unhappiness or depression, lack of enthusiasm for work, lack of energy, distancing from clients or colleagues, psychosomatic conditions such as headaches, backaches, and lack of energy, and the excessive use of alcohol or drugs (Zabel and Zabel, 358).
42. I'm writing these words as I sit at my computer in Fort Worth, Texas, three weeks after returning from Moscow.
43. The effect of seventy-five years of repression, persecution, suspicion, and mistrust does not end quickly. Trusting others comes slowly in the former Soviet Union.

Chapter 8
1. Woolfolk, 143–144.
2. See Gary D. Borich and Martin L. Tombari, *Educational Psychology: A Contemporary Approach* (Boston: Addison-Wesley), 519; Dembo and Oja, 519; Eggen and Kauchak, 205; and Sprinthall, Sprinthall, 587.
3. Some writers call this "mainstreaming," though "inclusiveness" is now the preferred term.
4. Wakefield, 269.
5. See *Created to Learn*, chapter 10, "Humanistic Learning Theory."
6. Borich and Tombari, 598–99.
7. Woolfolk, 133.
8. Dembo, 403–405.
9. Ibid., 405.
10. Eggen and Kauchak, 191.
11. Ibid., 192.
12. Dembo, 406.
13. Ibid.; Eggen and Kauchak, 192.
14. Eggen and Kauchak, 193.
15. Borich and Tombari, 593.

16. Adapted from Deborah Bainer and Jeffrey Peck, "Effective Teaching and Multicultural Religious Education" in *Multicultural Religious Education*, ed. Barbara Wilkerson (Birmingham: Religious Education Press, 1997), 297–298.

17. Borish and Tombari, 590.

18. See *Created to Learn*, chapter 7: "Albert Bandura."

19. (In 1986.) See Borich and Tombari, 589.

20. Ibid., 590.

21. Ibid.

22. Ibid.

23. Based on material in Bainer and Peck, 303–304.

24. Biehler and Snowman, 263.

25. Ibid., 259–260.

26. All of the educational psychology texts I consulted for this chapter included "deafness" or "hearing impairment" under the category of physical impairment. Educators of the deaf no longer consider deafness as much a physical impairment as a language or culture group (a multicultural issue). Much of our discussion of multicultural issues applies directly to teaching deaf students, as you will see in the deafness section.

27. Wakefield, 281.

28. Woolfolk, 125.

29. Dembo, 512–13.

30. See Woolfolk, 136–37, and Dembo, 505.

31. Woolfolk, 137.

32. Dembo, 507.

33. Woolfolk, 137.

34. Ibid., 135–36.

35. Ibid., 136.

36. Dembo, 502; Wakefield, 282.

37. Wakefield, 282; Woolfolk, 138.

38. Dembo, 502.

39. Woolfolk notes that the diagnosis of "learning disability" increased 119 percent between 1977 and 1985 (143).

40. Woolfolk, 141–143.

41. Borich and Tombari, 562.

42. Woolfolk, 140; Eggen and Kauchak, 216.

43. Eggen and Kauchak, 216; Woolfolk, 141.

44. Wakefield, 282. Terminology differs slightly among authors. You might see ADHD called ADD-H (Attention Deficit Disorder with Hyperactivity).

45. Eggen and Kauchak, 216.

46. Borich and Tombari, 568.

47. Wakefield, 294.

48. Dembo, 516.

49. Wakefield, 294.

50. Ibid., 298.

51. Borish and Tombari, 539.

52. Ibid., 540.

53. Woolfolk, 146.

54. Eggen and Kauchak, 239.

55. Dembo, 508.

56. Ibid., 534.

57. Jews, Samaritans, Gentiles.

58. Palestinian, Roman.

59. Pharisees, Sadducees, scribes, pagans.

60. Rich or poor, clean or unclean.

61. Healthy or sick, able-bodied or lame.

Chapter 9

1. Paul Eggen and Don Kauchak, *Educational Psychology: Classroom Connections*, 2nd ed. (New York: Mcmillan College Publishing Company, 1994), 647. See also William Yount, *Research Design and Statistical Analysis in Christian Ministry*, chapter 8: "The Measurement Triad" (Fort Worth: Southwestern Baptist Theological Seminary Printing, 1988–1998).

2. Content validity is one of four major types. The others are predictive, construct, and concurrent validity.

3. See Borich and Tombari, 442.

4. Slavin, 509.

5. Hamachek, 374.
6. Gage and Berliner, 709.
7. LeFrançois, 369.
8. Nunnally, 160.
9. Dembo, 581; Behler and Snowman, 582.
10. Payne, 105.
11. Dembo, 581.
12. Payne, 105.
13. Woolfolk, 160; Dembo, 581.
14. Slavin, 512; Payne, 108.
15. Dembo, 581; Hamachek, 376.
16. Dembo, 581; Nunnally, 162; Payne, 106.
17. Dembo, 581; Payne, 107.
18. Kubiszyn and Borish, 73.
19. Dembo, 581.
20. Hamachek, 376.
21. Dembo, 581.
22. Payne, 107.
23. Hamachek, 374; Payne, 108.
24. Hamachek, 374.
25. Dembo, 581.
26. Biehler and Snowman, 582; Payne, 108; Kubiszyn and Borish, 73.
27. Payne, 108.
28. Not all authors agree with the 60-40 split. Biehler and Snowman (p. 582) and Hamachek (p. 377) both suggest an equal number of true and false items.
29. Supply items demand a higher degree of recall than the simple recognition of true-false items. Having students correct false items adds this higher level of difficulty.
30. Kubiszyn and Borish, 77.
31. Biehler and Snowman, 584.
32. Nunnally, 172; Kubiszyn and Borish, 86–87.
33. Dembo, 583.
34. Ibid., 581.
35. Biehler and Snowman, 584.
36. Payne, 110.
37. Slavin, 510.
38. Kubiszyn and Borish, 87.
39. Nunnally, 180; Payne, 112.
40. Biehler and Snowman, 584; Payne, 112.
41. Dembo, 578; Hamachek, 375; Nunnally, 174.
42. Nunnally, 174.
43. Kubiszyn and Borish, 87.
44. Nunnally, 173; Payne, 113; Slavin, 512.
45. Hamachek, 374.
46. Dembo, 579; Nunnally, 174.
47. Biehler and Snowman suggest listing the responses alphabetically (p. 584).
48. Nunnally, 176.
49. Ibid., 174.
50. Payne, 113; Kubiszyn and Borish, 87.
51. Slavin, 511.
52. Payne, 116–126; Kubiszyn and Borish, 84–87.
53. Hamachek, 378.
54. Biehler and Snowman, 581.
55. Hamachek, 378.
56. Payne, 112.
57. Hamachek, 378.
58. Nunnally, 164.
59. Dembo, 581.
60. Payne, 104.
61. Biehler and Snowman, 581; Nunnally, 166.
62. Payne, 128.
63. Nunnally, 167.
64. Biehler and Snowman, 583.
65. Dembo, 580; Kubiszyn and Borish, 77.
66. Payne, 129.

67. Nunnally, 167.
68. Kubiszyn and Borish, 77.
69. Nunnally, 167.
70. Ibid.
71. Payne, 129.
72. Kubiszyn and Borish, 74.
73. Dembo, 580.
74. Kubiszyn and Borish, 75.
75. Ibid., 77.
76. Ibid., 98.
77. Kubiszyn and Borish, 103.
78. Ibid., 104.
79. Eggen and Kauchak, 661.
80. Dembo, 582.
81. Kubiszyn and Borish, 105.
82. Dembo, 582.
83. Biehler and Snowman, 586.
84. Kubiszyn and Borish, 106.
85. Nunnally (p. 182) suggests that a "short answer" cover a half-page. If your testing period is one hour, it would be better to ask six ten-minute essays than two thirty-minute essays.
86. Payne, 143.
87. Biehler and Snowman, 587; Kubiszyn and Borish, 106.
88. Nunnally, 182.
89. Ibid., 184.
90. Dembo, 584.
91. Ibid., 585.
92. Biehler and Snowman, 587.
93. Ibid., 592–594; Glover, 421–423; Nunnally, 186–196; Payne, 274–276; Kubiszyn and Borish, 122–130.
94. TestPALII, an MS-DOS program I wrote in 1985, eliminates the tedium of computing discrimination indices. Comes on a 3.5-inch IBM-compatible diskette. Send a self-addressed, postage-paid diskette mailer to me at: Rick Yount, Box 22428, Fort Worth, Texas 76122, and I'll send your free copy to you—my way of saying *Thanks!* for your commitment to evaluate, and if necessary improve, your tests.
95. LeFrançois, 382ff; Wakefield, 616ff; Woolfolk, 553ff; Borich and Tombari, 497ff.
96. Wakefield, 616.
97. Woolfolk, 552.
98. Wakefield, 620.
99. "Command and Conquer" emphasizes human death in war, complete with blood and screams. "Total Annihilation" increases the degree of destruction but removes all reference to human death and suffering by employing only robots and machines.
100. Wakefield, 622; Woolfolk, 553.
101. Woolfolk, 555.
102. LeFrançois, 382–383.
103. Woolfolk, 556.
104. My statistics class also uses problem sets and a take-home examination to reinforce analytical skills.
105. See Wakefield, 619–20.
106. LeFrançois, 375.
107. Ibid.
108. These suggestions based on Woolfolk, 568.

Chapter 10

1. *Vine's Expository Dictionary*, #3101, "mathetes."